D0882813

Black Itinerants of the Gospel

And it shall come to pass in the last days, saith God, I will pour out of my spirit unto all flesh: and your sons and your daughters shall prophesy, and your young men shall see visions: And on my servants and on my handmaidens I will pour out in those days of my Spirit; and they shall prophesy.

—Acts 2:17–18

BLACK ITINERANTS OF THE GOSPEL

The Narratives of John Jea and George White

Edited with an introduction by
Graham Russell Hodges

MADISON HOUSE

Madison, 1993

Hodges, Graham Russell, ed.
Black Itinerants of the Gospel: The Narratives of John Jea and George White

Printed in the United States of America.

LIBRARY OF CONGRESS CATALOGING-IN-PUBLICATION DATA

White, George, b. 1764.
[Brief account of the life, experience, travels and Gospel labours of George White, an African]
Black itinerants of the Gospel: the narratives of John Jea and George White / edited with an introduction by Graham Russell Hodges.— 1st ed.
p. cm.
Includes bibliographical references and index.
Contents: A brief account of the life, experience, travels and Gospel labours of George White, an African / George White — The life, history, and unparalleled sufferings of John Jea, the African preacher / John Jea.
ISBN 0-945612-32-X (alk. paper)
1. White, George, b. 1764. 2. Jea, John, b. 1773. 3. Afro-American clergy—United States—Biography. I. Hodges, Graham Russell, 1946- . II. Jea, John, b. 1773. Life, history, and unparalleled sufferings of John Jea, the African preacher. 1993. III. Title.
BR563.N4W49 1993
287' .6'0922—dc20
[B] 92-39713
CIP

ISBN 0-945612-32-X

Designed by William Kasdorf
Printed on acid-free paper by Edwards Brothers, Inc.

Published by Madison House Publishers, Inc.
P. O. Box 3100, Madison, Wisconsin, 53704

FIRST EDITION

Contents

Illustrations

Acknowledgments

I owe substantial debts to scholars and friends who helped me reconstruct the worlds of George White and John Jea. Mechal Sobel of the University of Haifa first taught me about George White in an excellent seminar at the Northeast Seminar on African-American Religion at the Schomburg Library in 1989. My first awareness of John Jea came through reading Henry Louis Gates's *Signifying Monkey: A Theory of African-American Criticism*. I learned of Jea's hymns in the useful anthology *Black Writers in Britain, 1760–1890*, ed. Paul Edwards and David Dabydeen. I have acknowledged other historical and literary debts within the text.

Many institutions enabled this project. I found valuable materials on John Jea in England at the Portsmouth Record Office, the City of Portsmouth Library, the British Museum and Library, the Public Record Office, the Methodist Historical Society, and the Bodleian Library at Oxford University. I learned much about White at the American Antiquarian Society, the Maryland State Archives, the New-York Historical Society, the New York Municipal Archives, the New York Public Library, the Rutgers University Library, the State Library and Archives of New Jersey, the Virginia State Library and Archives, and the Library of Congress. Mr. Alva R. Caldwell, librarian at the United Library of Garrett-Evangelical and Seabury-Western Theological Seminary was immensely helpful in obtaining a copy of the frontispiece of George White's narrative.

A number of foundations, state and federal grant programs, and university councils generously provided support for research on this study. They include the American Council of Learned Societies Major Grant Program, the New Jersey Historical Commission, the National Endowment for the Humanities Summer Stipend and Travel-to-Collections Program, and the Colgate University Dean of Faculty, and Faculty Research Council.

Numerous students at Colgate and my stepchildren James B. and Celeste B. Creel listened patiently to my excited words about unknown preachers. Special help came from Colgate students John D. Ruppert III and Alan Brown. Alan prepared the table which appears as Appendix 2.

Several scholars have helped enormously with this task. Marcus Rediker of Georgetown University read the first draft of the introduction and made many cogent suggestions. John Wigger of Notre Dame University and Phillip Richards of Colgate University, made several excellent suggestions. Steve Kaplan and Daniel Baugh of Cornell University helped me avoid mistakes in tracing Jea's travels. Dewey Mosby, director of the Picker Gallery at Colgate University, generously supplied me with information about Henry Osawa Tanner's painting, *Lazarus*. Thanks also to John P. Kaminski and his staff at Scholars Editorial Services, Inc. for their excellent proofreading. Gregory M. Britton of Madison House proved to be a supportive, patient, yet exacting editor. My father and mother, the Reverend Graham R. and Elsie R. Hodges, helped identify biblical quotations in the two narratives. Reverend and Mrs. Hodges, like the two preachers inscribed in this work, personify devotion to the profession of parish ministry.

As always, my greatest debt is to my wife and intellectual companion, Margaret Washington.

Introduction

Black Itinerants of the Gospel: The Narratives of John Jea and George White

I

The narratives of John Jea and George White, reprinted here for the first time since the early nineteenth century, speak to us in many different ways.[1] They amplify our knowledge of a threefold intellectual transformation sweeping the Atlantic basin during the revolutionary era. The autobiographies inform us of the Methodist evangelicalism that overwhelmed orthodoxy and ignited a democratic revolution in American religion. In the late eighteenth century, Methodism hit America at the point of its greatest vigor. Evangelists and itinerants, aided by lay ministers and enthusiastic converts, proselytized throughout the country. As Nathan O. Hatch has indicated, early American religion deeply affected American revolutionary ideals. These narratives illuminate the radical republicanism that charged the American, French, and Haitian revolutions.[2] Both Jea's and White's stories reveal evidence of a third revolution, the creation of African-American Protestant denominations and theologies, spurred by Methodist evangelicalism, revolutionary egalitarianism, and a nascent black nationalism. Radical black denominations appeared in the United States, Nova Scotia, Sierra Leone, England, and the West Indies. Black preachers, who combined political and spiritual leadership, shared this transformation with their parishioners. Like their better-known counterparts, Absalom Jones, Richard Allen, and John Marrant, Jea and White were members of the first generation of free African-American ministers who harvested souls in the early decades of the American republic.[3]

In this introduction, I hope to place the narratives of John Jea and George White in the context of sweeping religious, political, and racial changes of their time. Second, I wish to shed light on the scant biographical information in the narratives. Because neither author was careful about dates and names, I spent many hours hunting for identifications of people mentioned in the book only to conclude that misspellings, inaccurate dates, and exaggerated distances made complete accuracy impossible. Because the ministers wrote their narratives for specific audiences, they sometimes omitted important details. Sponsors may have required White, for example, to omit his years organizing the first African Methodist Church in New York City. Third, because their work is little known or studied by modern scholars, I hope to fix the importance of the two narratives within the tradition of African-American autobiography.

To appreciate the works of Jea and White, we must first understand the tumultuous societies in which they lived. John Jea and George White spent much of their lives within the decaying system of slavery in New York and New Jersey. Slavery, the substructure of the small-farm, artisan, and mercantile economies of the North, came under ideological and moral attack following the American Revolution. In New England, where black populations were small, slavery died quickly. In Pennsylvania, where the Society of Friends continued their colonial antislavery appeal, gradual emancipation began by 1780. Of all northern states, only in New York and New Jersey did slavery flourish after the American Revolution, and, despite rising demands for abolition, remain a potent force in the two economies.[4]

In 1785 the New York state legislature prohibited the sale of slaves and lifted the requirement in place since 1712 requiring masters to post a £200 bond before freeing a slave. The law greatly liberalized manumissions but did not immediately produce massive numbers of emancipations. These reforms did not undermine the legal framework of slavery. In 1788 the New York legislature reaffirmed colonial slave codes, granting a single concession to the New York Manumission Society by making it illegal to buy or receive slaves with the intent to export them.[5] In New Jersey, Governor William Livingston, frustrated by pro-slavery forces during the Revolution, pushed through a ban in 1786 on the importation of slaves from Africa or the West Indies, although slaves could still enter New Jersey from other states.[6]

New York and New Jersey cautiously approached gradual emancipation in the 1790s. Part of their recalcitrance was a complacent belief that their brand of slavery was milder than that in the American South or in the West Indies. One anonymous New Yorker, writing in 1796, denounced slavery in America as "abominably unjust, inconsistent and ridiculous," showing that the revolution in America, "tho truly great and glorious, is by no means so thorough." Still, argued the immediatist, slavery in New York and New Jersey was "mild (if any slave can be said to receive mild treatment), compared with what they receive in the southern states." Blacks in the North were "better clothed and fed and could avoid excessive whipping." Probably in no part of the world, concluded the author, "do slaves live so comfortable as here."[7]

After much debate, legislators in 1799 in New York and in 1804 in New Jersey passed gradual emancipation laws which freed no one, but which promised gradual liberty to slaves after more than twenty years of service. New York, however, did not completely end servitude until 1827. New Jersey's slaves were not entirely free until the Thirteenth Amendment in 1865.

Facing limited economic and political freedom, African-Americans pressed their energies into building separate institutions. This was especially evident in their religious practices. Because at first blacks were members of northern Protestant denominations, their early activities occurred within the ideological boundaries of those churches. While post-revolutionary egalitarianism opened Protestant church doors to blacks, membership remained sporadic and power restricted. The reorganized Episcopal church remained the vanguard of black conversion. Disestablished by the new American states, Anglicans continued their colonial benevolence toward blacks and added important new services, such as education, marriages, and funerals. Although hampered by legal and doctrinal disputes, Trinity Church, for example, became the center for black education in New York City. After a brief hiatus following the Revolution, Trinity Church reopened its charity school for blacks in 1787, renaming it the African Free School.[8]

Despite reforms, black roles in white churches were limited. Clientage characterized race relations in Episcopalian, Dutch Reformed, and Presbyterian churches. Postwar religious liberalism barely extended outside the household. Black members were usually servants of white members. Except for the Methodists, few blacks listed on church rolls lived in independent households.[9]

Spurning institutions they associated with slavery, blacks flooded into the rising Methodist denomination. The church of John and Charles Wesley appealed to ambitious, intelligent, young African-Americans for several reasons. First, it had few colonial ties with slavery. Many Methodist ministers in the United States were openly antislavery. The Methodists combined revolutionary egalitarianism with their own evangelical "conscience" concerns. In 1782, Methodists passed an exclusionary rule against slaveholders and openly espoused immediate emancipation of southern slaves. In Virginia, for example, Thomas Coke was nearly lynched for his antislavery prayers.[10]

Politically, Methodists combined antislavery activism with loyalist attitudes which set them apart from patriotic denominations. This combined loyalist and antislavery stand made the denomination attractive to blacks seeking alternatives to the new American government that condoned slavery. British army appeals to blacks during the war which offered independence in exchange for military service made loyalism an ironic symbol of freedom for African-Americans. Methodist Charles Wesley's own poetry echoes the close ties between the denomination and loyalism.[11]

Methodism, along with Baptism, was already an umbrella for the aspirations of black nationalist denominations. In Nova Scotia and Sierra Leone, loyalist African-Americans established a radical fusion of Christianity, republicanism, and black nationalism while in exile. Inspired by Henry Alline and the Countess of Huntingdon Connection, black preachers John Marrant, David George, and Moses Wilkinson led a potent Christian revival emphasizing a democratic group conversion not dependent on education or the availability of a trained minister. When disenchanted blacks in Nova Scotia migrated to Sierra Leone in 1791, they perceived their hegira, which was widely discussed around the Atlantic basin, as fulfillment of biblical prophecies. Word of this new black nationalism reached New York while White and Jea were part of the African Methodist community. In the early years of the nineteenth century, black Methodists, including White, hosted Paul Cuffe who extolled the black political and religious liberty of Sierra Leone during his visits to New York City.[12]

Second, the Methodist church was receptive to blacks during the late colonial era and continued to accept them after the war. Peter Williams, Sr., and his wife, Mary Durham, for example, were among many blacks prominent in the New York Methodist community. Because black men and women held separate classes in the church, this separation enhanced the development of female leadership. Women constituted nearly eighty percent of the black converts by 1791.[13]

Methodist itinerants preached to interracial audiences—such as this one in Brooklyn—throughout the late eighteenth century.

On a personal level, Methodism offered blacks a sympathetic ear. Methodist divines treated blacks better than other denominations and listened sincerely to the words of blacks for inspiration. In New York City, Methodist Thomas Rankin, upon hearing New York blacks deliver accounts of their religious experience, commented "If the rich in this society were as devoted to God as the poor are, we should see wonders done in this city." As James Essig has remarked, white Methodist evangelicals beheld in pious free and enslaved blacks, persons who conformed to their spiritual ideals. Blacks were the downtrodden, despised humanity, alienated from centers of power and social prestige, but favored by God. Their sincere qualities made blacks irresistible to Methodists, and Methodism irresistible to blacks.[14]

Third, Methodism's widespread use of itinerants enhanced black religious practices and services. Methodism did not require stationary preachers and churches, a necessary convenience to blacks whose assemblages were still restricted by law. An evangelical ministry attractive to the least educated, itinerancy developed out of the earlier crusades of George Whitefield. Methodist clerics Francis Asbury and John and Charles Wesley prepared the way for legions of itinerant ministers who tramped the roads of England and America, bringing God's word and salvation to the masses. Itinerancy offered the traveling preacher a special rapport with his temporary audience. The itinerants convinced audiences to listen of their own free will. By the 1780s, Methodist itinerants Thomas Coke, Freeborn Garretson, Thomas Rankin, Joseph Pilmore, and Joseph Whatcoat preached in egalitarian settings to blacks and whites and sparked the spectacular growth of Methodism from New York down through the Delmarva Peninsula.[15]

Methodist and Baptist itinerants spread their messages more easily in post-revolutionary America through the flood of democratic pamphlets. In the United States, dozens of short, crudely printed life stories reinforced the union of republican political ideology with a resurgence of evangelical religion. Standard Methodist themes—including political egalitarianism meshed with Arminian conceptions of free choice, personal salvation, and disdain for luxury—appear regularly in the narratives. Presented first by fiery itinerants at camp meetings, personal accounts of salvation sparked connections between preacher and audience. These accounts were often published in both England and America as confessionary epistles or narratives of tragedy and triumph.[16]

Methodists allowed blacks to hear, learn, and preach God's word but not necessarily in an egalitarian setting. Henry Hosier, a famous black exhorter, earned a superior reputation traveling with Methodist ministers Francis Asbury and Freeborn Garretson. Hosier delivered his sermons "with great zeal and pathos and his language and connection is by no means contemptible."[17] Hosier, however, never rose beyond the rank of exhorter, held back by Methodist paternalism. In contrast, as itinerants, Jea and White took Methodist doctrine and preached it with few of the restraints imposed by the Anglo-American religious community. White's services were in the forests and fields, docks and streets of Virginia, Delaware, Maryland, New York, and eastern New Jersey. Jea's ministry encompassed the world.

Methodists proselytized without regard to previous religious experience. Jea and White had backgrounds, for example, which crossed many denominational boundaries. Like many unlicensed itinerants, Jea, using any theology which appealed to him, immersed himself in several denominations before accepting Methodism as his creed. Raised on plantations in the upper South, where African folkways remained potent, George White received his earliest formal instruction in the Church of England. He was reborn as a Methodist during a "memorable watch-night" on the Bowery in New York City in 1795. White henceforth worked within the Methodist hierarchy, inspiring critic William L. Andrews to refer to him as the first black religious organization man. Because Methodists would not accept black preachers as equals, White was forced to wander for over a quarter of a century. Later he split from the local African Methodists to join Richard Allen's dissident African Methodist Episcopal church, and worked the streets of New York City and the fields and forests of New Jersey in the late 1820s.[18]

Black membership in the Methodist church was primarily an urban phenomenon. In 1788, the first tally of black communicants counted fifty-four in the city with only a handful in rural areas. After jumping to 154 in 1793, black membership stagnated, then dropped over the next decade. Not until 1809 did African-American membership in the New York conference extend to over 500 souls. The zenith occurred in 1817 when 843 blacks belonged to New York City Methodist churches. Even then, rural membership was no larger than in other denominations. In 1820 when the African Methodist church cut all ties with the parent church, black membership declined sharply to the 1788 level.[19]

There were limits to Methodist racial liberalism. As Nathan O. Hatch has argued, the Methodist church's position towards blacks was torn by the paradox of its egalitarianism and its racism. Increasing white discomfort with black membership cooled post-revolutionary tolerance. By the 1790s, Methodist slaveholders were able to soften the earlier injunction against the institution by amending the Methodist constitution to apply only when slavery was "contrary to the laws of the state." Soon, Methodist ministers and their flocks in the South and West welcomed masters and excluded their slaves.[20]

Methodist recalcitrance over licensing for black preachers became a major reason for African-American formation of their own churches. Methodists were unwilling to share power with blacks or to promote qualified leaders. Not until 1809 did Francis Asbury, for example, promote Richard Allen, the preeminent black Methodist, and New Yorkers Abraham Thompson and James Varick, to the modest post of deacon. George White, too, applied five times before his licensing as a Methodist minister.[21]

Hatch has noted that white evangelical religion "unwittingly enhanced the leadership potential of black preachers, both slave and free." Several examples indicate, however, that if blacks used Methodist theology as a cover for their beliefs, the movement towards a black ministry was self-motivated.[22] Those exclusive attitudes helped spawn independent black congregations which emerged as intrinsic parts of the developing urban, black community. Independent, black churches softened the pain of socially-imposed segregation among the economically disadvantaged and anchored the construction of benevolent societies, literary and political forums, and occupational structures within the communities.

A final and very important reason for independence was that the black ministry was engaged in the struggle to end slavery, a process which brought cooperation from few sympathetic whites. Blacks warmly embraced the radical views of man's destiny and duty which characterized evangelical Christianity in this era. Unlike in the South, however, where Methodist theology taught blacks to endure slavery through doctrine which promised eventual deliverance without the demands of resistance, blacks in the North employed their beliefs as proof of equality and requisite liberty.[23]

Long after white clergy abandoned abolition, black Methodists kept a steady drumbeat against slavery. James Varick, who led African-Americans out of the parent Methodist church in 1796, resolutely opposed slavery. William Hamilton, an early member of the New York African church and reputed to be the son of Alexander Hamilton, wrote John Jay on March 8, 1796, describing slavery as human theft, and asked the governor to end the "scandal of the country." There is no record that Jay, a prominent member of the New York Manumission Society, responded.[24] Although the parent church gradually lowered its once-strident antislavery position, black Methodists were unceasing in their opposition. The African-American church movement fostered the stream of itinerant black preachers after 1800 who carried abolitionist messages out of New York City into the more conservative rural regions.

As African-American churches and licensed preachers were rare outside of the cities, itinerants were often the sole purveyors of God's word to black audiences. Jea and White made excursions to Long Island and eastern New Jersey which had very few black parishes and where white congregations were slow to integrate. There, the two itinerants led massive assemblages of black worshippers. Both showed remarkable courage speaking to black audiences in regions where abolition was a hotly contested issue.

Both authors were quick-witted, powerful narrators. To a religious audience, their biblical references had potent emotional qualities. Their chanted sermons enunciated the spiritual contact of the preacher and audience. Repetition pounded forth the message, spellbinding listeners with the impact of God's message. Both men used hymns to expand their sermons and, in Jea's case, to identify his personal struggle with the world. Such dynamic qualities were common in oral cultures where the performance is the creation. One can imagine Jea's hymns and White's stump sermons varying slightly with each audition. If their words seem formulaic or saturated with biblical references, it is because words were only a baseline for composition. Unlike white autobiographies of the time, which were created for public confession or private meditation, Jea's and White's books read like transcriptions of camp meeting sermons. As a result, both narratives are oral as well as written documents and help trace the elusive transition between oral and written culture.[25]

Black orators learned their methods in Africa, or among the African-American community in North America. As Viv Edwards and Thomas J. Sienkewicz have recently shown, itinerant "good talkers" roamed the West Coast of Africa in search of experience, inspiration, and audience. In America, fugitive and free blacks became strolling preachers. On Long Island in 1769, for example, Mary Cooper observed that "some Indians and one black man came from Montauk," and preached all day. Major Prevost of Bergen County, New Jersey, advertised in 1774 the escape of slaves Mark and Jenney. Prevost described Mark as "a preacher, short, black, and well set, speaks slow." Jenney was "smooth-tongued and very artful." In 1793, a Maryland slave master advertised the flight of a slave Methodist preacher, who was "raised in a family of . . . Methodists, and has lived with them . . . on terms of perfect equality." After his new master refused to continue these terms, the slave, "accustomed to instruct and exhort his fellow creatures . . . in religious duty," escaped.[26]

Jea and White, in short, worked within a political and religious milieu in the 1790s which shaped their careers and theologies. Brave African-American Methodists extricated themselves from the paternalist, white churches and started their own congregations. They did so within a very uncertain, hostile, political environment. Although gradual emancipation was on the horizon, slavery persisted in both states. Laws still permitted slave catchers free rein to retake fugitives. It was within this environment that both Jea and White struggled to make their mark.

II

Because of the marginality of itinerant black preachers, the detail of their careers often remain sketchy. The available information about George White is greater than usual. He was born in Accomack, Virginia, in 1764 and sold eighteen months later to a slave master in Essex County, Virginia. When he was six years old, he was sold to a master in Somerset County, Maryland. Resold at fifteen to a Suffolk County, Maryland, planter, White remained there until his dying master granted his freedom in the sweep of increasing manumissions in the 1780s. Other slaveholders, alarmed by the burgeoning free black population that rose through this period, petitioned the legislature in 1782 to stop this trend. White won his freedom just prior to these restrictions.[27]

White's initial religious exposure while in Virginia was to the Church of England, but he also experienced the growing wave of Methodism. During the last years of the American Revolution, itinerant Methodists swept across the Delmarva Peninsula. Benjamin Abbott and Freeborn Garretson, Methodist itinerants, were influential in Virginia and Maryland during White's early manhood. Garretson canvassed the Maryland shore during the first years of the 1780s, preaching to mixed audiences and denouncing slavery as unchristian. While other Methodists rescinded their antislavery messages, Garretson convinced some owners to emancipate their bondspeople. White's master may have been among those touched. White, listening among the throngs of worshippers, must have been impressed with Garretson's interracial, antislavery ministry.[28]

White spent several of his early years of freedom in search of his mother. Failing to learn of her fate, in 1787 at the age of twenty-five, he began his migration to the North with a pass from his ex-master. This document saved him when a Trenton, New Jersey, sheriff arrested him on September 27, 1787, as a suspected fugitive slave. "Gailor" David Wrighter of Trenton advertised in the local newspaper that he was detaining White for four weeks to give a pursuing master time to claim him. Wrighter noted that White "says he is free man, was born at New-Weesey in Virginia, and has lived the greatest part of his time with Colonel William Johnson." Wrighter assumed White's pass was forged and that he was a "Runaway Slave." After four weeks, Wrighter freed his prisoner.[29] White then spent the next three years as a rural laborer in

ON Thurſday the 27th inſt. was committed to my cuſtody, a certain NEGRO or BLACK MULATTO, who calls himſelf GEORGE WHITE, and ſays he is a free man, was born at New-Weeſey in Virginia, and has lived the greateſt part of his time there with Colonel William Johnſon. When apprehended he produced a kind of paſs, ſigned with that name, which it is ſuppoſed was forged, and that he is a RUNAWAY SLAVE. He appears to be about 25 years of age; had on a round hat, blue broadcloth coat and brown breeches; had ſeveral articles of clothing with him, but none very valuable. His maſter, if he has any, is requeſted to take him away, within four weeks from the date hereof, or he will be diſcharged.

DAVID WRIGHTER, *Gaoler.*

Trenton Gaol, Sept. 29, 1787.

Constables and sheriffs commonly arrested unfamiliar African-Americans without a pass or manumission statement. The lawmen then advertised a description to alert owners seeking return of fugitive slaves. If the prisoner remained unclaimed, the sheriff would either auction off or release the captives. This advertisement from the *Trenton Mercury and Weekly Advertiser,* October 9, 1787, provides us with the only known physical description of George White.

New Jersey where he had further opportunity to hear Garretson and Abbott, who worked the region extensively in the 1780s.[30]

In New York City, attracted by the antislavery radicalism, White fully embraced Methodism. In 1795, a Methodist minister named Stebbins converted White "on a memorable watch-night, held in the Bowery Church." White's rebirth occurred in a trance, a common practice which crossed ethnic and denominational boundaries. White's conversion experience was typical, fraught with profound emotional turmoil. He "experienced such a manifestation of the divine power, as I had before been a stranger to and under a sense of my amazing sinfulness in the sight of God, I fell prostrate on the floor, as one wounded or slain in battle."[31]

White then joined the African "Class #31" at the John Street Methodist Church. Despite Methodist liberalism in the 1790s, the church regularly organized its black parishioners into segregated classes. White's fellow students included such future leaders of black New York as James Varick, Abraham Thompson, William Miller, William Hamilton, Thomas Miller, and George Moore.[32]

Chafing under the constraints of racist paternalism, blacks began to leave the Methodist church. White joined the first separatist "African Society" of New York City. That body of free blacks petitioned the New York City Common Council in 1795 for assistance to purchase land in the Seventh Ward for a burial ground. The group's leadership, who referred to themselves as the "Managers of the Business of the said Association," complained that they were not allowed to incorporate as a religious body. They petitioned for assistance to "procure a place for the erection of a place of divine worship and the interment of the People of Colour." This last request hit a positive note with the city government which for seven years had been vexed by speculators' encroachments on the Old Negro Burial Ground behind the Alms House on Bowery Lane. Land investors had chipped away at the cemetery, in operation since the 1640s, and the city was anxious to be done with the problem. It, therefore, granted £100 to the African Society to create a new graveyard at Potter's Field in Greenwich Village.[33]

In 1796 Williams, White, and other black Methodists, angered by negative white attitudes toward the Haitian Revolution, and by the unending irritation of "black pews" in Methodist churches, left the John Street Church to hold separate meetings. In 1799 the group held several meetings on Cross Street and decided to build a separate church. Known as the African Methodist Episcopal Church, it remained under the control of the parent Methodist Episcopal Conference. This meant that only white ministers could preach to the black congregations. In 1801 White was among the trustees of dissident black Methodists who built the African Methodist Episcopal Zion Church on a lot at Church and Leonard streets after gaining a charter from the New York legislature.[34]

As White became a presence in the African Methodist church, he established himself in the community. On July 24, 1799, White married Mary Henery at the John Street Methodist Church.[35] The city directory for 1800 lists White, his wife, and two daughters living at 123 Cherry

Street. The following year White and his family moved to 33 George Street in lower Manhattan. This would be the family residence for the remainder of his life.

Like other working-class New Yorkers, White used several means to earn a living. White started his own business as a fruit seller, a common occupation for blacks and poor whites in early nineteenth-century New York. White combined preaching with his travels to purchase fruit in rural communities. By 1805, he opened an oyster shop at 209 Water Street. Again, his preaching coincided with work. Oystermen worked a circuit from northern Virginia to Boston. By 1810, White and his family opened their house to nine boarders. Perhaps intending to start an independent black publishing business, he also rented a printing office at 109 Water Street.[36]

His call to preaching came in 1804 after a camp meeting. That night White dreamt of Hell. "It was a pit . . . a lake burning with fire and brimstone. . . . The descent into this place of misery, was by a series of steps, the top of which was near the surface of the earth." In his dream, White saw "multitudes of souls, suffering the torments . . . out of whose mouths and nostrils issued flames of fire; and from those flames an impenetrable cloud of smoke." White beheld a "coach, with horses richly furnished, and full of gay, modish passengers, posting to this place of torment. . . ." When the coach approached the pit, "their countenances changed, and awfully bespoke their surprise and fear." White received a message to "Go, and declare what you have seen."[37]

White frequently had emotionally charged dreams and spiritual visits common among evangelicals. White's dream was quite similar to one which Freeborn Garretson described in his sermons in eastern Maryland in the early 1780s. Lorenzo Dow, whose early troubles over ordination mirrored White's, had innumerable dreams which amplified his convictions of personal grace.[38]

White describes two other spiritual experiences, trances and shouts, that combined African-American pastoral methodology with Methodist techniques.[39] White's descriptions of "shouts" are among the first instances recorded. Primarily associated with southern African-American religion, "shouts" have been recorded in Delaware, but were not previously known in New York City. As Sterling Stuckey explains in *Slave Culture*, the "ring shout" practiced in Africa and North America was a counterclockwise dance ceremony, usually for purposes of mourning, in which dancing and singing were prayers directed to the ancestors and gods, the tempo and revolution of the circle quickening during the course of the movement. As expressed in funereal practices in Sierra Leone, Dahomey, and the Kongo region, the ring was a means of achieving oneness between the mourners and the dead. [40] During White's itinerant tours in Delaware, he visited the developing African Union Church, which used "shouts" as a regular part of the service.[41] In New York, White used the shout during Sister Henery's final moments in 1809. At her bedside, White and Sister Henery began shouting to prepare for her meeting with God. As the "shout" intensified, Sister Henery achieved oneness with God.

White's theology is best expressed in his funeral sermon for Sister Henery recorded in the narrative. Sister Henery, he argued, demonstrated the correct path to the "strait gate" through her life and repentance. For each person, repentance meant "self-denial, mortification, self-renunciation, conviction, and contrition of sin." Sister Henery's faith, he compared, was superior to the cynical disbelief of another recently departed black New Yorker. This man, according to White, died in "mental anguish" because he denied the collective happiness of faith in God. Breaking from Methodism, White forecast a millennium in which each person would be chosen or rejected. Acceptance of God, said White, was the only way to true happiness, for God was a friend that "sticketh closer than a brother." Improvement of one's fortunes was only possible through acceptance of Scripture.

Throughout his life, White considered himself a Methodist, yet his difficulties securing a preaching license from the Methodists betray the strained relations between blacks and the Methodist hierarchy. After the quarterly Methodist meeting refused to license White as a preacher, he returned to the road as an exhorter on Long Island and in New Jersey.[42] He specialized in prayer-meetings at which "many of my African brethren, who were strangers to religion before, were now brought to close in the offers of mercy." At this time, there were no counterparts in New Jersey to the black churches of New York City. Religious blacks had to rely on the uncertain hospitality of white churches or the infrequent visits from itinerants.

George White appeared on April 12, 1807, for the fifth time before the elders of the Methodist church in New York City, seeking a license as an African Methodist minister. He had failed the examination four times before and had only limited hopes on this occasion. American Methodists had become very conservative about licensing poorly-educated itinerants. Ironically, the Methodist hierarchy, so contemptuous of clerical authority themselves, became in White's mind, an entrenched theocracy. White's painful negotiations with the Methodists bore heavily on his spirit. At one point he "passed several months in a most gloomy and distressing state of mind, deprived, both of slumber and appetite." Only his inner contact with God, who advised him in prayer to "Go—warn the wicked to flee from the wrath to come," kept his spirit afloat.[43]

In spite of its importance to White, the Methodist Quarterly Meeting did not record his difficult negotiations. It is probable that none was kept because his application was as an African-American preacher. Despite opposition from other black preachers and the hostility of white Methodist clerics who informed White that the devil was pushing him to apply for a license, he finally succeeded in earning the coveted permit.

The Methodist church carefully defined each of the positions White would hold. He began as an exhorter or a licensed, religious public speaker. He later became a licensed local preacher, "a higher order of licentiates . . . to preach as local clergymen." It was not until 1800 that the Methodist church decided to ordain blacks as deacons and local ministers. Much later in 1815, after years as a preacher, White eventually ascended to the post of deacon, elected by the annual conference, and ordained by the elders and bishop. As deacon, White could assist in the administration of communion, baptize and administer matrimony, and try disorderly persons in the absence of the elder. These were the highest offices to which White ascended, or, for that matter, any black within the Methodist church at this time.[44]

After the Methodists licensed him as a "coloured preacher." White traveled on Long Island and in New Jersey as an itinerant. The quarterly meeting renewed his license in 1808. White indicates that opposition came from Daniel Coker, a brilliant young, black minister, who later would become active in Richard Allen's Bethel African Methodist Church in 1820 and led a ship of New York City blacks into exile in Liberia. Despite Coker's opposition, he listed White as a local minister in one of his publications.[45]

It was at this time that White probably began his autobiography. As William L. Andrews observes, White is the first black narrator to compose and write his life on his own, demonstrating White's perseverance in a hostile world. White's production of a narrative just three years after the Methodist church licensed him is indicative of his strong determination and courage. He confronted slaveholders and suspicious

Methodist clerics by "putting my trust in God and obeying his will, under all these trials, infinite goodness has caused all events to turn to my account at last." White's unselfish orientation and institutional identity allowed him to succeed. In his negotiations with the Methodists, he accepted a rigorous and disappointing trail to his goal. Although he was troubled by Methodist refusals, his persistence was at last rewarded.[46] White, by placing public service ahead of his own needs, showed republican virtue.

In 1810, the New York City printer, John C. Totten, published White's narrative, "Written by himself," and revised by an anonymous friend. Totten specialized in children's and religious books. In 1808 he published a Methodist magazine, *The Moral and Religious Cabinet*, which included numerous biographical and conversion accounts. The next year, Totten compiled the first edition of a Methodist hymnal and later printed issues of the Methodist Tract Society. He was an important member of the Forsyte Methodist Church in New York City, serving as a class leader and steward. Located near the Bowery, slightly north of the main group of early nineteenth-century New York City publishers, Totten's firm made additional money publishing the sermons and commemorative speeches of numerous black leaders over the next few years.[47]

By 1811, White applied for promotion to the post of deacon. The Methodist Quarterly Meeting rejected him three times before approving his petition on May 15, 1816, as the sixth black Methodist deacon in America.[48] In 1817, White remarried to Mary Ann Forsyte, also a Methodist; and they bore a son, Robert George White, on January 5, 1820.[49] By then White had retired from the arduous task of mining oysters from the sea to became a shoemaker.[50]

In 1820 White left the factionalized New York African Methodist Church and aligned with Richard Allen's Bethel African Methodist Episcopal Church. Allen's church initially attracted a number of black preachers and worshippers in New York City, but White was the only area minister to remain with the Allenites. His first constituency was in Flushing, Long Island, where White had frequently visited during his preaching tours. White informed this congregation that "all the members of the Zion church decided "to join the Allenites, except one or two." Alarmed, William Miller and George Collins from Zion traveled out to Flushing to correct White's account. They found, however, that

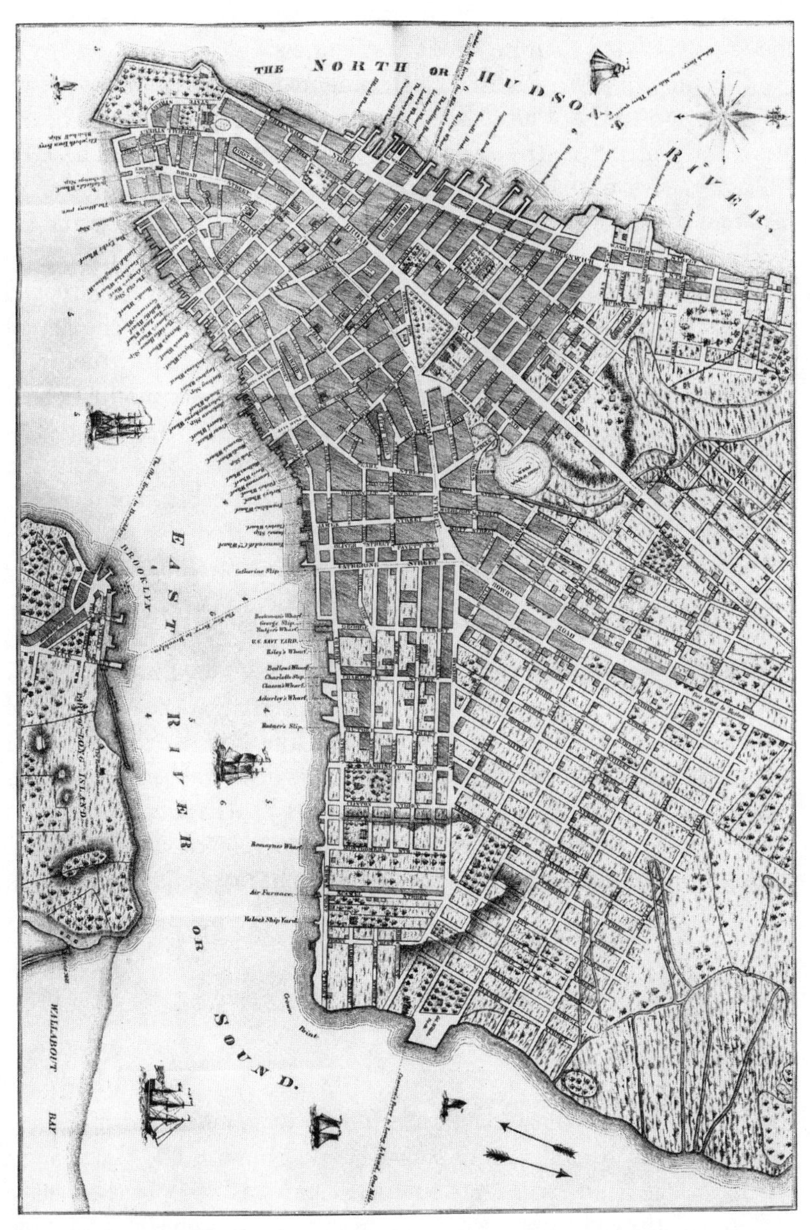

This map of New York City from 1797 is useful in locating the African-American community. The African Methodist Church was located on Cross Street just below the Collect Pond; the burial ground stretched from Broadway and Chambers Street to just below the pond. White's home at 33 George Street was several blocks to the east.

the people in Flushing were "under the influence of . . . George White, they were induced to unite with the Allenites."[51]

On June 8, 1822, Richard Allen ordained White as a deacon and assigned him to the White Plains circuit at the first Conference of the New York district of the African Methodist Episcopal Church. [52] By 1828, at the age of sixty-four, White undertook the last itinerant tour of his career, working in the Trenton, New Jersey, A. M. E. Zion circuit. He worked there until expelled from the circuit for unknown reasons in 1829. He then returned to 33 Spruce Street in New York City and worked as a shoemaker. He died on January 12, 1836, at the age of seventy-two, and was buried in St. Philip's African Church Cemetery. [53]

Much of White's importance lies in his careful reconstruction of clerical politics between African-Americans and white Methodists. Important as well are his evocations of African-Methodist rituals and folkways. What White does not mention in his autobiography are the swirling controversies in New York over abolition of slavery and the slave trade, and the unceasing irritants of slavecatching, clandestine slave sales to the South, and the denial of black civil rights. Contemporaries of White, Peter Williams, Jr., William Hamilton, Daniel Coker and others around New York made the issue of slavery a regular part of their discourse. White's reticence in mentioning slavery may well have come from his fear of institutional or personal retribution. By this reticence White suggested that he deferred to the Methodist establishment for his position and for publication of his memoirs. Blacks who confronted slavery more directly were either part of the burgeoning African-American abolitionist movement or were true religious independents like John Jea.

III

While George White sought acceptance within Methodist institutions, John Jea expanded from them. He was born in Old Callabar, in southern Nigeria, in 1773. Although Callabar was a well-known slave port during the eighteenth century, European traders preferred to avoid it because slaves of Efik or Ibibio origins, the principal nations in the area, were so fierce and rebellious.[54] Despite the brevity of his references to Africa , Jea's nationality remained important throughout his life and his narrative. He referred to himself continually as a "poor African," an "African Preacher," and a " black African."[55]

By the time of Jea's birth, there was ample evidence of the luxurious profits of the slave trade in Old Callabar. Its chieftains traded humans for clocks, watches, and sofas; porcelain cabinets were common in the homes of principal dealers in flesh. Old Callabar slave traders used "trust trade" by which a European trader gave merchandise to a native chief of good reputation, who would then use them to purchase a specified quota of slaves. Items which could have been exchanged for the Jea family included copper bars, knives, rum, gin, basins, tankards, beads, locks, mirrors, guns, powder, and shot. Traders expected "dashes" or tips to complete the deal. A man was worth thirty-eight copper bars and a woman, thirty-seven.[56]

Jea's father, Hambleton Robert Jea, and mother, Margaret Jea, and their children, including two-and-a-half-year-old John, came to America in a slave ship and were sold to the New York Dutch family of Oliver and Angelika Triehuen.[57] In New York, Jea and his family worked as field slaves for the Triehuen family. Life in rural New York for black field hands was harsh. Agricultural depression and high land prices meant scarce profits for Dutch slave masters concomitantly poor treatment for their slaves.[58]

Jea's masters were members of the conservative Dutch Reformed church that, during the colonial period, strongly resisted the practice of slave conversion. Segregated since the 1660s, the Dutch Reformed church in New York City began accepting black communicants in the reformist wake after the Revolution. Most of the black members at that time were servants or slaves of white worshippers. As part of a very gradual acceptance of black members, the church constitution of 1792 resolved that "no difference exists between bond and free in the Church of Christ; slaves or blacks when admitted to the church possess the same privilege as other members of the same standing; their infant children are entitled to baptism and ministers who deny them any Christian privilege are to be reprimanded." In its new-found openness the Dutch Reformed church celebrated marriages among slaves, between slaves and free blacks, and between free black couples. A few blacks were even buried in Dutch Reformed cemeteries. In spite of this new liberalism, black membership in the Dutch Reformed church remained small and churches remote from New York City still excluded blacks.[59]

In the postwar period a leadership shortage caused rural Dutch

Reformed parishes to scramble for ministers. In 1784 the Dutch Reformed General Body found that only fifteen of its ninety congregations in New York and New Jersey had their own minister and thirty-eight more had to share their pastors.[60] In this absence of institutional control, church members altered their worship to fit their own community situation. Such conditions meant that rural Dutch slave masters often worshipped with slaves and used less-frequent rituals to replace weekly Sabbath services. Holiday services, of which the most popular was *Pinkster*, the Dutch version of Pentecost, became the most common occasion for religious celebration and conversion.

In the Old Testament, Pentecost (or Shabuoth) brought together Jews from the Diaspora into Jerusalem to celebrate the revelation of the Ten Commandments; Christians adopted the term and holiday to celebrate the descent of the Holy Spirit upon the apostles and disciples.[61] Upon this holiday, African-Americans grafted their own religious meaning. Pinkster celebrations featured Dutch and African dances, music, gambling, and debauchery. As a youth living on a Dutch farm, Jea undoubtedly took part in the festivity, but later rejected it by turning to its more spiritual messages.[62]

Whether discussing the celebration as an African survival or as a means of social control, historians have neglected its spiritual qualities in favor of its more vulgar aspects. Pinkster was also a deeply private religious ceremony which took place in the home. Religious comprehension of Christ's sacrifice and resurrection occurred when the Holy Spirit rushed through the heart or home on a "holy wind," and provoked speaking in tongues by masters and servants. Holy wind could consist of powerful preaching, or prophetic speech and could cross race, gender, and class boundaries. What was important was the ecstatic moment when the participant, whether master or slave, became a "mouthpiece of God." Private observance of Pinkster appealed to the Dutch, who, losing public authority, retreated into the privacy of their tight-knit communities.[63]

Pinkster created a temporary equality and community among Africans and Dutch, and, it may be argued, a safety-valve for household tensions. The ecstatic moments of the holy wind served as replacements for church baptisms and acted as spiritual conversion. At Pinkster, the church of Jesus' time united with the church contemporary with Jea and his masters. Through the Holy Spirit, Dutch slave owners could accept their slaves into the sanctity of their homes without the anxiety of the emancipating effects of Anglican baptism. Among slaves, moreover, Pinkster ceremonies sustained promises of sacred equality. Unlike Anglican ceremonies, where literacy and comprehension of theology was paramount, Pinkster services permitted spiritual rebirth on the communicants' own terms and without regard for education.[64]

Pinkster was important to Jea's life for two reasons. First, it prepared him for miraculous religious events. Ecstatic and hallucinatory in effect, Pinkster set the stage for future developments of his doctrine and ministry. Its overwhelming religious experience translated well at camp meetings and with the potent individual conversions of evangelical sects. Although Jea, like virtually every former slave of the Dutch, quickly abandoned the Reformed church for more egalitarian denominations, he took with him the religious combination of African and Reformed traditions learned during his childhood.[65]

Second, *Whitsuntide*, or Whitsunday, the English counterpart of Pinkster, was very important to Wesleyan Methodist theology. Charles Wesley, whose hymns Jea abundantly included in his collection, traced his own rebirth to Whitsuntide in 1738. In several hymns published in 1739, Charles and brother John celebrated his rebirth on Whitsuntide. It is very likely that Jea easily linked Wesley's vision of the ascension with his own childhood Pinkster experiences.[66]

Jea's early influences by the Dutch Reformed culture partially obscured his African experience and behavior. Efik cosmology, however, translated well into Jea's Christianity. The Efik believed in a supreme being, known as *Abasi* who dwells in the sky, created the world, and discountenances all injustice and evil—all beliefs that would sustain Jea during enslavement.[67]

Before comprehending his mission on earth, as a young man Jea underwent a bitter conversion process. As Jea struggled with a deep depression characteristic of African conversion into Christianity, his master sought to instill docility in his dissatisfied slave by sending him to a church school, which Jea strongly rejected: "My hatred was so much against going to the chapel that I would rather have received one hundred lashes." Despite his recalcitrance, Jea came to grips with his faith by praying in a secret place in the woods. To stop this unauthorized meditation, his master beat him unmercifully. Failing to channel the slave's piety, he sold Jea to another master who in turn passed him on to two others. By this time Jea accepted Christianity sufficiently to steal away and be baptized without permission. Furious, his master attempted to deny Jea's conversion; the minister insisted that Jea be taken before magistrates who examined his knowledge of Christianity. Jea made a public affirmation that "God, for Christ's sake had pardoned my sins and blotted out all mine inequities," and testified "that there is no other Name under Heaven, given to Man, whereby he shall be saved, but only in the name of Jesus Christ." Jea reported that, satisfied with his conversion, the magistrates freed him. Jea mistakenly believed this emancipation was the law of New York State. In reality the magistrates probably only validated his baptism and conversion.

Slave misconceptions about the liberating qualities of baptism dated back to 1706 when Elias Neau, founding instructor at Trinity Church's famous school for slaves in New York City, lobbied successfully for a law which declared that Christian baptism did not alter civil condition. Neau designed the law to assure Anglican, Dutch, and Huguenot slave owners that his school would not breed rebellious slaves. Throughout the colonial period, however, many New York slave owners refused to permit slave attendance in schools. African-Americans viewed the cultural and legal dissention as proof that baptism mandated freedom despite the law.[68]

Muddy interpretations in English law caused further confusion. Even Blackstone could not state clearly the law concerning baptism and freedom for slaves. In England, blacks frequently cited baptism as proof of their freedom. As English abolitionism emerged, a slave's Christian status strengthened his or her case for emancipation.[69]

Despite Jea's claim, his master refused to emancipate him. Frustrated, the illiterate Jea took the Bible and "held it up to my ears, to try whether the book would talk with me or not, but it proved all to be in vain." His master laughed at him, troubling Jea further. After six weeks of prayer, he dreamt that he was in a dungeon with a Bible "illuminated with the light of the glory of God, and the angel standing by me, with the large book open . . . and said unto me *'Thou hast desired to read and understand this book . . . in English and Dutch.'*" God then gave Jea the ability to read the Book of John. After he read the whole chapter he looked up and "the angel and the book were both gone." For advice about this remarkable dream, he went to a Presbyterian minister, Peter Lowe, who gave him a Bible, which Jea read successfully. The story of Jea's miraculous literacy spread through New York City, and this time the magistrates insisted that the young man receive his freedom.[70]

As Henry Louis Gates, Jr., has explained, Jea's miraculous attainment of literacy reveals the "trope of the talking book among Africans." Gates argued that Jea's narrative is the culmination of a literary tradition beginning with early eighteenth-century African writers Jacobus Captetein, Francis Williams, Wilhelm Amo, and Ignatius Sancho and running through the narratives of Albert Ukawsaw Gronniosaw, John Marrant, Ottobah Cugoano, and Olaudah Equiano. These early black writers shared traditions and efforts "intent on placing their individual and collective voices in the texts of Western letters," and did so by reflecting upon each other's works. Literacy, instilled in African slaves by missionaries and paternalistic slave owners, became "the ultimate parameter by which to measure the humanity of authors struggling to define an African self in Western letters." Protestant denominations in America were highly reliant on words and books. At the same time, American pietism accentuated emotional use of texts. The works of Gronniosaw, Marrant, Cugoano, and Equiano were steps in the transformation from an oral into a literate culture. Jea's narrative made the trope literal by placing it directly within his plot structure. God's gift to Jea, then, is emblematic of the African-American's transformation and legitimization of self.[71]

Jea prayed fervently that God give him the power to read, understand, and speak the language of the Gospel of John in "the English and Dutch languages." By reading the Gospel of John, Jea was able literally and figuratively to find God, and, by his own claim, gain literacy, an understanding of God's work, and his own true freedom. The same passages which narrate Jea's literacy are equally imbued with discussion of his evolving faith and his personal mission. For Jea, literacy and faith were fused into one powerful force.[72]

While both the Jea and White narratives owe much to oral culture, they are written reflections of the deep African-American devotion to literacy. Despite extensive illiteracy and pressures against learning by slave masters, there was an impressive amount of literacy among blacks and a high correlation of reading with liberty. Both Jea and White connected biblical reading with personal, as well as spiritual, liberty.[73]

After his miraculous attainment of literacy, Jea received his freedom. The narrative does not give a date, but in one of his hymns, Jea indicated that his conversion occurred in 1788 when he was fifteen. His manumission, although unrecorded, presumably occurred sometime in the next year or so. Literacy, conversion, and freedom were all powerful forces in Jea's life. Jea fully equated his Christianity and literacy with freedom from slavery. In one of own compositions, Jea wrote:

> I thank God, that did set
> My soul at liberty;
> My body freed from men below
> By his almighty grace.
>
> I will be slave no more,
> Since Christ has set me free,
> He nail'd my tyrants to his cross,
> And bought my liberty.[74]

Literacy as God's miraculous gift became a significant part of Jea's theology. As an African preacher, Jea believed in the power of revelation. Because African ministers could not enforce a uniform cosmology, their position was precarious. Itinerants required constant validation of their ability to receive revelations and transmit prophecies. Jea, whose credentials were frequently challenged by both clerics and heretics, called upon God's intervention to bring him the miracle of literacy and silence his critics.[75]

After liberation, Jea married a Native American slave. After a period of happiness and the birth of a child, his recently freed wife fell victim to a deep depression. Newly freed domestics often had the stressful choice between remaining in near-bondage in their former mistresses' residences or setting up independent households with little money. Citing his own example, Jea encouraged his wife to learn how to read and gain her freedom. Her mistress, however, worked equally hard to convince her to remain in servitude. Maddened by the pressure, Jea's wife killed her mother and child and threatened to murder her husband. The ensuing trial and execution were unreported in the press or court records of the period. Jea related these sensational events in a flat, almost impersonal manner which has caused one critic to regard him as lacking in any "common sympathy for common cheerfulness, laughter, song, and sexual love."[76]

This is a misreading of his narrative. During the portion of his career of which we have knowledge, Jea lost three wives and all of his children. In his hymns, Jea expresses his deep sorrow over the passing of loved ones.[77] Whether the references were to his first wife, or another, Jea was very capable of love, and identified personal affection with the love of

God. Further, Jea may have omitted these emotional details as inappropriate for this audience.

Free and recovering from personal disasters, Jea began his career as a minister. In the late 1790s, he traveled throughout rural New York and eastern New Jersey as an itinerant minister. With an assistant he conducted major evangelical rallies which lasted from Saturday night through Sunday evening. Jea's services were held "out of doors in the fields and woods; which we used to call out large chapel." These meetings were based loosely on Methodist "love feasts" at which any person could speak of their experiences to a supportive audience. As slavery was dying slowly in New York and New Jersey in the late eighteenth century, few slave masters welcomed black evangelists with messages of freedom and Christian baptism. Black itinerancy was dangerous. Holding all night vigils in New York's rural environs, Jea skirted laws against unlicensed assemblages.

Jea brought Christian messages to slaves who had limited access to church. In his sermons he instructed the slaves not to do evil and learn to do well for "the end of all their troubles was near at hand." He warned them to be careful of the company they kept and not to desire any of the "dainties of the world." Jea promised the throngs that "God had promised to deliver them that call on him in time of trouble." [78]

As a roving preacher, Jea gradually pushed up the Atlantic coast to Boston, where he signed up as a cook for the first of his many ocean voyages. The booming ports of New York and Boston in the late eighteenth century attracted many newly freed or fugitive blacks. During the eighteenth century blacks worked as sailors on whalers from eastern Long Island and Nantucket, and during the Revolution then regularly joined the crews of British warships.[79] African-Americans held about eighteen percent of the seamen's posts on ships out of New York City between 1800 and 1825, with as many as sixteen percent of the 120 ships out of New York in 1818 using all black crews.[80] Yet few blacks were willing to ship out on long voyages for fear of being kidnapped and sold in the West Indies. Jea showed courage by accepting posts to Europe, South America, and the Far East.

Jea 's position as ship's cook was a common choice. As on land, there were institutionalized obstacles to blacks' advancement on ships. The United States Navy, for example, refused to enlist blacks after 1799. With the rare exception of Paul Cuffe, blacks could not captain or hold petty officer posts even on small vessels. Despite such discrimination, seafaring provided black sailors with more autonomy than on land. Black sailors lived in the fo'c'sle (or forecastle), a part of the ship by custom off-limits to the captain and his officers. Similarly, the dog-watch at twilight time was free from managerial interference. A third such area was the kitchen. Because blacks virtually always held the post of cook, with many from Africa, shipboard fare was black controlled.[81]

For blacks, following the sea brought an income, personal freedom, and importantly for these early narratives, mental and spiritual enrichment by association with other sailors. Among the most republican of laborers, white and black sailors formed dyadic relationships. Such friendships went far beyond the antislavery pronouncements of early Methodist leaders to inspire genuine racial equality. Shipboard often became a place of open exchange, of teaching and learning. This exposure to the currents of transatlantic religious radicalism shaped Jea's theology. Its wake is evident in his narrative.[82]

Seafaring figures prominently in the narratives of Britton Hammon, John Marrant, Ottobah Cuguano, Oludah Equiano, James Albert Ukawsaw Gronniosaw, and Venture Smith. For Africans, the sea had material and magical powers. As Melville Herskovits relates, in "ceremony after ceremony witnessed among the Yoruba, the Ashanti, and in Dahomey, one invariable element was a visit to the river or some other body of 'living water.'" Among African tribes from Jea's birthplace, Callabar, water deities were the most powerful.[83] Jea transformed this African cosmology about the sea into God's power. Echoing similar stories of Gronniosaw and Hammon, Jea initially had difficulty with irreligious sailors, but after God intervened, he was able to impress upon them the power God's grace. The sea, as a representation of eternity, was the locus of God's retribution on sinners.[84]

In his narrative and in several of his hymns, Jea describe his seaborne adventures. On every occasion Jea preached the gospel to disbelieving crews. On his first miserable sea voyage, Jea's shipmates castigated him as Jonah, the symbol of bad luck, and threatened to heave him overboard. A providential God assured Jea of his chosen position by smashing his doubters with terrible vengeance. Struck by lightening or cast into the sea, Jea's doubters suffered God's awesome anger.[85]

Seafaring brought Jea to Ireland and England, where his travels retraced closely the itinerancy of Lorenzo Dow in 1805 and 1806. Estimates of Jea's visits place him virtually on Dow's heels as he burned his way across these outlying, poorly churched districts. Jea's years on the road and at sea nearly matched John Wesley's indefatigable efforts.[86]

During a period of receding Anglican influence and rising republican radicalism, unlicensed and unpaid itinerants made special efforts to fill gaps in working-class society and preached their way across the length and breadth of England. The results were an alloy of popular and often mystical beliefs with radical Methodism. Parishioners, who increasingly disliked educated clergy, preferred itinerants who spoke of wondrous signs and prophetic dreams.[87] Itinerant preachers electrified their British audiences with hallucinatory visions, trances, and direct supernatural activities. These early manifestations of Primitive Methodism veered into Pentecostalism, a radical form of ecstatic Christianity. For Jea, however, the Pentecostal moments recalled his childhood Pinkster celebrations.[88]

Rebirth was a recurrent theme in Jea's sermons. In a heated dispute with a conservative Methodist in Sunderland, England, Jea poured out his identification with Lazarus. The story of Lazarus of Bethany, chiefly found in John 11:1–44, was the last of Jesus' miracles and was key to both Jea's and White's theology. Lazarus was the brother of Martha and Mary, and intimate friend of Jesus, who raised him from the dead. It was the act of raising Lazarus that gave Jesus much support among the Jews and raised the demands that he be put to death.[89]

The parable of Lazarus was a staple of Methodist hymns and camp-meeting sermons and was introduced into the religion by Charles Wesley. In Wesley's vision, Lazarus represents the resurrection of humanity and forgiveness of its sins.[90] The story of Lazarus is the climax in a series of signs of Jesus' power and love. Previously exhibited as the fountain of living water, as the light of the world, and as the good shepherd, in the Lazarus parable Jesus set forth the ultimate gift of resurrection and eternal life, an image especially attractive to African-Americans.[91]

Jea's use of Lazarus was an early manifestation of an important intellectual tradition. Black religious narratives, in company with Methodist accounts of salvation, commonly identified themselves with biblical figures. John Marrant identified with Christ, Jonah, and the Prodigal Son. Britton Hammon envisioned himself as the biblical hero, David embattled with the Philistine giant. James Albert Ukawsaw Gronniosaw found scriptural parallels between his own life and that of Isaiah.[92]

Unlike the heroic personifications in other black narratives, Jea's choice was one of the most abject figure in the Bible. Jea, who identified with Lazarus, made constant references to physical and spiritual rebirth, an image undoubtedly attractive to poor blacks. Methodist clerics even referred to blacks as Lazarus.[93] In reaction to being told by his master that he had no soul, Jea equated his own rebirth with Lazarus' revival.

Jea also referred to Lazarus the Leper, the true Christian in a parable of rich and poor. In a dramatic narration in Luke 16:19–31, Christ compared a wealthy man with his fine linen of purple, who spends each day in carousing, to a beggar, covered with sores, cast helpless at the other man's gate. The beggar yearned for crumbs that fell from the rich man's table, but received none and was left to the dogs. In the hereafter, Lazarus the beggar sat at the heavenly banquet while the rich man waited desperately for a drop of water.[94] This parable of the virtuous acceptance of poverty and the eternal punishment of the greed was a familiar one to republican-minded black and white Methodists in early nineteenth-century America.

In a debate in Liverpool, Anglican ministers, anxious about the incursions of radical itinerants, openly questioned Jea's ability to interpret the Bible. Jea again used the image of Lazarus to reply. He asked "are you laying in the grave of sin and wickedness? For many have been laying in that state . . . stinking in the nostrils of the Almighty God. . . ." In his debate with the Anglican Mr. Chittle, Jea defeated his opponent by arguing that God "has opened his grave in which he had once lain stinking in the nostrils of God."

The rebirth of Lazarus was a symbol of the slave's emergence both in God's grace, but also into Western society. Orlando Patterson's theory of slavery as social death helps us understand Jea's evocation. Patterson argued that the "slave was ritually incorporated as the permanent enemy on the inside—the domestic enemy." As a product of a hostile, alien culture, the slave was an intruder in the sacred space. Marginality characterized the slave's existence. At the same time, eighteenth-century European-American denominations agonized over means for incorporating the slave into society. As Frank Klingberg commented, catechism and baptism for the slave were ascending steps into white society. Even after acceptance into the church, however, blacks remained peripheral and were relegated to "negro pews."[95]

The master's power rested in the institutionalized marginality of the slave. By regarding the slave as incapable of full comprehension of

God's word, slave owners gained religious sanction. Such "social death" is precisely what Jea contested in his sermons about Lazarus. The power of God through the mystical actions of Jesus was so omnipotent that any person, no matter how lowly or "dead," could be raised into salvation and eternal life. Even slaves received God's grace. Even a "lowly African preacher," as Jea described himself, could minister His message and through God be legitimized in society.

Later African-Americans used the parable of Lazarus to combine Christian redemption with their hope that after death as slaves, they would be reborn home in Africa. A Port Royal slave women idealized the death of Lazarus:

> I want to die (Titty 'Ritta die like-a Lazarus die)
> [I want to] like-a Lazarus die;
> I want to die like-a Lazarus die
> like-a Lazarus die, like-a Lazarus die.[96]

This theme culminates in Henry Ossawa Tanner's masterpiece, *The Resurrection of Lazarus*. Tanner, an African-American whose father was a minister, fervently believed that artists could adapt biblical parables to illustrate the hopes and struggles of African-Americans. In *The Resurrection of Lazarus*, Tanner, by portraying onlookers as both black and white, celebrated the black rebirth in the Emancipation Proclamation.[97]

After his heated exchanges with Anglican orthodoxy, Jea returned to the sea. In 1807, his ship was part of the English fleet involved in the disastrous invasion of Buenos Aries.[98] In 1810, a French privateer captured Jea, working as a cook aboard the British ship, *Iscet of Liverpool*, near the English port of Torbay. First placed in ship galleys, Jea was later imprisoned in Brittainy. In the prison at Morlaix, an American consul, seeking sailors for warships in the War of 1812, offered freedom to Jea and others in exchange for their labor. Jea, describing himself as a "poor black African, a preacher of the gospel," refused. Asked to minister to the American crew, he declared "far be it for me to ever fight against Old England, unless it be with the sword of the gospel, under the captain of our salvation, Jesus Christ." Using the republican language of early American Methodism and echoing a loyalism that harkened back to the Revolution, Jea condemned the American vessel as a "floating hell," under the "banner of the tyrants of the world."[99]

The American consul vowed to "cool [Jea's] negro temper," but failed because Jea, as a radical Methodist and firm opponent of slavery, felt that persecution had a salutary effect on a godly life. Republicanism gave a political message to Jea's staunch faith and cognizance of sin. To Jea, restoration of true Christianity required the abolition of slavery. His sharp confrontation with American officials conveys how deeply felt was his African-American liberation Christianity. Decades before David Walker and Frederick Douglass, Jea used slavery to divide good and bad Christians. He believed that God punished slaveholders and insured freedom for the oppressed.[100]

An important secondary feature of Jea's message was that England was a better friend to blacks than the new democracy of the United States. Discounting the earlier role England played in the slave trade, African-Americans combined the enticements England used to secure black military service in the American Revolution with the liberalism of Granville Sharp, John Clarkson, and the Clapham Group which sought the legal extinction of slavery in England and, eventually, the international slave trade. Reinforced during the War of 1812 by British promises of freedom to slaves who rebelled against their American masters, by the second decade of the nineteenth century, England was dearest in the hearts of African-American leaders. The black radical David Walker declared the English "the best friends the coloured people have."[101]

A third and highly unique aspect of Jea's uncompromising defiance is the strong hint of anarchist pacifism. Jea made plain his respect for the English, but identifies himself as "a poor black African, *a preacher of the gospel*" and declares that he "would rather suffer any thing than fight or kill any one," except with "the sword of the gospel." Jea's antiauthoritarianism was common among sailors, but his pacifism was unique.[102]

After gaining his freedom without compromising his opposition to serving on an American ship, Jea eventually found succor in the ancient neighborhood of Portsea in Portsmouth, England. He apparently desired to retire from seafaring and initiate the arduous task of converting the population of this brawling seaport. Portsea was a scruffy, dangerous harbor rife with religious and political radicalism in the early nineteenth century. Later known as the birthplace of Charles Dickens, whose family lived near Jea, Portsmouth attracted a picaresque clientele of sailors and prostitutes. One observer in this period wrote that Portsmouth was "not only filthy and crowded, but crowded with a class of low and abandoned beings, who seem to have declared war against every habit of common decency and decorum." He noted that "the riotous, drunken, and immoral scenes of this place, perhaps exceed all

Generally recognized as African-American artist Henry Osawa Tanner's masterpiece, *The Resurrection of Lazarus*, painted in 1896, portrays the theme of rebirth that Jea invokes in his narrative. Tanner portrays the gathering of onlookers as interracial.

others." Life in Portsmouth was not only immoral but highly dangerous. Prostitutes, preying upon sailors, relieved them of the "wages of a long and dangerous cruise." Press gangs operated frequently in the town and unsolved murders and robberies were common.[103] As in most ports, black sailors were common in Portsmouth and seen by some as the cause of much trouble. Newspaper stories of a notorious murder in 1815 reported that blacks were "latterly seen in great numbers in this town."[104]

The city's immorality attracted itinerant clerics intent upon saving desperate souls. George Whitefield visited Portsmouth several times in the 1750s, but the most attentive was Methodist divine John Wesley who preached in Portsmouth more than thirty times over a forty year period. He, for example, inspired the local itinerant John Pounds who taught children to read with discarded bits of paper, newssheets, hand-bills, and posters.[105]

As a hotbed of religious activity, Portsmouth and nearby communities became arenas of religious crisis within the Methodist church. Francis Asbury and John Wesley never desired a permanent rupture from the Church of England and as a result, Methodism had become increasingly hierarchical and less evangelical. This was in contrast with pietistic Methodism practiced in the United States where the chief conciliation to changing times was softened opposition to slavery. In England, however, splinter groups disgruntled with increasingly mainstream Methodism continued to push God's work through revivals and camp meetings. The absence of censorship and the easy availability of cheaply printed newspapers, magazines, and pamphlets insured the circulation of an astonishing range of religious beliefs.[106]

As Wesleyan Methodism entered a decade of increasingly rigid conservatism after 1810, numerous splinter groups emerged. Methodists dissatisfied with hierarchy in the church could turn to Bible Christians, Tent Methodists, Methodist New Connection, Independent Methodists and, the most influential, Primitive Methodists. Founded by the Englishman Hugh Bourne and the American charismatic, Lorenzo Dow, Primitive Methodists relied upon visions, glossolalia, constant reference to the Bible for revelation of truth, and reliance on female preachers. Less charitable observers criticized the Primitive Methodists for their emotional excesses and the interminable length of their sermons.[107]

Historians have long associated the Primitive Methodists and other splinter groups with working-class radicalism.[108] As the Methodist church constructed standards for preachers, forbade use of unofficial hymnals (like Jea's), and banned camp meetings, more radical Methodist attracted large followers seeking the church of Wesley's day. These splinter Methodists continued the use of camp meetings and held the door open to unlicensed preachers like Jea.[109] Like evangelicals in America, their principal means of recruitment was the camp meeting with its day-long sermons and personalized hymns.[110] Many of these hymns reflect a spirit of openness and acceptance of all people. One hymn used frequently at camp meetings urged Christians be "united and free from bigotry." A second hymn entitled "The New African Hymn" emphasized "The Pleasant Road to Canaan" where despite a tedious journey and many dangers, "The Lord has brought us through."[111]

The Wesleyan church in its growing conservatism rarely sanctioned marginal preachers like Jea. But in the intellectually tumultuous atmosphere of Portsmouth, Jea found the audience for his theology, his hymns, and his narrative. He, of course, differed from English itinerants by race, background, and critical social attitudes; and sponsorship of his work undoubtedly came from one or more radical Methodists seeking to reinvigorate the denomination's attack on slavery.

Political attitudes in England during the first decades of the nineteenth century encouraged publication of black memoirs. English society had long debated the place of Africans and slavery in society and the narratives contributed to this debate. There were two types of African narratives printed in England in the eighteenth century. First were works by elite servants, "student princes," whose demonstrated mental abilities, as Keith Sandiford has observed, helped ameliorate English attitudes toward blacks. In this class fell Ignatious Sancho, Julius Soubise, Philip Quaque, and the American poet, Phyllis Wheatley.[112]

As liberal English society prepared its brief against slavery, a second type of African-English writer gained acceptance and publication. With the growth of the British abolitionist movement and as blacks demonstrated in the American Revolution and in the migration to Sierra Leone keen interest in republican egalitarianism, more militant, antislavery black writers appeared. Ottubah Cuguano, for example, used the Bible to refute pro-slavery arguments, found slavery inconsistent with Christianity, and argued that God's favor tilted towards Africans because of the grave injustices slavery imposed upon them.[113]

Olaudah Equiano, a black sailor, whose work most closely anticipates Jea's, used his emergence from slavery as proof of his Christian value. Reversing pro-slavery ridicule of blacks, he compared the humility, cleanliness and modesty of African men and women with the vulgarity of slaveholders.[114]

Cuguano and Equiano gained legitimacy through education and Christianity, and publication through the patronage of whites. By the early nineteenth century less reputable blacks published work in England. Robert Wedderburn, for example, son of an English merchant and a black slave, balanced a career between crime and Wesleyan ministry, and published numerous pamphlets between 1800 and 1820.[115]

Because Jea was too poor and transient to be listed in any tax roles in this period, it is unclear how he could finance his two publications within the same year.[116] In the Preface to his book of hymns, Jea makes an oblique reference to his situation: "For many years I have been importuned by a number of respectable and religious friends to publish such a book of hymns." Patrons of enthusiastic ministers were common, and it is likely that Jea found someone (or a number of people) to sponsor his publications. Who that person or group was remains unknown.[117]

Although Jea acknowledges an amanuensis, it is unlikely that it was the publisher. James Williams of Portsea specialized in lottery tickets, cheap paperbacks, and children's books. Selling most of his productions at six pence, Williams printed plagiarized versions of *Fanny Hill*, *Moll Flanders*, *Robinson Crusoe*, and assorted dream books, jest books, and accounts of famous murders.[118]

There is some dispute about the publication date of Jea's narrative. The British Museum and the Bodleian Library at Oxford University list 1800 as the date of initial publication long before Jea arrived in England. Also, Williams printed a catalog on the back of *The History of the . . . Murders of Mr. William Galley and Mr. Daniel Chater,* printed about this time, which does not list either of Jea's works. The British Library copy has a better indication of date of publication. A Portsea baker, grocer, and bookseller, T. Saunder, stamped sale of the book to an unknown person and inscribed it with an illegible name "his book, Portsea, 1817." This suggests, at least, that Jea's narrative was still in print in at that time.

How long Jea remained in Portsmouth is unclear. Two brief announcements punctuate our knowledge of his career. In the first, on October 28, 1816, John Jea, "African Preacher, of Portsea," announced his fourth marriage to Jemima Davis of Frackwell Heath in Hempstead County, England. The following year, John and Jemima Jea baptized their child Hephzabah on September 25, 1817, at St. John's, an Anglican chapel in the parish of Portsea.[119]

These fragments are the last we know of John Jea. His poverty may have forced him back to the sea despite his age. Blacks worked as ordinary mariners far longer than whites. There is no way to speculate whether Jea found the watery grave which he feared or made his way to some distant port where he could preach the gospel. Black life expectancy was not much beyond forty in the early nineteenth century; and for itinerants, the hardship of the road, bad food, and illness meant he had little expectation of old age. By the time history swallowed Jea, he was an old man by standards of his time and profession.[120]

IV

Since their first efforts in the late 1940s, scholars writing on African-American autobiography have concentrated on two aspects: the greater exposure of the genre and, second, the development of an African-American identity. Although scholars uncover new narratives annually, many of the over six thousand examples remain undiscussed and much critical energy remains concentrated on better-known antebellum works.[121]

The narratives of Jea and White provide firm evidence of developing African-American theology; and analysis of the texture of their beliefs greatly amplifies our understanding of that theology in this period. Grafted onto Protestant tenets, Jea's and White's ideological positions on slavery, baptism, resurrection, and death are all couched in biblical terms and represent a nascent, African-American religious doctrine. Their examples demonstrate that blacks, turning away from increasingly racist white congregations, sustained an African-American syncretism of early Christianity. This particular amalgam of antislavery politics and religion presages a form of liberation theology.

The two works must be considered in the evolution of the black American intellectual tradition. Their extensive biblical quotations and their religious tone clearly mark the two autobiographies as bridges between eighteenth-century spiritual narratives and the politically motivated, abolitionist works of the antebellum period.

Although the techniques used by Jea and White are similar to those of other early African-American narrators, Francis Foster has argued that late colonial black autobiographies differ from earlier black writings by showing remarkable independence. The late colonial narrators placed themselves at the center of the narrative and used their lives to make observations about their world. Such authors related a chronological sequence of personal experiences liberally spiced with religious, philosophical, and political observations. Reflecting the mutual influences of the Great Awakening and the American Revolution, the narrators asserted themselves as Christians and as individuals with personal liberties. Denial of these rights by the institution of slavery was unfair and unchristian in their cosmology. God's instructions sanctioned rebellion against such restrictions. This focus on the struggle for freedom shows the beginning of the authors' identification as rebellious and independent.[122]

In his autobiography and, later, in his book of hymns, Jea melds African spiritualism and American Protestantism. Jesus Christ was his lens for interpreting the world. Jea used biblical imagery and the popular evangelical language of radical Methodism to define his life and the world around him. White, in turn, used a combination of formal Methodist language with highly charged evangelical methods to convey his cosmology. When speaking to the Methodist hierarchy, White used what Russell Richey has termed episcopal language; but, in his preaching, he resorted to popular, evangelical language and its methods of shouts, trances, call and response, and jerks associated with the religion of Lorenzo Dow and with African-American Christianity.[123]

Both Jea's and White's narratives also fit within four broader literary traditions: New England hagiography, John Bunyan's parables of life, the picaresque tradition, and African autobiography. Calvinist writers of early New England assembled evidence of God's favor toward them and spent much of their work on the question of divine grace. In Puritan autobiography, personal chronology was less important than descriptions of acts of providence, God's tests of the sinner, and the author's eventual salvation.[124] Other similarities between Puritan autobiography and that of Jea and White included the shared metaphors of Christian salvation and personal freedom, direct admonitions to the reader, and a spiritual interpretation of both personal and worldly events. Invariably this typology worked within an interpretive framework emphasizing the significance of the Scripture and the ubiquity of God's providence.

A second, if indirect, Puritan influence on their work was John Bunyan. Bunyan recreated the vision of life's pilgrimage for the ordinary man and woman. Using dream-visions, as Thomas Cole has argued, Bunyan portrayed the universal quest for salvation amidst the local settings of daily life.[125] Jea and White illuminate the African-Christian search for truth in the fields and streets, on shipboard, and in the marketplace. Their personal tales become metaphors for life's pilgrimage toward salvation.

Although White's narrative has elements of the picaresque, John Jea is a much better example of how blacks reworked this genre. In picaresque accounts the narrator builds a compelling portrait of realistic detail designed to illustrate the brutality and inhumanity of the victim's life.

Events are episodic and coincidences underscore the chaos and decadence of the world. Except for references to divine intervention, there is little regard for causality. The picaresque allows the narrator, who is engaged in a desperate battle for survival, to put on a deceptive mask, and express contempt for the hypocrisy in society. As Charles H. Nicolls has argued, the slave narrator as picaroon punctures the inflated rhetoric and empty boasts of the slave master. Most slave narrators, Nicolls points out, use comic irony to help the reader grasp the bitterness and intensity of their struggle for existence. In his struggle for God's grace and human dignity in a racist world, Jea employs anger and indignation in the effort to resurrect and legitimize himself.[126]

Echoing these European literary traditions does not diminish the African qualities of Jea and White. As James Olney has observed, although most narrators were quite young when they were captured into slavery, they had already embraced African religious tenets. Jea, who left Africa when very young, lived, for most of his early life, among his African family and among a dynamic African-American community. White lived on southern plantations, which were replete with surviving African ways. Despite the Christianized, half-removed character of their lives, African theological methods imbued their narratives. There is a communality of existence unknown in the western world evident in their stories. Explaining the gaps in personal detail, their individual chronologies have less meaning than the shared events and fabulous adventures which illustrate God's direct intervention with his people. As Olney notes, Africans wrote autobiographies to preserve a disappearing world, to describe the African milieu for outside readers, and to describe a representative case of a particularly African experience. Their messages were located in individual experiences and in shared and universally comprehended rituals. Meaning existed only in God. Such stories have a social as well as historical meaning.[127]

Further, Jea and White incorporated into their ministry the concept of Christ's second coming. These millennial thoughts and political ideals coalesced into a single revolutionary ideology. Historians have argued that blacks were disinterested in millennial thought. Jea and White, however, demonstrate that African-Americans could combine antislavery ideology with the perfectionism of revolutionary millennialism. Black Americans adopted the jeremiad by combining the belief that they were a chosen people with the hope that social liberation and redemption awaited them.[128]

White and Jea traveled contrasting paths toward an African-American fusion of Methodist evangelicalism, radical republicanism, and black Christianity. White's narrative tells much about the trials of black preachers seeking acceptance within the institutionalized Methodist clergy. He lived and worked among the first generation of organized African-American Christians and took part in the construction of the African Methodist church. His theological emphasis on the "Strait Gate" anticipates the development of middling rank black Christians striving to assimilate in an Anglo-American society. At the same time, White brings to Methodism the African spiritual gifts of visions, trances, and shouts.

John Jea's career and theology were far less institutional than White's. Jea was rarely associated with a church, and it is doubtful that he ever attempted to become a licensed preacher. His combination of bible-oriented, visionary pietism and magic emphasized the supremacy on earth of God's word and intervention. Jea transformed this personal evangelism into a radical republican attack on slavery. His vision of the rebirth of Africans using the parable of Lazarus is a prelude to the black Pentecostalism associated with radical evangelists later in the century. The narratives of Jea and White lead in many directions; and their modes of salvation and belief extend from African folkways through Methodism to the roots of modern Pentecostalism.[129]

Jea and White were highly pietistic, desiring in their theologies to return to the sincerity, beliefs, and methods of the early church. As Methodists, both experienced what Clarke Garrett has described as the paradox of pietism. Pietism expected the divinely induced regeneration to be collective and universal, and at the same time absolutely personal, through God's entering the heart of the individual believer. Further, as Nathan O. Hatch has demonstrated about American pietism, collective beliefs gradually gave way to authoritarian structures. Jea and White, as African-American itinerants, worked within a church originally noted for its egalitarian views of salvation, but which hardened on the question of slavery and black representation. Eventually, the Methodist church in America would fracture over slavery. Blacks retained Methodist abolitionist attitudes long after the church had parted from earlier positions on slavery. Jea and White identified themselves as Methodists because the church originally offered room for their theologies, and they left when racism offended their nationalism.[130]

The direct influence of the two narratives on subsequent African-

American autobiographies is more elusive. There are no references to either work in the many narratives of fugitive blacks written during the antebellum period. Jea's books, published in England, were probably unknown to American readers; and there were no subsequent reprintings of White's narrative. The two works, however, exist within a tradition of African-American ideology and experience. White's travails with the Methodist church anticipate the later works of James W. C. Pennington, Samuel Ringgold Ward, and Frederick Douglass' second autobiography.[131] Jea clearly anticipates Douglass' brilliant discussion of Christianity and slavery; and Jea's experiences with his masters are earlier versions of Douglass' classic confrontation with Mr. Covey, the pious Methodist and vicious slavedriver. A less obvious comparison with Jea is the narrative of Sojourner Truth.[132] Jea and Truth spent their early years as slaves of Dutch Reformed slave masters in New York. Both were deeply pentacostal and experienced literacy as an emancipating miracle. Through literacy and religion, Jea and Truth found salvation and liberty.

Jea and White fused the religious quests of colonial African-American narrators with the secular pursuit of freedom exemplified by antebellum slave autobiographers. In the early nineteenth century the messages of revolutionary republicanism and evangelical Protestantism created a theology and politics of liberation. The narratives of Jea and White signify how African-Americans both adopted these powerful forces and charged them with the historical experiences of Africa, the Diaspora, and the ascent from slavery. They stand as testament to the African experience in America.

In preparing this edition of the two narratives I have endeavored to remain true to John Jea's wishes not to "allow alterations to be made by the person whom I employed to print this narrative."[133] Thus I retained the original wording, syntax, punctuation, and composition. Where the text was illegible, I have inserted brackets to indicate the missing word or phrase. Misspellings remain uncorrected, and I have tried to indicate inaccurate dates and distances in footnotes. Whenever possible I have identified individuals, places, hymns, and biblical verses that appear in the narratives.

Notes

1. [John Jea], *The Life, History, and Unparalleled Sufferings of John Jea, the African Preacher* (Portsea, England, c.1815). Copies are in the collections of the British Library, Bodleian Library at Oxford University, and Columbia University. For excerpts from Jea, see Henry Louis Gates, Jr., *The Signifying Monkey: A Theory of African-American Criticism* (New York, 1988), 158–69 and Paul Edwards and David Dabydeen, *Black Writers in Britain 1760–1890* (Edinburg, 1991), 117–27. [George White], *A Brief Account of the Life, Experience, Travels and Gospel Labours of George White, An African Written by Himself and Revised by a Friend* (New York, 1810). Copies of White's narrative are at Columbia University, the New-York Historical Society, Howard University Library, and the United Library of Garrett-Evangelical and Seabury-Western Theological Seminaries in Evanston, Illinois. White's narrative was reprinted on microfilm in 1980.

2. For transformation of American republicanism, see Nathan O. Hatch, *The Democratization of American Christianity* (New Haven, Conn., 1989) as well as Roger Finke and Rodney Starke, "How the Upstart Sects Won America: 1776–1850," *Journal for the Scientific Study of Religion*, 28 (1989), 27–44. For the latest summary of republicanism, see Gordon S. Wood, *The Radicalism of the American Revolution* (New York, 1992). The work of Marcus Rediker and Peter Linebaugh has influenced my understanding of Atlantic basin radicalism. See Rediker, "Good Hands, Stout Heart, and Fast Feet: The History and Culture of Working People in Early America," and Linebaugh, "All the Atlantic Mountains Shook," both in *Labour/Le Travialleur*, 10 (1982), 87–144 and Marcus Rediker and Peter Linebaugh, "The Many-Headed Hydra: Sailors, Slaves, and the Atlantic Working Class in the Eighteenth Century," *Journal of Historical Sociology*, 3 (1990), 225–52. For an earlier period, see John Thornton, *Africa and Africans in the Making of the Atlantic World, 1400–1680* (New York, 1992). For the impact of the Haitian Revolution on black Methodism, see Bishop William J. Walls, *The African Methodist Episcopal Zion Church: Reality of the Black Church* (Charlotte, N.C., 1974), 42. For a general treatment, see Robin Blackburn, *The Overthrow of Colonial Slavery, 1776–1848* (London, 1988), 161–265.

3. For coverage of Jones and Allen, see Carol V. George, *Segregated Sabbaths: Richard Allen and the Rise of Independent Black Churches, 1760–1840* (New York, 1973); Gary B. Nash, *Forging Freedom: The Formation of Philadelphia's Black Community 1720–1840* (Cambridge, Mass., 1988), 100–34, 192–99; for Marrant, see Margaret Washington Creel,*"A Peculiar People": Slave Religion and Community-Culture Among the Gullahs* (New York, 1988), 104–06.

4. For revision of historical attitudes towards slavery in the North, see Shane White, *Somewhat More Independent: The End of Slavery in New York City, 1770–1810* (Athens, Ga., 1991), 24–56.

5. Arthur Zilversmit, *The First Emancipation: The Abolition of Slavery in the North* (Chicago, 1967), 146–52; Rhoda Golden Freeman, "The Free Negro in Antebellum New York" (Ph.D. diss., Columbia University, 1966), 17–21.

6. For the ban on external slave trade and the end of manumission bond in New Jersey, see *Acts of the General Assembly of the State of New Jersey, 1786* [10th Session] (Trenton, 1786), 239–40.

7. *Reflections on the Inconsistency of Man Particularly Exemplified in the Practice of Slavery in the United States* (New York, 1796), 8, 15; White, *Somewhat More Independent*, 81–113.

8. "Register of Marriages," Trinity Church Archives, I, 104, 107, 149–295. Charles W. Andrews, *History of the New-York African Free Schools* (New York, 1830), 8–9, 31; "African Free School Records," 4 vols., Manuscripts, New-York Historical Society, I:4–10; Raymond A. Mohl, "Education as Social Control in New York City, 1784–1825," *New York History*, 51 (1970), 219–38.

9. Point made by comparison of church memberships with census listings and with Alice Eicholtz and James M. Rose, *Free Black Heads of Households in the New York State Federal Census, 1790–1830* (Detroit, 1981).

10. Sylvia Frey, *Water from the Rock: Black Resistance in a Revolutionary Age* (Princeton, N.J., 1991), 193–94, 245–46 and Frank Baker, "The Origins, Character, and Influence of John Wesley's 'Thoughts on Slavery,'" *Methodist History*, 22 (1984), 75–86.

11. For Wesley's poems, see S. T. Kimbrough and Oliver Beckerlegge, *The Unpublished Poems of Charles Wesley*, 3 vols. (Nashville, 1988–1992), I: 59–167; and Frank Baker, *Representative Verse of Charles Wesley* (Nashville, 1962), 310–40. For Methodism as alternative to American slavery, see Blackburn, *The Overthrow of Colonial Slavery*, 96–101.

12. For accounts of the black identification with the British and Methodism, see Ellen Wilson, *The Loyal Blacks* (New York, 1976), 82–83, 120–30; James W. St. G. Walker, *The Black Loyalists: The Search for a Promised Land in Nova Scotia and Sierra Leone* (New York, 1976), 65–74; and Lamont D. Thomas, *Rise to Be a People: Paul Cuffe Black Entrepreneur and Pan-Africanist* (Urbana, Ill. 1986), 77–78, 104–10.

13. Reverend J. B. Wakeley, *Lost Chapters Recovered in the Early History of American Methodism* (New York, 1858), 440–83. For black women, see Doris Elizabeth Andrews, "Popular Religion and the Revolution in the Middle Atlantic Ports: The Rise of the Methodists, 1770–1800" (Ph.D. diss., University of Pennsylvania, 1986), 227.

14. For Rankin quote and comments, see James D. Essig, *The Bonds of Wickedness: American Evangelicals Against Slavery, 1770–1808* (Philadelphia, 1982), 33–38.

15. For the most recent discussions of itinerancy in America, see Harry S. Stout, *The New England Soul: Preaching and Religious Culture in Colonial New England* (New York, 1986), 193–94. William Henry Williams, *The Garden of American Methodism: The Delmarva Peninsula, 1769–1820* (Wilmington, Del., 1984), 25–40; Hatch, *The Democratization of American Christianity*; Stephen A. Marini, "Evangelical Itinerancy in Rural New England: New Gloucester, Maine, 1754–1807," in Peter Benes, ed., *Itinerancy in New England and New York* (Boston, 1986), 65–76; and Timothy David Hall, "Contested Boundaries: Itinerancy and the Reshaping of the Colonial American Religious World" (Ph.D. diss., Northwestern University, 1991). For itinerancy in England, see Deryck W. Lovegrove, *Established Church, Sectarian People: Itinerancy and the Transformation of English Dissent, 1780–1830* (New York, 1988).

16. Hatch, *The Democratization of American Christianity*, 11, 17–36, 40–58.

17. For a description of Harry Hosier at camp meetings, see Reverend G. A. Raybold, *Reminiscences of Methodism in West Jersey* (New York, 1849), 165–68; *History of American Methodism*, 3 vols. (New York, 1964), 2:601–5; for comments on Hosier, see Hatch, *The Democratization of American Christianity*, 10; Donald G. Mathews, *Slavery and*

Methodism, A Chapter in American Morality, 1780–1845 (Princeton, N.J., 1965), 5, 9–10; Richard R. Wright, Jr., *The Centennial Encyclopedia of the African Methodist Episcopal Church* (Philadelphia, 1916), 13–15; and Lewis V. Baldwin, *"Invisible Strands in African Methodism": A History of the African Union Methodist Protestant and Union American Methodist Episcopal Churches, 1805–1980* (Metuchen, N.J., 1983), 24, 27.

18. William L. Andrews, *To Tell a Free Story: The First Century of African-American Autobiography, 1760–1865* (Urbana, Ill., 1986), 52–56. For similar comments on White's mission, see Marion Wilson Starling, *The Slave Narrative: Its Place in American History* (Washington, D.C., 1988, reprint edition), 87–88.

19. See Appendix 2 for membership.

20. Hatch, *The Democratization of American Christianity*, 106–8.

21. See for example the prescient points in Carter G. Woodson, *The History of the Negro Church* (Washington, D.C., 1921), 78–83. For an update on these ideas, see Hatch, *The Democratization of American Christianity*, 103–10.

22. Hatch, *The Democratization of American Christianity*, 107.

23. Gary B. Nash, "Forging Freedom: The Emancipation Experience in the Northern Seaport Cities, 1775–1820," in Ronald Hoffman and Ira Berlin, *Slavery and Freedom in the Age of the American Revolution* (Charlottesville, Va., 1983), 3–48; Timothy L. Smith, "Slavery and Theology: The Emergence of Black Christian Consciousness in Nineteenth Century America," *Church History*, 41 (1972), 497–98 .

24. Hamilton quoted in Walls, *African Methodist Episcopal Zion Church*, 138–40. For possible relation to Alexander Hamilton, see C. Peter Ripley et al., *The Black Abolitionist Papers*, 5 vols. (Chapel Hill, N.C., 1985–1992), III:359n.

25. For these comments, see Bruce Rosenberg, *Can These Bones Live? The Art of the American Folk Preacher* (Urbana, Ill., 1988 2nd ed.), 11–12, 28–19, 45–47, 50–53, 70–75; and Viv Edwards and Thomas J. Sienkewicz, *Oral Cultures Past and Present: Rappin' and Homer* (Oxford, 1990), 37–39, 58–74.

26. For "good talkers," see Edwards and Sienkewicz, *Oral Cultures*, 35. For Long Island preachers, see Hall, "Contested Boundaries," 1–2, 237–41. For Mark and Jenney, see *New York Gazetteer*, June 8, 1775. For another preacher, see *Pennsylvania Gazette* (Philadelphia), September 4, 1746. For the Maryland slave and several others, see Woodson, *The History of the Negro Church*, 62.

27. In the text, White mistakes "Essex" for "Esther." Ira Berlin, *Slaves Without Masters: The Free Negro in the Antebellum South* (New York, 1974), 45–49. For the petition, see Legislative Petition, Accomack County, June 3, 1782.

28. John Lednum, *A History of the Rise of Methodism in America from 1736 to 1785* (Philadelphia, 1859), 342–46. See also Williams, *The Garden of American Methodism*.

29. *The Trenton Mercury, and the Weekly Advertiser* , October 9, 1787.

30. For discussion of labor in rural New York and New Jersey, see Graham Hodges, "'Root and Branch': African-Americans in New York and Eastern New Jersey, 1613–1863," forthcoming, ch.9. For Methodists, see Reverend John Atkinson, *Memorials of Methodism in New Jersey* (Philadelphia, 1860), 125–30.

31. Clarke Garrett, *Spirit Possession and Popular Religion from the Camisards to the Shakers* (Baltimore, 1987), 20–21. For discussions of trances, see Gilbert Rouget, *Music and Trance: A Theory of the Relations between Music and Possession* (Chicago, 1985), 2–12. For the quotation, see White, *A Brief Account,* 53.

32. For class lists, see Methodist Episcopal Records, vol. 80, New York Public Library. For discussion, see Walls, *The African Methodist Episcopal Zion Church,* 44–48.

33. "Petition of the African Society on the Subject of Two Lots Purchased for a Burial Ground," June 22, 1795, New York Muncipal Archives; and *Minutes of the Common Council of the City of New York 1784–1831,* 21 vols. (New York, 1930), II: 112, 151, 158. For problems over the Negro Burial Ground, see I: 554, 598, 610, 663, 709–10, 739, 769; II: 22, 134, 218, 221, 252, 264. The burial ground has recently been rediscovered. For the fullest accounts, see *The New York Times*, October 9, 1991 and August 9, 1992.

34. For creation of the church, see Record of Religious Incorporation of the City of New York, March 9, 1800, vol. 1:28, New York Muncipal Archives. See also [Christopher Rush], *A Short Account of the Rise and Progress of the African Methodist Episcopal Church in America* (New York, 1843), 15, 21–23; Roi Ottley and W. J. Weatherby, *The Negro in New York* (New York, 1967), 55; W. E. B. DuBois, *The Negro Church, A Social Study* (Atlanta, 1903), 20, 45; Daniel A. Payne, *The Semi–Centenary and Retrospective of the African Methodist Church in the United States of America* (Baltimore, 1866), 20–21 and Wright, Jr., *The Centennial Encyclopedia*, 13.

35. "Methodist Marriage Register for the City of New York 1799," Methodist Episcopal Church Archives, vol. 72:1, NYPL.

36. See *Longworth's Directory of New York City in the United States of America* (New York, 1800–1834) and *Elliot's Improved New York "Double Directory" for 1812* (New York, 1812). In this latter directory White is listed as "coloured." For boardinghouses, see Elizabeth Blackmar, *Manhattan For Rent, 1785–1830* (Ithaca, N.Y., 1989), 60–63, 134–35.

37. White, *A Brief Account,* 54–56.

38. For Garretson, see Lednum, *A History,* 414. *The Dealings of God, Man, and the Devil as Exemplified in the Life, Experience, and Travels of Lorenzo Dow, in a Period of over Half a Century: Together with his Polemic and Miscellaneous Writings Complete to which is added the Vicissitudes of Life by Peggy Dow* (New York, 1852), 15, 16, 17, 22, 29. Dreams became motivating forces later for Rebecca Jackson, the black mystic and Shaker. See Jean McMahon Humez, *Gifts of Power: The Writings of Rebecca Jackson, Black Visionary, Shaker Eldress* (Amherst, Mass., 1981), 89–102, 108–14.

39. Robert Farris Thompson, *Flash of the Spirit: African and Afro–American Art and Philosophy* (New York, 1983), 180–81; Thornton, *Africa and Africans*, 242–45.

40. For shouts, see Sterling Stuckey, *Slave Culture: Nationalist Theory and the Foundations of Black America* (New York, 1987), 12, 24, 36, 43, 79, 89, 96; Creel, *"A Peculiar People,"* 297–302. For example of cultural adaptation in the New World, see the essays in Sandra T. Barnes, *Africa's Ogun, Old World and New* (Bloomington, Ind., 1989).

41. Baldwin, *Invisible Strands in African Methodism*, 138–40.

42. For Sister Henery's eulogy, see White, *A Brief Account,* 77–83; for White's attempts to receive a license, see 56–67. For discussion of black churches in one New Jersey county, see Graham Hodges, *African-Americans in Monmouth County, New Jersey, 1784–1860* (Lincroft, N.J., 1992), 13–16.

43. White, *A Brief Account*, 57. For Methodist anticlericalism, see Hatch, *The Democratization of of American Christianity*, 9, 12, 14, 22, *passim*.

44. These titles and others are summarized in Walls, *African Methodist Episcopal Zion Church*, 102–6.

45. For the list, see Daniel Coker, *A Dialogue Between a Virginian and an African Minister* (Baltimore, 1810), 41. For Liberia, see *Journal of Daniel Coker, A Descendant of Africa from the time of Leaving New York in the Ship Elizabeth, Captain Sebor, on a Voyage for Sherbro in Africa in Company with Three agents and about Ninety Persons of Color* (Baltimore, 1820).

46. Andrews, *To Tell a Free Story*, 48, 53–54.

47. For Totten's productions, see *The Moral and Religious Cabinet, Containing Short Accounts of Christian Experience Together with Instructions and Useful Extracts Intended to Promote Happiness of Pious Minds,* vol. 1 #1–26 (January–June, 1808); *A Collection of the Most Admired Hymns and Spiritual Songs, with the Choruses Affixed as usually Sung at Camp–Meetings &ct with others Suited to Various Occasions* (New York, 1809). Later editions appeared in 1811, 1813, 1815, 1818, and 1821. *New–York Methodist Tract Society*, #1–37 (New York, 1821–). See also John C. Tebbel, *A History of Book Publishing in the United States*, 4 vols. (New York, 1972), I: 165, 263, 327. For examples of Totten's publication of black writers, see Dorothy Porter, *Early Negro Writing, 1760–1837* (Boston, 1971), 42, 365, 459.

48. "New York State Methodist Episcopal Conference Journals, 1811–1815," 61, 66, 82, 96, Methodist Episcopal Church Records, vol. 2, NYPL.

49. Methodist Marriage Register for the City of New York, June 4, 1818, Methodist Episcopal Records, v. 72: 26; "Records of Baptisms," Hudson Street Methodist Church, March 5, 1820, Methodist Episcopal Record, v. 232, NYPL.

50. For discussion of shoemaking in this period, see R. Sean Wilentz, *Chants Democratic: New York City and the Making of the American Working Class, 1788–1850* (New York, 1984), 124–27; and Howard B. Rock, *Artisans of the New Republic: The Tradesmen of New York City in the Age of Jefferson* (New York, 1979), 248–68.

51. Rush, *A Short Account*, 35, 54 and Harry V. Richardson, *Dark Salvation: The Story of Methodism as it Developed Among Blacks in America* (Garden City, N.Y., 1976), 135–36.

52. Daniel A. Payne, *History of the African Methodist Episcopal Church* (Nashville, 1891), 31–34, 38.

53. "Trenton, New Jersey Circuit of the African Methodist Church, 1828–1848," Carter Woodson Papers, Library of Congress. For his expulsion, see "Thirteenth Annual Conference of the New York African Methodist Episcopal Church . . . 1834" in Porter, *Early Negro Writing*, 197. For his death, see New York County Deaths, X, New York Municipal Archives.

54. Daryll Forde, ed., *Efik Traders of Old Callabar* (London, 1956), 5–7.

55. Dabydeen, *Black Writers*, 117; and Gates, *Signifying Monkey*, 159.

56. Forde, *Efik Traders*, 20–21.

57. There are no listings for this Dutch couple in the 1790 or 1800 census. After much searching, I have concluded that Jea's owners were Albert and Anetje Terhune of Flatbush in Kings County (Brooklyn). Jea's corruption is fairly close to their name; their location and family size fits his description. For the Terhunes, see *Population Schedules of the Second Census of the United States, 1800*, National Archives (M32 r24 p4). Another clue is the presence nearby of Peter Lowe, the Presbyterian minister.

58. For discussion of slavery in Kings County, see White, *Somewhat More Independent*, 51–53.

59. For the constitution, see *Tricentenary Studies of the Reformed Church in America* (New York, 1918), 401; John Pershing Luidens, "The Americanization of the Dutch Reformed Church," (Ph.D. diss. University of Oklahoma, 1969), 331. For discussion of Dutch Reformed attitudes towards slaves in this period, see Hodges, *"Root and Branch,"* chs. 7–9. For a good recent discussion of the conservative nature of the Reformed church, see David G. Hackett, *The Rude Hand of Innovation: Religion and Social Order in Albany, New York, 1652–1826* (New York, 1991), 90–91, 146–47, 181–82.

60. For postwar staffing problems see Richard W. Pointer, *Protestant Pluralism and the New York Experience: A Study in Eighteenth-Century Religious Diversity* (Bloomington, Ind., 1988), 107–8.

61. For discussion of European religions and Pentecost, see Francis X. Weiser, *Handbook of Christian Feasts and Customs: The Year of the Lord in Liturgy and Folklore* (New York, 1974) and Bob Bushaway, *By Rite Custom, Ceremony and Community in England, 1700–1880* (London, 1982), 16–18, 37–47, 260–64. For folklore background of Pinkster, see Joel Munsell, *Annals of Albany*, 10 vols. (Albany, N.Y., 1855), V: 232–33.

62. A key description of Pinkster is in *Zenger's Weekly Journal* (New York), March 7, 14, 21, 28, 1737. Differing sides in the debate over Pinkster may be found in Stuckey, *Slave Culture*, 80, 142, 144, 160, 227, 296 and White, *Somewhat More Independent*, 95–106.

63. The key biblical passage on Pinkster is Acts 2:17–18. For a full discussion of the holiday, see A. C. Barnard, "Die Pinksterfees in Die Kerklike Jaar" (Ph.D. diss., University of Amsterdam, 1954), 14–22, 24–25, 32, 40, 45–46, 48, 54, 57. For Dutch traditions, see A. G. Roeber, "The Origin of Whatever is Not English among Us": The Dutch–Speaking and German–Speaking Peoples of Colonial British America," in Bernard Bailyn and Philip D. Morgan, *Strangers within the Realm: Cultural Margins of the First British Empire* (Chapel Hill, N.C., 1991), 220–84 and Roderic H. Blackburn and Ruth Piwonicke, *Remembrance of Patria: Dutch Arts and Culture in Colonial America, 1609–1776* (Albany, N.Y. 1988), 55–58.

64. Bernard, "Die Pinksterfees," 106; Sobel, *"Trabelin' On,"* 15–20; Hodges, "Root and Branch," chs. 5, 11. For union of Old and New Testament, see George A. Buttrick, ed., *The Interpreter's Bible: The Holy Scriptures in the King James and Revised Standard Versions. . . .* 12 vols. (Nashville, 1952–1964), IX: 39–42.

65. For discussions of the ecstatic nature of Pinkster, see Hodges, "Root and Branch," ch. 9. For hallucinatory methods in radical Methodism see E. P. Thompson, *The Making of the English Working Class* (New York, 1963), 42–52.

66. For this account, see John R. Tyson, ed., *Charles Wesley, A Reader* (New York, 1989), 92–111 and Kimbrough and Beckerlegge, *Unpublished Poetry*, II: 286–88.

67. Forde, *Efik Traders*, 22–25.

68. For discussions of the law regarding baptism and subsequent cultural disagreements, see Hodges, "Root and Branch," chs. 5, 11. For background on this law, see Albert J. Raboteau, *Slave Religion: The "Invisible Institution" in the Antebellum South* (New York, 1978), 98–99, 123–24, 227–28 and A. Leon Higginbotham, *In the Matter of Color, Race & the American Legal Process: The Colonial Period* (New York, 1978), 125–29.

69. For a good discussion of English cases and the development of this controversy, see F. O. Shyllon, *Black Slaves in Britain* (London, 1974), 17–19 and Blackburn, *Overthrow of Colonial Slavery*, 81–83.

70. Jea, *Life, History,* 112–16. For a discussion of this revelation of the "talking book," see Gates, *The Signifying Monkey,* 158–61. For a similar account of literacy through prayer, see Humez, *Gifts of Power,* 108.

71. Gates, *Signifying Monkey,* 131, 163–64. For comments on words and books, see Garrett, *Spirit Possession and Popular Religion,* 23–24, 106–8.

72. Dabydeen, *Black Writers,* 119–26.

73. See Harvey J. Graff, *The Legacies of Literacy: Continuities and Contradictions in Western Culture and Society* (Bloomington, Ind., 1987), 362–66; Cathy Davidson, *Revolution and the World: The Rise of the Novel in America* (New York, 1986), 56, 59 and Janet Duitsman Cornelius, *When I Can Read My Title Clear: Literacy, Slavery, and Religion in the Antebellum South* (Columbia, S.C.,1991), 59–85.

74. [John Jea], *A Collection of Hymns, Compiled and Selected by John Jea, African Preacher of the Gospel* (Portsea, England, 1816), 169. The only extent copy is in the collection of the Bodleian Library at Oxford University, England.

75. For a good discussion of the miracles and the African priest, see Thornton, *Africa and Africans,* 246–47.

76. For comment on Jea's lacking in common sympathy, see Dabydeen, *Black Writers,* 117. For flat impersonal nature of most narratives, see Francis Smith Foster, *Witnessing Slavery: The Development of Antebellum Slave Narratives* (Westport, Conn., 1979), 49.

77. Jea, *A Collection of Hymns,* 169, 175, 177.

78. Jea, *Life, History,* 117–18. For discussion of love feasts, see Jonathan Crowder, *A True and Complete Portraiture of Methodism or the History of the Wesleyan Methodists* (New York, 1813), 242–43 and Richey, *Early American Methodism,* 4–5.

79. For New Jersey seamen in Philadelphia, see Ira Dye, "Early American Merchant Seafarers," *Proceedings of the American Philosophical Society,* 120 (1976), 351; Billy G. Smith, *The "Lower Sort" Philadelphia's Laboring People, 1750–1800* (Ithaca, N.Y., 1990), 156–59. For black life in Boston and other New England ports, see William D. Piersen, *Black Yankees: The Development of an Afro-American Subculture in Eighteenth-Century New England* (Amherst, Mass., 1988), 14–25.

80. W. Jeffrey Bolster, "'To Feel Like a Man': Black Seamen in the Northern States, 1800–1860," *Journal of American History,* 76 (1990), 1173–99.

81. Bolster, "'To Feel Like a Man,'" 1179–85.

82. For comments on the relationships between white and black sailors, see Peter Linebaugh, *The London Hanged: Crime and Civil Society in the Eighteenth Century* (New York, 1992), 352–56.

83. Herskovits quoted in Stuckey, *Slave Culture,* 34. See also Rosalind I. J. Hackett, *Religion in Calabar: The Religious Life and History of a Nigerian Town* (Berlin, Germany, 1989), 26–30.

84. For sailor's irreligion, see Marcus Rediker, *Between the Devil and the Deep Blue Sea: Merchant Seamen, Pirates, and the Anglo-American Maritime World, 1700–1750* (Cambridge, England, 1987), 173–79, 185, 189, 201.

85. Jea, *A Collection of Hymns,* 173–74.

86. For Wesley's travels, see, among many sources, A. R. Ward, *Religion and Society in England, 1790–1850* (London, 1972), 76–88; Thompson, *The Making of the English Working Class,* 37–50; Lovegrove, *Established Church, Sectarian People,* 16, 31. For transat-

lantic revivalism, see Richard Carwardine, *Transatlantic Revivalism: Popular Evangelicalism in Britain and America, 1790–1865* (Westport, Conn., 1978).

87. For irreligion and rise of Primitive Methodist itinerants in the Midlands, see Ward, *Religion and Society in England, 1790–1850*, 39–43, 47–51; John Kent, *Holding the Fort: Studies in Victorian Revivalism* (London, 1978), 18–24, 40–41; David Hempton, *Methodism and Politics in British Society* (Stanford, Calif., 1984); Garrett, *Spirit Possession and Popular Religion*, 144–46.

88. Kent, *Holding the Fort*, 44–50.

89. For commentary on Lazarus, see Rev. Dr. R. Dunkerly, "Lazarus," *New Testament Studies*, 5 (1959), 321–27; F. L. Cross, ed., *The Oxford Dictionary of the Christian Church* (London, 1974), 806–7.

90. Kimbrough and Beckerlegge, eds. *The Unpublished Poetry of Charles Wesley*, 246–49; Tyson, *Charles Wesley*, 19, 162, 170, 296.

91. Buttrick, *Interpreter's Bible*, 9: 638–53 and Mark W. G. Stibbe, *John as Storyteller: Narrative Criticism and the Fourth Gospel* (New York, 1992), 78–84.

92. Angelo Costanzo, *Surprizing Narrative Olaudah Equiano and the Beginnings of Black Autobiography* (Westport, Conn., 1987), 94–109. See p. 63 for Equiano's similar problems with antagonistic sailors.

93. For studies of rising bigotry based on personal characteristics, see White, *Somewhat More Independent*, 56–79; Nash, *Forging Freedom*, 172–212 and Dana D. Nelson, *The Word in Black and White: Reading "Race" in American Literature, 1638–1867* (New York, 1992), 22–38. For clerical references, see *Methodist Magazine*, 26 (1803), 369.

94. Charles G. Herbermann, et al., *The Catholic Encyclopedia*, 16 vols. (New York, 1907–14), IX: 96.

95. For social death, see Orlando Patterson, *Slavery and Social Death: A Comparative Study* (Cambridge, Mass., 1982), 44–47; and for acculturation, see Frank Klingberg, *Anglican Humanitarianism in Colonial New York* (Philadelphia, 1940).

96. William F. Allen, ed., *Slave Songs of the United States* (New York, 1867), 98.

97. Dewey E. Mosby, ed., *Henry Ossawa Tanner* (Philadelphia, 1991), 135–39. See also Henry Osawa Tanner's fascinating article on Lazarus in *A.M.E. Church Review* (1898), 359–61. My thanks to Dewey Mosby for this reference.

98. For discussion of the invasion of Buenos Aires, see entry for "John Whitelock," in *Dictionary of National Biography*, 62 vols. (London, 1885–1900), LXI:119.

99. For republican language, see Richey, *Early American Methodism*, 84–88. For quotation, see Jea, *Life, History*, 155–57.

100. For republicansim and antislavery, see Essig, *The Bonds of Wickedness*, 43–52, 62, 94.

101. For recent commentary on English abolitionism in this period, see Blackburn, *Overthrow of Colonial Slavery*, 131–61. For Walker's quote, see Herbert Aptheker, ed., *"One Continual Cry": David Walker's Appeal to the Colored Citizens of the World. . .* (New York, 1965), 106.

102. There is very little work on pacifist anarchism in the early nineteenth century. For the anarchism of sailors, see Rediker, *Between the Devil*, 240–46.

103. For Dickens, see Michael Allen, "The Dickens Family at Portsmouth, 1807–1814," *The Dickensian*, 77:3 (1981), 131–44. For descriptions of conditions at Portsmouth, see William G. Gates, *Illustrated History of Portsmouth* (Portsmouth, England,

1900), 484–88, 542–46; W. H. Saunders, *Annals of Portsmouth* (London, 1850) and Alistair Geddes, "Portsmouth During the Great French Wars 1770–1800," *Portsmouth Papers*, 9 (1970), 18–20. For murders, see "Hants Newspaper Clipping File," 6 vols., Portsmouth Central Library.

104. *Hampshire Telegraph* (Portsmouth, England), August 23, 1815.

105. Laurence Isherwood, *Christianity Comes to Portsmouth* (Havant, England, 1975), 35–38.

106. Garrett, *Respectable Folly*, 147–50; Julia Stewart Werner, *The Primitive Methodist Connexion: Its Background and Early History* (Madison, Wis., 1984), 6–10.

107. For the Primitive Methodists, see Hugh Bourne, *History of the Primitive Methodists: Giving an Account of Their Rise and Progress up to the Year 1823* (Bemersley, England, 1823), 14–35; [John Walford], *Memoirs of the Life and Labours of the Late Venerable Hugh Bourne by a Member of the Bourne Family* (London, n.d.); John Petty, *The History of the Primitive Methodists Connexion from Its Origin to the Conference of 1859* (London, 1860). For recent work, see Werner, *The Primitive Methodist Connexion*; Ian Sellers, *Nineteenth Century Nonconformity* (London, 1972), 9–11; Kent, *Holding the Fort*, 38–52; Anthony Armstrong, *The Church of England, The Methodists and Society, 1700–1850* (London, 1973), 198–213; Ward, *Religion and Society*, 87–95; Thompson, *The Making of the English Working Class*, 388–97.

108. See especially Thompson, *Making of the English Working Class*, 44–50 and Iain McCalman, *Radical Underground Prophets, Revolutionaries and Pornographers in London, 1795–1840* (New York, 1988), 128–52.

109. Hatch, *The Democratization of Christianity*, 50; Kent, *Holding the Fort*, 58.

110. Bourne, *History of the Primitive Methodists*, 44–50 and Petty, *History of the Primitive Methodist Connexion*, 12–14.

111. Hugh Bourne, *A General Collection of Hymns and Spiritual Songs for Camp Meetings, Revivals, &ct, New Edition* (Bingham, England, 1819), hymns 41 and 42.

112. Keith Sandiford, *Measuring the Moment Strategies of Protest in Eighteenth-Century Afro-English Writing* (Selinsgrove, Pa., 1988), 38–42.

113. Sandiford, *Measuring the Moment*, 93–109. For an early example of this, see [Thomas Day], *The Dying Negro: A Poetical Epistle from a Black Who Shot Himself on Board a Vessel in the River Thames, to his Intended Wife* (London, 1774, 2nd ed.).

114. Sandiford, *Measuring the Moment*, 136–43. See also Catherine Acholonu, *The Igbo Roots of Qlaudah Equiano* (Owerr, Nigeria, 1989).

115. McCalman, *Radical Underworld Prophets*, 50–58. For the work of Robert Wedderburn, see *Horrors of Slavery and Other Writings*, ed. by Iain McCalman (Princeton, N. J., 1992).

116. In a baptismal announcement Jea lists his address as Spring Street, although there is no record of his habitation in any of the city tax lists from 1814 to 1820. See Rate Book, Portsmouth, 1814–1820, Portsmouth City Record Office.

117. Jea, *A Collection of Hymns.*

118. R. W. Wheeler, "The Booksellers and Booktrade of Portsmouth and Portsea, 1700–1850" (Diploma thesis, Portsmouth Polytechnic School of Social and Historical Studies, 1987), 29, 35–36, 66, 73.

119. For the marriages, see *Hampshire Telegraph*, October 28, 1816, in Marriage file in Portsmouth Central Library. For the baptism, see "Baptisms Solemnized in the St.

John's Chapel in the Parish of Portsea in the County of Southampton, in the year 1817," 268, Portsmouth City Record Office. For St. John's, see John Offord, *Churches, Chapels and Places of Worship on Portsea Island* (Portsmouth, England, 1989), 52.

120. Hatch, *The Democratization of American Christianity*, 87–89.

121. For review of the scholarship about black narratives, see William L. Andrews, "African-American Autobiography Criticism: Retrospect and Prospect" in Paul John Eakin, *American Autobiography Retrospect and Prospect* (Madison, Wis., 1991), 195–216. The major new synthesis of the African-American intellectual tradition is Stuckey, *Slave Culture.*

122. Foster, *Witnessing Slavery*, 43.

123. For the sources of my interpretations of Jea's Methodist techniques, see S. T. Kimbrough, Jr., "Charles Wesley as a Biblical Interpreter," *Methodist History*, 26 (1988), 139–53. For popular language of Methodism, see Richey, *Early American Methodism*, 87. For syncretic African–Christianity, see Creel, *"A Peculiar People,"* 259–76.

124. Daniel B. Shea, *Spiritual Autobiography in Early America* (Princeton, N.J., 1968), 87–91, 124–27, 146–50. Christopher Hill, *A Tinker and a Poor Man: John Bunyan and His Church, 1628–1688* (New York, 1989), 63–75.

125. Thomas R. Cole, *The Journey of Life: A Cultural History of Aging in America* (New York, 1992), 31, 40–42.

126. For the insights in this paragraph, see Charles H. Nicolls, "Slave Narrators and the Picaresque Mode," in Charles T. Davis and Henry Louis Gates, Jr., *The Slave's Narrative* (New York, 1985), 283–98.

127. Costanzo, *Surprizing Narrative*, 20–27 and James Olney, *Tell Me Africa: An Approach to African Literature* (Princeton, N.J., 1973), 27, 38, 47, 57–62 and Olney, *Metaphors of Self: The Meaning of Autobiography* (Princeton, N.J., 1972), 1–25, 39–40. A similar point about African preachers is made in Rosenberg, *Can These Bones Live?*, 50–53.

128. Costanzo, *Surprizing Narrative*, 11–12, 16–20; Wilson Jeremiah Moses, *Black Messiahs and Uncle Toms: Social and Literary Manipulations of a Religious Myth* (University Park, Pa., 1982), 30–31. For discussions of millenialism, see Ruth Bloch, *Visionary Republic: Millenial Themes in American Thought, 1756–1800* (New York, 1985), 45–47, 67–70, 80, 130–33.

129. Donald W. Dayton, *Theological Roots of Pentacostalism* (Metuchen, N.J., 1987), 35–63; Vinson Synan, *The Holiness–Pentacostal Movement in the United States* (Grand Rapids, Mich., 1971), 34–53.

130. Garrett, *Spirit Possession and Popular Religion*, 75.

131. James W. C. Pennington, *The Fugitive Blacksmith or Events in the History of James W. C. Pennington, Pastor of a Presbyterian Church, New York* (London, 1849, 2nd ed.); Samuel Ringgold Ward, *Autobiography of a Fugitive Negro: His Antislavery Labours in the United States, Canada & England* (London, 1855); Frederick Douglass, *My Bondage and My Freedom. Part 1. Life as a Slave. Part II. Life as a Freeman* (Auburn, N.Y., 1855).

132. [Olive Gilbert], *Narrative of Sojourner Truth, a Northern Slave, Emancipated from Bodily Servitude by the State of New York in 1828* (Boston: Yearlington, 1850).

133. Jea, *Life, History*, 159.

A

BRIEF ACCOUNT

OF THE

LIFE,

EXPERIENCE, TRAVELS,

AND

GOSPEL LABOURS

OF

GEORGE WHITE,

AN AFRICAN;

WRITTEN BY HIMSELF, AND REVISED BY A FRIEND.

God hath chosen the foolish things of the world to confound the wise: and base things of the world, and things that are despised, hath God chosen, yea, and things that are not, to bring to nought things that are: that no flesh should glory in his presence. St. Paul.

New-York:

PRINTED BY JOHN C. TOTTEN,

No. 155 Chatham-street.

1810.

George White

A Brief Account of the Life, Experience, Travels, and Gospel Labours of George White, An African

To The Reader.

As reading the account of the lives, and religious experience of others, has often quickened and comforted my own soul, and encouraged me in the way to heaven, I feel it my duty to present the friends of Jesus with a short detail of the dealings of God towards me; in my conversion, temptations, religious conflicts, call to preach, and sufferings therein; hoping to adminster some of those benefits to them, which I have derived from the writings of others on the same subject: to which I have subjoined with the same view, an account of the extraordinary death of two persons of my own acquaintance, the one very pious, and the other very wicked: as also some remarks on the subject of true happiness.

When I consider the station in which I am placed, and the obligations I am under, especially to my African brethren, I rejoice at every opportunity of facilitating their spiritual welfare and happiness. And should the present undertaking prove conducive thereto, the reader will do me the pleasure, to ascribe the honour and glory to God; while he enjoys the proposed benefit.

And that, whoever reads the following relation, may be blessed of God, and eternally saved in Jesus Christ, is the most affectionate and fervent prayer of their sincere friend and brother, in the kingdom and patience of Christ Jesus,

George White.
New-York, April 10, 1810.

Brief Account, &c.

My mother was a slave, belonging to an estate in the township of Accomack, state of Virginia, where I was born in the fall of 1764: but at the age of one year and a half, was torn from her fond embraces, and carried by my owner into Esther county; where I was kept until six years of age; being treated with a degree of indulgence, uncommon to the children of Virginian slaves. However, about this time, my master, for reasons best known to himself, sold me to a person in Sommerset county, state of Maryland; from whom I received much better treatment than is usual for Africans to meet with, in this land of human oppression and barbarity. Here I continued in servitude, until the fifteenth year of my age; when I was again made merchandize of, sold, and sent into Suffolk; where I continued under all severities of the most abject slavery, till I arrived at the twenty-sixth year of my age.

When about nineteen, the sympathy of nature, awakened in my mind, such a sense of filial affection, that the thoughts of my enslaved, but loving parents, deprived me of my necessary rest; and my frequent inquiries about, and earnest entreaties to visit them, though very offensive to my master, yet at length prevailed with him, to give me permission to return to the place of my nativity, to see my mother, who, as I was informed by one of her acquaintance, was yet living.

As my mother knew not what had become of me, the reader will easily imagine the affecting nature and circumstances of the scene of the first meeting, of a parent lost, and a child unknown; and both in a state of the most cruel bondage, without the means, or even hope of relief. But our joyful interview of mingling anguish, was of but short duration; for my condition, as a slave, would not admit of my prolonging the visit beyond the day appointed for my return: therefore we were obliged to undergo the painful sensations, occasioned by a second parting; and I, to return to my former servitude, in despair of ever obtaining an emancipation.

However, an infinitely wise disposer of all events, called my master to the world of spirits, when I was about twenty-six: and so far humanized his heart, that he left me free at his death; although it was with great difficulty, that I saved myself from the renewal of my thraldom, which was attempted by the heirs to his estate.

Perhaps nothing can be more conducive to vice and immorality, than a state of abject slavery, like that practised by the Virginia planters upon the degraded Africans: For being deprived by their inhuman masters and overseers, of almost every privilege and enjoyment, in their absence, without much restraint or reserve, fall into those practices, which are contrary to the well-being of society, and repugnant to the will of God, whenever opportunity offers.

By after I had obtained my freedom, (a blessing quite unexpected) I began to think, that as God in his providence had delivered me from temporal bondage, it was my duty to look to him for deliverance from the slavery of sin; that I might be prepared to make him suitable returns for so great a favour.

I had often attended public worship in the Church of England, but without any sufficient evidence of being benefited thereby. The Methodists happening about this time, to hold a quarterly meeting in Annimissick I repaired thither; and was considerably alarmed with a sense of my sins, and enabled to form resolutions for life, very different from those I had before.

Having now, no other master but him, whose protecting care had brought me to the present period, and had inspired my mind with a desire to seek his face, I felt anxious to become more acquainted with Christian people; and hearing that the Africans were treated with less severity and contempt in the northern, than in the southern states, I resolved to evade these scenes of brutal barbarity, which I had so long witnessed in my native land, and so set off for the city of New-York: which place, however, I did not reach till about three years after; finding good employ in the interim, at Philadelphia, and in the state of New-Jersey, which induced me to tarry at those places.

In the year 1791, it pleased my Almighty preserver, in his good providence, to bring me in safety to this place, where I resided several years before I set out with my whole heart to seek a saving interest in Jesus Christ; yet was not without the strivings of the Divine Spirit. But under the preaching of the Rev. Mr. Stebbens, from. "The axe is laid unto the root of the trees,"[1] (on a memorable watch-night, held in the Bowery Church) I experienced such a manifestation of the Divine power, as I had before been a stranger to: and under a sense of my amazing sinfulness in the sight of God, I fell prostrate on the floor, as one wounded or slain in battle; and indeed I was slain by the law, that I might be made alive by Jesus Christ.

The distress of my mind at this time, was such as no language can describe, and can only be apprehended by those who have laboured under the same weight and burden of sin, conscious of their own just condemnations, as rebels against the righteous government of God. However, I soon found a degree of encouragement and relief to my sin-sick soul, though not the clear evidence of my acceptance in the beloved. Soon after this I joined the Methodist society.

The followers of the despised Jesus now became more than ever the excellent of the earth in my view, and in their society I took great delight. But the enemy of my soul, by whom I had so long been enslaved, unwilling to lose his prey, beset me on every side, and brought me into a new scene of distress. Had not the Lord sustained my feeble mind under the sore conflicts I endured, I must have fallen a victim to the rage of the infernal foe.

But thanks be to God, his grace was sufficient for me; and I may truly say, his strength was made perfect in my weakness;[2] and by the light of his Spirit, shining upon my disconsolate soul, he cheered my heart with his love, and revived my languid hope, which encouraged me to persevere in the way of righteousness.

In the year 1804, I attended a Camp-Meeting, being one of the first held in this district. A large concourse of people, of all descriptions, convened on the occasion, of which, many were made the subjects of saving grace, and believers were filled with perfect love. At this meeting, the Lord, in a more powerful manner than ever, made known his salvation to me, by the influences and witness of his Holy Spirit; so that, when the exercises were over, I left the hallowed place with a glow of heavenly joy, which none but God himself can inspire.

Sometime after this, I had the following most affecting, interesting, and frightful dream, or night vision. After the usual religious exercises in my family, I retired to rest at the late hour of about two in the morning; and falling to sleep, the place of the future torment of the wicked was presented to my view, with all its dreadful horrors. It was a pit, the depth and extent of which were too vast for my discovery; but perfectly answering the description given of it in holy writ—a lake burning with fire and brimstone;[3] which has enlarged her mouth without measure, and is moved from beneath, to meet the wicked at their coming.

The descent into this place of misery, was by a series of steps, the top of which was near the surface of the earth. In it, I saw vast multitudes of souls, suffering the torments of the damned; out of whose mouths and nostrils issued flames of fire; and from these flames an impenetrable cloud of smoke continually ascended; and being attended

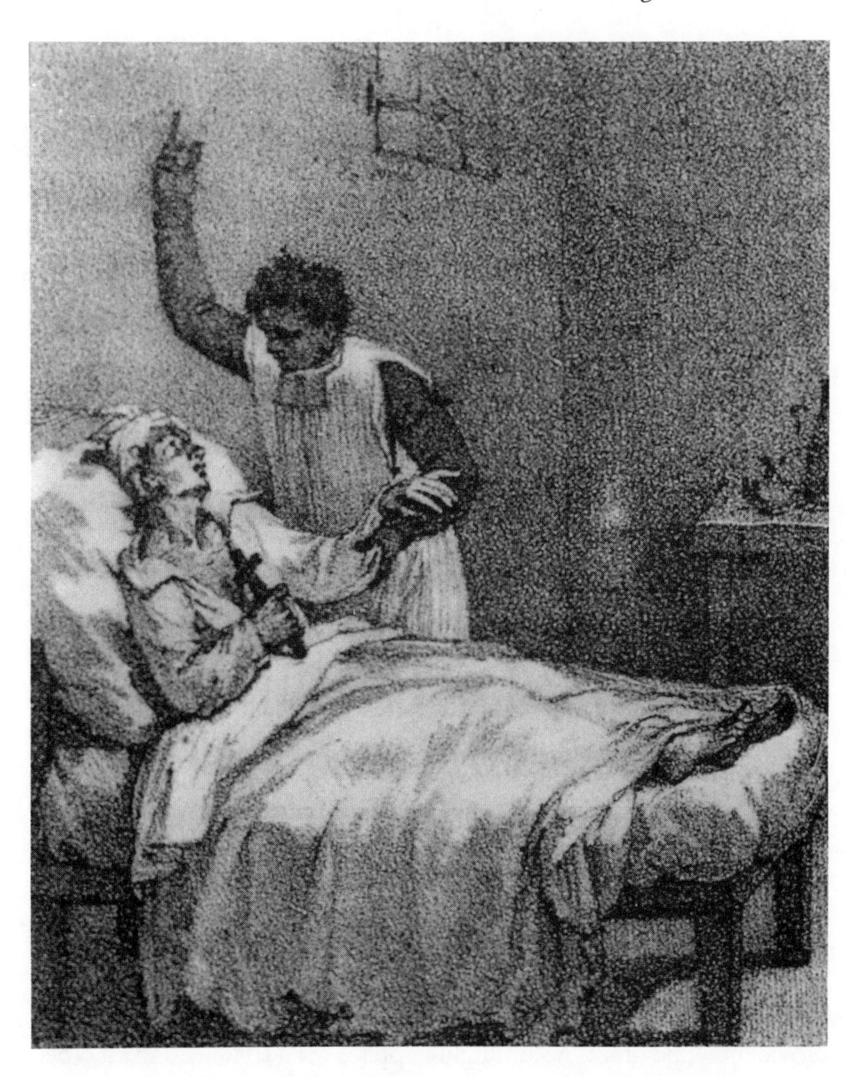

Slaves knew their last chance for freedom might be at their master's deathbed. Even in the post-revolutionary era, very few gained their liberty the way White did.

by a guide, he bade me take particular notice of what was passing, in, and about this hedious gulph; upon which I beheld an host of evil spirits, continually employed in leading human souls to the place of descent into this bottomless pit; at which they were received by other devils, who awaited their coming, and dragged them headlong down the steps, to meet their final doom.

But one, which I particularly observed, and doubted from its smallness and singular appearance, whether it was a human being, had no sooner arrived at this place of misery, than it assumed the features and size of a man, and began, with all the other newcomers, to emit flames of fire, from the mouth and nostrils, like those I had seen there at first.

I next beheld a coach, with horses richly furnitured, and full of gay, modish passengers, posting to this place of torment; but, when they approached the margin of the burning lake, struck with terror and dismay, their countenances changed, and awfully bespoke their surprise and fear.

But having myself, while engaged with my conductor, stepped upon the top of the descent, and apparently burnt my feet, which he observing, said to me, "Go, and declare what you have seen." Upon which I awoke; but so overcome by the effect of what I had seen, that it was a considerable time before I was able to speak.

Having recovered a little from the anguish of my mind, occasioned by this distressing scene, I related the whole to my bosom companion; who, having heard it with astonishment, and much affection, was desirous to know what I thought would be the result; concerning which, I gave her my opinion in full; and we covenanted together from that time, to be more faithful to God than ever, and to escape, if possible, the torments I had seen.

From a belief, that it was my duty to call sinners to repentance, I communicated my exercises on the subject, to my christian brethren:—But person of long experience in the way of godliness, from whom I expected encouragement, said, If you are going to preach, I will quit.

However, I thought with myself, that the best and safest method I could persue, was, to yield obedience to the command of him, who I believed had called me to this duty; trusting alone in his promises, providence, and grace. Accordingly I applied for a trial hearing, in order to obtain license as an exhorter; to which the brethren consented, and I made my first attempt to speak in public in the month of April, 1805; but with much fear and trembling; being sensible of my inability and ignorance: for at this time I had not so much learning, as even the knowledge of the English alphabet; but in my broken way could talk of Christ, and his love to sinners, which I did according to the best of my abilities. But the brethren, after hearing what I had to say concluded that it would be improper to give me license, which brought fresh trials upon my mind: yet I endeavoured to keep what the Lord had committed to me.

From a conviction that God had called me to labour in public, and the distressing fear, lest the enemy of souls should take an advantage of my neglect, and entirely rob me of my confidence, and undo me forever, I passed several months in a most gloomy and distressing state of mind, deprived, both of slumber and appetite.

My only consolation, during this season of trials, was derived from reflecting upon the greatness, goodness, and power of God; as being adequate to the accomplishment of whatever seemeth him good; which encouraged me to place my whole dependance upon him; in hope that he would clear my way before me: for he still seemed to say, "Go—warn the wicked to flee from the wrath to come."

Under these exercises, in the month of July, I solicited the brethren to give me a second hearing; with which they complied, and the Lord gave us a powerful and happy season, while waiting upon him; by enabling me to speak, and blessing his word to them that heard. After consulting on the subject, the brethren agreed that I should have license to exhort; which was matter of no small joy to my soul, being thereby relieved from my former embarrassment, and at liberty to do the will of God, without transgressing the order of his church.

The importance of the work assigned me now, engrossed all my thoughts, and I resolved to improve what ability the Lord had given me, to exhort all, both men and women, to repent and turn to that God who had set my own soul at liberty.

Having a desire to travel, I left New York and proceeded to Long-Island, where I went from village to village, exhorting the people to seek the Lord, for I soon found there was but little religion among them, which, though it gave me much sorrow, engaged me the more in urging them to seek it, not only by argument, but by giving them a narrative of my own experience, in the love of God.

But to do justice to the inhabitants of this island, even those who appear to be destitute of religion, are, nevertheless, generous and kind.

Having now fixed the limits of my rout, I continued my exhortations among them. While in this exercise, at a place called New-Lots, the word so reached the heart of a woman in the congregation, that she cried aloud for mercy, and though opposed and ridiculed by some professed deists who were present, she professed to find peace with God.

Travelling to the eastward, I stopped at Babylon, where a meeting had been appointed for me, at the house of Mr. Conklin. This gentleman is not only hospitable, but a friend to religion. My congregation here consisted of about fifty persons, among whom a deep solemnity reigned during the exercises; and numbers of them, I have no doubt, are now happy in the Savior, having caught the holy fire at that meeting; which was astonishingly manifested at the time.

During this tour of the island, I saw more of the manifestations of the power and love of God, and the different means, by which he effects the work of grace in the souls of men, than I had known before.

Many who knew not Christ, were awakened and converted, in a most extraordinary manner, being smitten to the earth by the power of God; which, with a number of other circumstances, led me more fully than ever, to reflect upon the importance of the work. I had undertaken for Christ's sake; which exercised my own mind to that degree, under a sense of the necessity of a clean heart, that I could not rest till God should sanctify my soul, and thereby, the better prepare me for his service.

Under these exercises, I returned to the city of New-York, and in the month of May, 1806, at a meeting held in my own house. I fell prostrate upon the floor, like one dead. But while I lay in this condition, my mind was vigourous and active; and an increasing scene of glory, opened upon my ravished soul; with a spiritual view of the heavenly hosts surrounding the eternal throne, giving glory to God and the Lamb; with whom, all my ransomed powers seemed to unite, in symphonious strains of divine adoration; feeling nothing but perfect love, peace, joy, and good-will to man, pervading all my soul, in a most happy union with God, my all in all—every doubt, fear and terror of mind were banished, and heaven opened in my bosom.

In this memorable hour, I have no doubts but God sanctifyed me to himself, by the power of the Holy Ghost; for, from this time, what had before appeared like insurmountable difficulties, were now made easy, by casting my whole care upon the Lord; and the path of duty was only the path of pleasure. I could pray without ceasing,[4] and rejoice evermore; and my stammering tongue was more than ever loosed, to declare the truth of God, with greater zeal, and affection. At the same time that I received this inestimable blessing, there were many others who were awakened, converted, and made happy in the pardoning love of Christ. The memory of that glorious day will never be erased from my mind.

After I received this divine manifestation of the power of sanctifying grace, I felt a greater desire than ever, to be able to read the scriptures myself, (for as yet I knew nothing of them, but from the reading of others), thinking that by this means I might become more useful. But how to begin to learn this art, at so late a period of life, and prosecute it with success was the difficulty. My children having learned to read and write, and my eldest daughter being now about sixteen years of age, I besought her to undertake her father's instruction; which she did with the utmost cheerfulness, and spared no pains to teach me all she learned at school; so that in three months from my first beginning, I was able to read the word of God for myself.

But what is most remarkable in this undertaking, was, that she could learn me nothing from the common spelling book; no, not so much as the alphabet; for my mind was so perfectly taken up with the notion of reading the bible, that I could think of nothing else:— therefore, from this sacred volume she had to instruct me, word by word. The first word of which I learn'd the letters, and how to spell it, was "And," but, by the blessing of God, I can now read any common book, so as to understand its meaning in general.

The latter part of this year she instructed me how to write, so far as to be able to keep my own accounts; and, though in a broken imperfect manner, to correspond with absent friends, and minute the travels of my own soul in the way to the kingdom, and the dealings of God towards me: a blessing I cannot too highly estimate.

Notwithstanding my illiterature, the Lord was with me in prayer and exhortation; and I trust, added his blessing to my imperfect, but well meant labours; and while persevering in this way, my mind was impressed with a belief, that God required me to preach his gospel in a more direct manner, than my license as an exhorter permitted me to attempt; by which I conceived that I might do more good, especially among my African brethren, many of whom I saw rushing head-long into those practices, which, if not repented of, must end in perdition and ruin.

From these views I requested, and was granted the privilege of being heard on trial; when I spake from, "Repent ye therefore, and be converted, that your sins may be blotted out, when the times of refreshing shall come from the presence of the Lord," Acts iv.19.—But after hearing me, the brethren in council, concluded I ought not to be licensed as a preacher.

Satisfied with this trial, for the present; in the spirit of Christian fortitude, I continued to exhort all sects and denominations of people, as opportunity offered, to repent of their sins; and the Lord, assisted me by his grace, and accompanied me with his holy Spirit wherever I went.

About this time I held an exhorting meeting on Long-Island, which was attended with unusual displays of the divine power. After the people were assembled, and began to pray, numbers of the neighbours came in, and loudly exclaimed against such kind of meetings, as being unnecessary, and prejudicial to society. Upon which I earnestly exhorted all present, who loved God and the souls of men, to unite in one general prayer for a revival of religion in that neighborhood; and God was pleased to hear and answer, by an immediate display of his power, which brought those very declaimers themselves prostrate to the ground, like men who had been shot, beside many others. And scarce could a sinner be in the assembly ten minutes, before he was in the same condition, crying for mercy: and so great was the work, that our meeting continued till ten o'clock next day; in which time, many who came there enemies to God, returned home, praising his name for pardoning mercy and saving grace.

Encouraged by this success attending my labours, I went to New-Lots, and appointed a meeting; and though I had but six hearers, yet perceiving them to be under religious concern, I continued my meeting among them, till God displayed his power, and raised about fifty, to witness his blessing upon my feeble endeavours. All glory to his holy name.

During this little excursion, I had many agreeable and happy prayer meetings; which frequently lasted till midnight; and were attended with peculiar blessings to many who were concerned for the welfare of their souls.

Still impressed with a sense of its being my duty to preach, I made a second application for license. And was permitted to preach another trial sermon; which I did August 22, from "Be not deceived; God is not mocked; for whatsoever a man soweth, that shall he also reap," Gal. vi. 7, but my petition was again rejected.

Soon after this a local preacher called to see me, from whose pious conversation, and account of his own call to preach, I took fresh courage to persevere. We parted in much union, love and fellowship, promising each other never to give up the cause we had espoused, while God continued to witness his divine approbation.

With increasing desires to advance the cause of my adorable Master, I visited the state of New-Jersey; and used my utmost endeavours to convince my African brethren in this part, of the necessity of repentance, in order to their salvation. To this work my whole soul and body were devoted; nor did I spare any pains or labour my capacity was capable of, to accomplish so desirable an object: nor yet, did God suffer me to labour and toil in vain, but gave me to witness many wonderful displays of his saving power, in persons of different ages, and even in children.

At one meeting where I was exhorting a numerous body of people, many of the aged of both sexes, fell prostrate under the divine power; acknowledged themselves sinners, and there remained until the Lord converted their souls, and gave them the witness of his Spirit: and little children, not more than ten years of age were wrought upon in the same manner; whose cries and prayers for the salvation of their own souls, and the souls of their brethren, for the conviction, and conversion of their ungodly parents, and neighbours; presented a most affecting scene to a feeling mind: at which my own heart glowed with inexpressible joy, and renewed resolution to proceed in obedience to my Master's command; exhorting to repentance all I met with.

The next meeting I attended was at a friend's house, where many assembled to hear. My feelings were much elevated from what I had so recently seen of the manifestations of the grace of God, so that, I spoke with greater confidence in my expectations, believing that more good would result from my labours under his blessing. While speaking, a woman of the neighbourhood fell on her knees, and cried aloud for mercy; to the great astonishment of the spectators, and all who were acquainted with her.

Thus I continued exhorting and holding prayer-meetings, and found, that thereby, many of my African brethren, who were strangers to religion before, were now brought to close in with the offers of mercy; among whom I yet hoped to preach the gospel of Jesus Christ, still believing God had called me to this work.

After my return to the city, I made a third application for license, but was told that it was not yet my privilege, and forbid to preach. However, I obtained liberty to preach another trial sermon; which I did from "Loose him and let him go." John xi, 44, yet the wisdom of God so ordered the consultation of the brethren on the subject, that they determined I should remain as I was, with only my license to exhort. But having previously given them an account of my exercises of mind, and anguish of soul concerning preaching, some of them pitied my condition.

This trial, among others, led me to a more scrutinous enquiry, respecting my own sincerity, and whether I had not been deceived. Under those afflictions and difficulties of mind, I could only vent my anguish and sorrow by crying aloud. I attempted to pray, but could not.

At length it appeared as though something said to my mind, "Remember Jonah." I then arose and went to a place where I had appointed to exhort. When I arrived I found the people assembled, and my soul willing to strive to do my duty. In the time of prayer the Lord revived my heart: and at this meeting, manifested himself to the assembly.

I now renewed my resolutions to do all the good I could as an exhorter: accordingly omitted no opportunity in complying with my duty in this respect; warning and beseeching all, whenever opportunity offered, to repent and turn from the evil of their ways, assuring them, from my own experience as well as from scripture, that there is a fulness of mercy in Jesus Christ, for all who will comply with the condition upon which it is offered to sinners: nor did I find sufficient reasons to discourage me from so doing; for my own soul was blessed, and many whom I thus exhorted embraced the Lord Jesus, and became his followers.

It is worthy of remark, however, that those, who from every appearance, set out the fairest for heaven, often turn back again to the world: while many, whose exercises we think but lightly of in their first beginnings, persevere in the way. I noticed an occurrence of this kind, which happened among those where I held a meeting in this city. Two young men, who had spent much of their early days in the vanities of the world; were convinced of sin, and manifested much contrition on the account of it; and both joined society. But the one who shewed the greatest signs of conviction, and could give a rational and affecting account of his situation; soon forsook the cause and people of God: turned again to folly, and is now in the high road to eternal ruin. While the other, who could say little more of himself than, that, he had a desire to serve God, has since experienced religion, and is now a faithful and useful member of society.

What added much to my happiness now was, that I could read the holy scriptures, and converse with my brethren on the important subjects contained therein, which became a source of great delight to my soul under all my trials and conflicts.

About this time, as I was lying in bed, about twelve o'clock at night, and ruminating upon the glories of heaven; all at once my room, which was before entirely dark, became exceeding light, and the appearance of three forms, like doves, presented themselves before my wakeful eyes, who, for some minutes looked me full in the face. A peculiar brightness, or light, surrounding each of them. Conceiving them to be angels, I was terrified with fear; but soon disappearing, and leaving the room dark as before, and me to reflect upon what I had seen, my mind was led to embrace the divine promises; and I considered this vision as an omen of good, and that, in due time, I should reap if I fainted not; for his angels are all ministering spirits, sent forth to minister to them that shall be heirs of salvation.

When upon my several little tours, to different parts of the Island, New-Jersey, and elsewhere, nothing so delighted my soul, as to see sinners turning to God, and Christians resolutely warring a good warfare. This, always gave me much encouragement, in pursuing the path of duty, which was pointed out for me by the great head of the church.

And as I generally found it to be attended with a good effect, I frequently declared, not only what I had experienced of the divine favour, but what I had seen of the rich displays of grace and power among others; and by this means encouraging all to trust in, and serve the living God. And I can truly say that many, who before were sitting in darkness, were brought into light and liberty.

But still impressed with the thought, that I was too much circumscribed in my privileges, in December following, I applied again for license to preach: and on the 31st day of the month, preached another trial sermon. My text was, "Let us therefore fear, lest a promise being left us of entering into his rest, any of you should seem to come short of it." Heb. iv. 1. and although the brethren found no fault with the doctrine I preached, nor offered any satisfactory reasons for rejecting my petition, yet they thought I had better remain as I was a while longer. However, I felt no ways concerned, but that, when I had fulfilled the time of probation, allotted me by the great Head of the Church, every objection would be removed from the minds of the brethren, who would then receive me into fellowship as a preacher.

After this, I again visited the people of New-Jersey, I had left so happy in the love of God a few months before; and endeavoured to encourage them to be faithful to the grace they had already received; by leading their minds to contemplate the glories which await the faithful in the world to come. And used all my efforts, to increase their numbers, by exhorting others to repent, and seek the salvation of their souls. The Lord crowned our meetings with success, and filled us with joy and gladness; while the spirit of love and Christian union, inflamed our hearts.

On my return to the city, I still pursued my usual practice among the brethren, by meeting with them for prayers and exhortation, and found great satisfaction therein. But under my impressions of mind, that God had called me to preach, which I could not resist, I again petitioned to be heard on trial, and obtained the privilege February 14, 1807, when I spoke from, "Behold I send you forth, as sheep, in the midst of wolves: be ye therefore wise as serpents, and harmless as doves." Matth. x:16:—and the Lord assisted me. But after consultation the preachers and leaders present, concluded I had better continue to exhort, and let preaching alone for the present: they were not unanimous however in their opinion, yet the majority carried the question against me. On being called before them, to hear their decision, I requested to know if they were dissatisfied with the discourse I had delivered; to which some of them answered in the negative. I then asked if there was any thing exceptionable in my character; to which they answered, no. Yet said, they thought it best that I should continue as I was. My mind being somewhat disaffected, at receiving no satisfactory reason, why I was rejected from receiving license to preach; I added; brethren, I have told you the exercises of my mind on the subject; and that I cannot rest without greater liberty than I now enjoy; for I believe God requires me to preach. I was then asked if I had license, whether I could preach any better for it? and what liberty I wanted more than I already had. To which I replied, that I wished to be at liberty to speak from a text, when presented to my mind for that purpose, and I thought God required it of me. But was finally told by one, (from whom I might have expected something more consoling) that it was the devil who was pushing me on to preach. And added, for he wants to raise you up, when he can get a fair shot at you. And his sentiment was seconded by another: at which my mind being extremely agitated with grief and anguish, I cried out; for God's sake, brethren, do not talk thus. And left the place without any to comfort me; my brethren viewing me in the same unfavourable light, that Job's friends did him.

Notwithstanding the great distress and conflicts of mind, occasioned by this last repulse, yet it did not in the least deter me from attending to my duty, but still continued as heretofore, to attend meetings appointed for prayer and exhortation, and constantly found the witness of the divine approbation, accompanying my improvements: for the Lord soon settled my ruffled mind, in a permanent and inviolable peace; which made me satisfied with all his dealings: and willing to suffer any, and every thing for his sake.

About this time one of the brethren called on me, and advised me to give up public speaking: for, said he, you will never obtain license to preach. I told him, as long as God would stand by me, I would never give it up. He strove to persuade me, that I was deluded, and said if I persisted, a stop would be put to my exhorting in public; with some other threats to the same nature.

But as I was convinced of his mistake and ignorance in the matter; as also, that God had called me to, and would finally enlarge me in the work; I charged him as in the divine presence, to take care what he did: for if by his opposition, he should become accessory to the loss of but one soul, the consequences to him, must be dreadful. So he left me as he found me, resolved to persevere in the work of God.

As I viewed myself almost friendless, I gave myself much to prayer; and my full heart was expressed in the following words of the poet, which very frequently dwelt upon my mind.

"O that I had a faithful friend,
"To tell my secrets to:
"On whose advice I might depend,
"In every thing I do.

"How do I wander up and down;
"And no one pities me.
"I seem a stranger quite unknown;
"A son of misery.

"None leads an ear to my complaint;
"Nor minds my cries and tears.
"None comes to cheer me though I faint,
"Nor my vast burden bears."

But although my conflicts and trials, from within and without, were so multiplied and great, as at one time to drive me to the very borders of despair; yet the Lord soon revived my soul again, by revealing himself, both in my private, and public devotions; which abundantly encouraged me to persevere, with increasing zeal in the good cause; placing my whole trust and dependence upon God.

And what seemed very much to urge me in the path of duty, was, reading in the holy scriptures, the threatenings denounced against the disobedient and unfaithful: and fearing, lest the enemy might take advantage of the state of trial I was under, as well as my bodily weakness, I neglected no means, which I thought would be beneficial to my own soul: but particularly fasting and prayer. And what I did myself, I exhorted others to do likewise: considering that they, with myself, must shortly stand before the judgement-seat of Christ, to give an account, for the deeds done in the body.

And I do most sincerely recommend the same practice, to all the followers of Jesus Christ; while they are travelling through this world of snares; especially in seasons of spiritual dullness, or barreness of religion; for at such times the enemy of souls, is always ready to take advantage of them; but by fasting, prayer, and faith, his designs may be defeated, and their souls escape, as a bird from the snare of the fowler.

"Lord of the harvest hear
"Thy needy children's cry:
"Answer their faith's effectual pray'r,
"And set them up on high.

"From hell's oppressive pow'r,
"Their struggling souls release:
"And to thy Father's grace restore;
"And to thy perfect peace."[5]

About this time I had another remarkable dream. In my sleep, a man appeared to me, having under his care a flock of sheep; from which, separating a few, requested I would stop them. But I told him I was no shepherd, still however, he went away and left them with me: I was going, I called after him to know his name: he replied that it was enough for me to know that he was a shepherd.

This dream encouraged me to hope, that I should find some of the fruit of my labours, in the flock of the great Shepherd of the sheep, at the last day; and inspired me earnestly to pray to God that it might be so.

Feeling it my duty to go abroad in quest of perishing sinners, and from the exercises of my mind fully believing the time was come, for me to obtain license to preach, I again made application for it; and on the 12th of April preached another trial sermon. My text was, "Cast not away, therefore, your confidence; which hath great recompense of reward. "Heb. x. 35 on this occasion, the president elder, and other official characters were present.

We had a comfortable meeting, and my own soul was much strengthened; believing that I was doing the will of God; and confidently relying on him for the result, fully resigned my cause to the divine disposal.

The Quarterly Conference was appointed to be held the ensuing evening, when my case must meet a final decision. When the question, whether I should be licensed to preach, was put to a vote, a majority of the Conference carried it in the affirmative. But a debate ensued between the president, and presiding elders respecting my preaching abilities. As also whether there was indeed a majority in favour of my being licensed. But by three times counting, it was at last determined that a majority in my favour was no longer disputable. Yet after all, the president elder could not prevail upon the Resident, to give me a license, who objected by saying, he did not believe I was called by the Spirit of God to preach; and if you license him said he to the other, the sin be upon yourself, and you will see before one year, that my words are true.

However the presiding elder had imbibed a more favourable opinion of me, and told him, that, as the Quarterly Conference had voted my licence, he should give it to me, for said he, I think better of George than you do, and hope that all his opposers may be disappointed in their predictions about him.

So he gave me a license to preach the gospel of Jesus Christ, and encouraged me to go on in the ways of God, and do what I could to bring sinners to repentance and a life of godliness, and to encourage believers, to run for the incorruptible crown of glory.

My mind was new led to a train of reflections, on the dealings of God towards me; in which I discovered so much wisdom and goodness, united with mercy and power, accompanying me through the many changes I had experienced, and effecting my deliverance in times of difficulty and distress; that my mind was overwhelmed with gratitude and love; which I have no language to express.

But this I have learned by experience, that omnipotence itself, is engaged on the side of those who put their trust in him, sincerely obeying the directions of his word and Spirit: and will, sooner or later, though it be through many tribulations, accomplish their deliverance from all their distresses. "O that men would praise the Lord for his goodness, and for his wonderful works to the children of men."[6]

Knowing that, although I had now obtained license to preach, its continuance depended entirely upon my upright conduct and usefulness, as a preacher; and being confident of the divine assistance, I resolved if possible to double my diligence. And that I might the better succeed, as far as possible, to cleanse myself from all filthiness of flesh and spirit; perfecting holiness in the fear of God: and to avoid giving any unnecessary offense; that the gospel might not be blamed through my means.

The better to approve myself, both to God and my brethren, I improved all opportunities while at home, to meet with them at their usual appointments, for prayer and exhortation; and God was with us of a truth; and gave us melting, refreshing times, while I strove in this way to sow the seed in sincerity.

But as it frequently happened, both in the city and country, that even many of the wicked, in the time of religious exercises fell to the earth, under great agitations of mind; I was led to enquire more particularly into the cause of it, from a fear lest some of those I often see fall under my own improvements, might pass through all those extraordinary, external exercises from some other cause than the power of God; and without being either convicted or converted. But upon examination, I could find no better cause to impute it to, than that assigned by St. Paul; who says, "If all prophesy, and there come in one that believeth not, or one unlearned, he is convinced of all, he is judged of all: and thus are the secrets of his heart made manifest; and so, falling down on his face, he will worship God, and report that God is in you of a truth."[7] And thus I have frequently witnessed it it be.

I again visited New-Jersey, and spent one week, in, and about Woodbridge. While preaching here, there was a man in the assembly, who was an avowed enemy to the doctrines taught by the Methodists, and had come to meeting it seems, to speculate upon the people, and look after his wife, who was smitten down by the power of God during the exercises, and his own soul so convicted of sin, that he never rested till he found peace, and is now happy in the Lord.

After my return from Woodbridge, I visited New-Town and Flushing on Long-Island and the adjacent villages, preaching at every place where I came: and the Lord was among the people in power, and gave us melting, and reviving sessions.

At a place called The Head of the Fly, a little out of Jamaica, I was invited to preach at the house of a coloured man, who was a professed deist. The circumstance much astonished his neighbours: but before I ended my discourse, the word reached his heart with such power, that he roared aloud in the assembly. He has since experienced religion, and is now happy in the love of God. Many others at this meeting, who were before strangers to the power of grace, united with us in prayer to God for mercy: and we parted in much love.

At New-Town likewise, I had a good time in preaching to a people, in whose hearts I believe the Lord has effected a gracious work.

The next morning being Sabbath, the white brethren having no preaching that day, I applied to one of the trustees for the privilege of the meeting-house, but was at first refused; being told that I had no authority to preach, or at least that if I had any it was only verbal, and that he had been so informed by D___ C___,[8] a coloured friend from New-York: but on shewing him my license, under the signature of the Presiding Elder, the objection was removed, and the use of the pulpit granted me. We had a gracious manifestation of the presence and power of God; and after preaching I met the classes, of both white, and coloured people, and found them happy in the Lord.

Thus I have found, that, although I have been rejected by some, opposed by others, and suspected by more, that by putting my trust in God, and obeying his will, under all these trials, infinite goodness has caused all events to turn to my account at last; which encourages me, with patience and resignation, to follow Christ, through all the conflicts of the christian warfare. Beside, I have ever found, that persecution, let it come from what quarter it may, serves only to make me more watchful and prayerful; and when I have endured it awhile longer, I hope, and expect to receive a crown of glory, at the right hand of God.

Having seen much good done this year, in the conversion and sanctification of precious souls, in the several parts where I had employed my time in the labours of the gospel, the period arrived, when I must undergo another examination before my brethren, for the renewal of my license.

At the Quarterly Conference, held in the city of New-York, April 13th, 1808, when my case was called, and some of the African brethren, had offered their animadversions upon my public performances, the Presiding Elder asked if the Conference was not agreed in giving me a license at first, and was answered that they were not all agreed.

Elder. Does he preach the gospel?

Brethren. Yes—we believe he does as well as he can.

Elder. And the best can do no more. But have you any objections against his moral character?

Brethren. Not any.

My license was then renewed, and the Elder exhorted the members of the Conference to union among themselves, and to avoid censuring and opposing each other.

The next appointment I attended, which was in this city, tended much to increase my conviction, that I was doing the will of God, as well as lead me to adore the riches of his goodness to sinners.

When I came to the place appointed for me to preach, I found but few assembled. But while waiting for an increase of my congregation, I entertained those present, with an account of my own experience in the things of God; which was so blessed to one of them, that she never rested till she found rest in Jesus, and I trust is now adoring the riches of his grace in a world of glory. Many others were blessed at this meeting, which was evidenced by their loud shouts and earnest prayers. Some of the wicked came to oppose us, but not being able to interrupt our devotions, went away in a rage.

I now visited New-Jersey again, and found in the several towns and villages where I stopped, that religion was in a prosperous way among the coloured, as well as the white people. But the former being my own blood, lay near my heart; so that my chief happiness consisted in seeking to promote their spiritual welfare, by preaching and exhortations among them; and by instructing them in class meetings.

After my return from this little tour, I was appointed to preach in the woods, a little south of New-town, on Long-Island. But before I went to the place where the people were assembling for meeting, the friends told me that a company of ill-disposed people, had collected for the purpose of attacking me on the ground; however I went to the place of appointment, with no other weapons for my defence but the Christian armour, willing to hazard my life thus panoply'd. The congregation was large, and the exercises attended with great power. The people of God were filled with joy and comfort, and many who were hitherto strangers to God, were awakened and converted.

While I was speaking, the company of opposers approached the place of worship, I raised my voice as high as possible, in order that they might hear me; and cried with all my might, "Satan is near the camp;" and exhorted all present, who loved the Lord, to unite in prayer that the designs of the enemy might be defeated. They immediately halted, took their seats upon a fence at a little distance; where they continued for a while, like men confused and ashamed, and then retired, mimicking each other: and left us to God and ourselves, to proceed in our devotions without disturbance. The wrath of man shall praise the Lord, and the remainder will he restrain.

Soon after this I returned to New-Jersey, which I had but recently left, in order to help forward the good work among my African brethren there, on this visit, much of my time was taken up in Brunswick, Shrewsbury, Middletown and Woodbridge; where I had good times, and the Lord attended my labours with much success.

After my return, I prepared for a journey to the south, with a view of visiting my native land, to see my parents, and how it fared with those of my own colour, who I left in a state of slavery a number of years before; in hopes of being beneficial to their souls; for my heart had often felt the keenest anguish for them.

With these views, I set off towards the last of this year, and arriving at Trenton, New-Jersey, I tarried two days, and preached twice from the following words, "Seek ye the Lord, while he may be found, call ye upon him while he is near." Isaiah lv. 6, and "For ye were sometimes darkness, but now are ye light in the Lord; walk as children of the light." Eph. v. 8.

My soul was much refreshed among the people in this place, who appeared united in the sanctified bonds of the purest friendship; and the work of God successfully advancing among them.

My next stage was the city of Philadelphia: where I spent two weeks. Here I found my coloured brethren much alive to God, and the interest of the Redeemer's kingdom. I preached in their churches, and was abundantly comforted.

From thence I went to Wilmington; state of Delaware; where I spent a week in visiting and preaching among my African brethren, who appeared to enjoy all the sweets of religion, and was much delighted with hearing them relate that experience in the things of God, and tell of his grace and goodness towards them, and leaving them engaged for heaven I set off for Baltimore.

Arriving there, I spent about two weeks in visiting the brethren; and was agreeably disappointed in finding many with whom I had been acquainted when a slave in Virginia; who were then in the broad road to misery: but had now become the children of the living God. At least, bore every appearance of being such; having become sober, honest and industrious, as well as professors of the religion of Jesus Christ: so that all appeared to be happy around them. During my stay among them, I preached frequently, and particularly urged upon the brethren as a duty, the necessity of using every means in their power, both by prayer, instruction and exhortation, to bring as many of their acquaintance as possible, who were yet in their sins, to the knowledge of the truth, as it is in Jesus Christ. I then preached a farewel discourse from, "The Lord direct your hearts, into the love of God, and into the patient waiting for Christ." Thess. iii. 5. I took my leave of them, commending them to God and the word of his grace, and pursued my journey to Somerset county.

But, when I reached this place, not finding as I expected, my aged parents, who had obtained their freedom, and removed to a great distance from this; nor more than half a dozen persons I had formerly been acquainted with, I spent but a short time among them; during which, I preached but twice, took my leave of them, and set out for home.

On my return, I revisited the brethren at Wilmington, with whom I tarried several days, which I spent in visiting, prayers, exhortation and preaching, and the Lord accompanied my labours with divine power, so that, at several of our meetings, much good was done in the name of the Lord Jesus.

From Wilmington, I came to Philadelphia; where I spent five days in the same exercises; and then left the followers of the Redeemer, in joyful hope of meeting them in heaven, if no more upon the earth.

I next stopped at Cranberry, state of New-Jersey; where I made a short stay; visited, and preached with the brethren, and parted from them in much love and friendship.

On my arrival at New-York, I found my family in good health: and the work of God prospering among my African brethren, in like manner as I had found it in the south.

After the rest and refreshment necessary from, so long a journey, I again visited the brethren upon Long-Island, where I renewed my labours with much success. The people here who had formerly been very unstable; from the many reproofs they had received, were now willing to unite with the children of God.

After preaching at a place called Little Neck, from "How shall we escape if we neglect so great salvation." Heb. ii. 3 a person of a different sentiment from the Methodists, came to me, and said, you have given us all to the devil (meaning his own denomination,) I told him that I gave no Christian of any denomination to the devil: but taught that the wicked would be damned if they did not repent, and endeavoured to convince him of the truth of what I had preached. After some time he became pacified, and he, with others of his own persuasion, invited me to preach among them at a place several miles distant from this, for which I gave them an appointment, and two weeks after preached to them from, "The last day, that great day of the feast, Jesus stood and cried, saying, if any man thirst, let him come unto me and drink." John vii. 37. the meeting was solemn and conducted with great order. The congregation was principally composed, of Africans and Indians. The Lord was present in power, and began a glorious revival of religion among this people, with whom I have since enjoyed many happy seasons of Christian intercourse and fellowship.

In the beginning of 1809, I made a little excursion to the northward of York Island, and spent about three weeks at Singsing, Westchester, and the adjacent villages; and found that many of the brethren in those parts, were much engaged with God, and determined, through grace to press towards the mark, for the prize of their high calling, in Christ Jesus. I enjoyed much satisfaction, in preaching, and other religious exercises among them, being accompanied with the refreshing manifestations of the divine power and presence.

After my return, I spent some time in attending the little meetings about the city, where God was carrying on his work, and gathering converts into the church. After which I went again to Long-Island, and found the cause of God advancing among the people, and sinners daily seeking shelter in the ark of safety, and uniting themselves with the followers of the Lord Jesus. At Jerusalem while preaching from, "Cry aloud, spare not, life up your voice like a trumpet, and shew my people their transgressions, and the house of Jacob their sins,"[9] the Lord attended his word with power, one woman was converted, and I had reason to believe much good was done. At this place and the neighbouring villages, I continued preaching and exhorting on all suitable occasions until the latter part of this year, and in the mean time assisted my Christian brethren in building an house for the Lord at Jerusalem.

On my return home, I was informed by my family that sister Mary Henery had been sick for some considerable time, and had repeatedly sent for me during my absence, to visit her. I went immediately to her master's house (for she was a slave) to see her, and found her extremely weak, and exercised with great bodily pain. On my entering her room she cried out, "Glory to God, brother, have you come?" Yes, said I, sister, for Christ's sake I have come.

I then inquired the state of her soul; to which she replied; I am as happy as I can be in the body. After which she sunk into a state of perfect insensibility to every outward object, and to all appearance lay entirely lifeless for some time. But after so far recovering as to be able to speak, she broke out in loud shouts of praise to God, and said, that while she was in that state she saw the gates of heaven opened, and a beautiful company of shining personages arrayed in white robes. And observed that she had often thought how delightful the singing was in the Methodist church, but that was incomparable with the singing of these angels in glory; with whom she expected shortly to join, and stated the moment her soul would leave the body for that purpose.

I asked if I should pray with her, she said, "yes, brother, pray that my faith fail not." While I was engaged in this exercise, she broke out aloud in prayer herself, for the welfare of her mistress and young master (his father being dead,) and earnestly besought the Lord to convert his soul, and to extend the same blessing to all mankind. The fervency of her prayer and the energy of the language with which it was clothed, so affected all present, that they were scarce able to stand.

I attended her on the day of her death, being October 28, 1809; three days after my first visit; and found her perfectly sensible, and resigned to the will of God. She said she was glad to see me, as she had something particular to say to her mother and me.

After intreating her aged mother in the most affectionate manner, not to weep on her account, as she was fully assured of arriving shortly at the place of eternal rest, she proceeded to give some advice respecting her own funeral preparations and solemnities, earnestly requesting that her corps might be dressed in a plain white shroud, without a ruffle, or any other ornament; and especially that there might be no spirituous liquor drank at her funeral, adding, that she had observed the practice of drinking, at a number of funerals which she had attended, and spoke of it in the highest terms of disapprobation, as being both improper and indecent.

Between eleven and twelve o'clock the following evening, she requested her mother to call the family together into her room. When they were come, she told them, that her soul, which was bound for heaven, would shortly quit the mortal body: but said she, "I shall give you the signal for my departure by shouting, being fully assured of dying triumphant in the faith."

Her father being present, she earnestly exhorted him to forsake the evil of his ways and turn to God, that he might meet her in a world of glory, to which she was now going. Her words much affected him, having reached his heart with convincing power; and from that moment he set out to seek the Lord, and is now a zealous member of Christ's Church, of which her mother was previously a pious member.

As she drew near the moment she had said she should expire, she asked her mother (who was quite feeble) if she would shout with the rest present, when she gave the word: who, although in great anguish of soul, on account of the prospect of parting with so excellent a child, told her she would, but not expecting the time was so near. But she soon repeated her request, and said, "Mother, help me all you can to praise God; I know you are weak, but come around my bed and get ready, for the chariot is coming—are you all ready? are you all ready? Now! now ! Here it comes. Glory! Glory! Glory! Shout! Shout! Mother, are you shouting? Jane, are you shouting?* Are you all shouting? And thus continued till she expired, which was at the very moment she had before said she should die.

Thus happy and triumphant died our dear young sister, the daughter of George and Sarah Henery, in the twentieth year of her age; and as she died, so she had lived after her conversion to God, which was but about two years before her death: during which time she had walked exemplary in all the ways of God, both towards her Redeemer, and her fellow-creatures; and to say the least of her that justice demands, she was modest, decent, sober, and diligent; in short, she possessed all the embellishments of the most chaste female character, to a degree seldom equalled, especially by those in a state of slavery. However, her master and mistress (Mr. and Mrs. Post,) had always treated her with much indulgence and great kindness, both in sickness and health; and when she died, the old lady and her son, as well as all present, were much affected with the scene.

She had experienced sanctification at the Croton Camp-Meeting, the year before her death; and the last time she met in class, she told one of the sisters, that she should meet with her no more in those religious exercises on earth; being fully persuaded that God, who had prepared her for a better world, was about to take her to himself.

To her case, the language of the poet is truly applicable.

* Jane was her fellow-servant.

"Happy soul, thy days are ended:
"All thy mourning days below.
"Go, by angel guards attended;
"To the sight of Jesus go.

"Waiting to receive thy spirit:
"Lo, the Savior stands above:
"Shews the purchase of his merit;
"Reaches out the crown of love.

"Struggle through thy latest passion:
"To thy dear Redeemer's breast:
"To his uttermost salvation;
"To his everlasting rest.

"For the joy he sets before thee;
"Bear a momentary pain.
"Die to live a life of glory.
"Suffer, with thy Lord to reign."[10]

I cannot but here remark, that while we see the souls of the righteous leaving the world, with loud shouts of joy and praise to God; that it is not to be wondered at, that individuals or whole assemblies of the people of God, in life and health, being filled with the joys of that hope which is full of immortality, should sometimes "Clap their hands, and shout unto God with the voice of triumph,"[11] as saith the Psalmist; or in correspondence with the sentiments of Isaiah, "should sing and shout because the holy one of Israel is great in the midst of them.[12] For that the upright in heart" should "shout for joy," while heavenly glory beams upon their ravished souls, can be nothing astonishing to the sincere Christian, who has "felt the powers of that world to come;"[13] where all the glorified host of God's elect continually cry with voices louder than many waters, and mighty thunders; glory "to him that has washed us from our sins in his own blood, and made us kings and priests unto God and the Father; to whom be glory for ever and ever."[14]

As God had made me instrumental in the awakening and conversion of this young sister, and being present at her death, her parents requested me to preach her funeral sermon; the substance of which, at their desire, I shall here insert; with an Elegy, composed on the death of their daughter. The defects of which, candor will find an easy apology for, considering the opportunities I have had to improve my mind in erudition.

The Substance of a Sermon, Preached on the Funeral Occasion of *Mary Henery.*

From *"Strive to enter in at the strait gate, for many I say unto you shall seek to enter in, and shall not be able."* Luke xiii. 34

The occasion on which we are assembled this day, is truly solemn, interesting and alarming; being met together to pay our last respects to the remains of our departed sister, who but recently filled her usual seat in this house; and rejoiced, on all religious occasions, to unite with you, my brethren, in chanting the songs of Zion, with an heart filled with the love of Christ, and exulting in the joys of his salvation.

But she is now no more: and though called to lament the loss of so worthy a member of the Church of Christ; yet we do not mourn as those without hope, for, "Them that sleep in Jesus, God will bring with him,"[15] at the last day; and our Saviour says, he "came to seek and save that which was lost:"[16] and in the chapter of which our text is a part, he intimates, that the chief of sinners may be saved who will repent; by preaching the doctrine of repentance, from the circumstance of the Gallaleans, whose blood Pilate mingled with their sacrifices; and that without repentance, none can be saved. But this blessing our departed sister had no doubt attained, with whom we hope to join in strains of immortal praise hereafter, when our bodies shall have endured the original sentence denounced against us for sin, "Dust thou art, and unto dust shalt thou return." For like her, through Jesus Christ we may obtain victory over death, hell and the grave, by complying with the terms of our text, which says "Strive to enter in at the strait gate, for many I say unto you, shall seek to enter in, and shall not be able."[17]

From which I shall take the liberty briefly to shew,

First, What we are to understand by the strait gate, and how we are to enter in thereat.

Secondly, Why it is called strait. And,

Thirdly, Who they are that shall seek to enter in, and shall not be able. And,

I. I am to shew what we are to understand by the strait gate, and how we are to enter in thereat. By their strait gate we are undoubtedly to understand, Jesus Christ himself, who has said, "I am the way, and the truth, and the life; no man cometh unto the Father but by me."[18]

And again: "Strait is the gate and narrow is the way that leadeth to life, and few there be that find it."[19] "I am," says he, "the door, by me if any man enter in he shall be saved, and go in and out and find pasture."[20]

Christ then being "the strait gate," and his doctrines the narrow way, and himself the only door of admission to the favour of God, and salvation; the scripture directs us how we are to enter in thereat, that is, by repentance, and faith in the merits of the atonement he has made for sinners, by the once offering of himself to God without spot.

By faith, then, we are to enter in at this gate: for although it is said, "Strive to enter in at the strait gate,"[21] yet we are to place no dependance upon our labours or strivings; for we can do nothing effectual in our own salvation, only as far as we are assisted by the all-sufficient grace of God; for it is written, "By grace are ye saved, through faith, and that not of yourselves, it is the gift of God."[22]

Yet although our strivings alone cannot prove effectual to our salvation, in this way, however, we must come to Christ, and receive him into our hearts. Therefore, "Strive to enter in at the strait gate, for many I say unto you shall seek to enter in, and shall not be able."[23] But,

II. Why is this gate called strait? I answer: from the example Christ has left us, that we should follow his steps, which is directly contrary to the corruptions of our own natures; and because repentance and faith, by which we must enter in thereat, are crossing, humbling and self-renouncing; in the attainment of which, the soul is brought into great inward straits of fear, terror and difficulty, but is always accompanied with hope of mercy, and followed with a revelation of Jesus Christ, as the all-sufficient Savior, to such as commit the care of their souls to him, trusting in his mercy alone for pardon and eternal salvation; and if adhered to, will lead to that eternal rest of glory, which our departed sister this day enjoys, in the presence of God and the Lamb. Therefore, "Strive to enter in at the strait gate, for many I say unto you shall seek to enter in, and shall not be able."[24]

I am 3dly, and lastly to shew, who they are that shall seek to enter in, and shall not be able.

There is no impediment to our entering in at the strait gate, but what originates in ourselves; for Christ has said, "He that cometh unto me, I will no wise cast out:"[25] and assigns it as the only reason why men are not saved, that they will not come unto him, that they might have life. And they do not come to Christ, because their hearts are opposed to his government, and his ways too crossing to their carnal inclinations.

But says the text, "Many shall seek to enter in, and shall not be able:" either because they do not seek aright, or in good earnest, by forsaking all their sins, resisting evil of every kind and degree; and by an agonizing, wrestling spirit, which refuses to be comforted, till Christ is formed in the heart the hope of glory.

Or lastly, because they seek too late; which is the reason Christ assigns in the words immediately following the text, "Strive to enter in at the strait gate, for many I say unto you shall seek to enter in, and shall not be able;" for, "When once the master of the house is risen up, and hath shut to the door, and ye begin to stand without, and to knock at the door, saying, Lord, Lord, open unto us; and he shall answer and say unto you, I know you not whence you are, depart from me all ye workers of iniquity."[26] How sad the disappointment, to seek for mercy too late to find it; even at the hand of him, who now says, "Behold, I stand at the door and knock; if any man hear my voice, and will open the door, I will come in to him, and will sup with him, and he with me.[27]

Improvement.

Whoever would go to heaven then, must repent, and believe in Jesus Christ, who is the only door of salvation, the way, the truth, and the life; and as our Lord said to Nichodemus, must be born again, or they cannot see the kingdom of God: for except renewed by the grace of God, in the very nature of things, no man can be happy; for the very nature of sin prevents the enjoyment of God, the only source and fountain of all happiness; so that, whoever dies without being renewed, must meet the just reward of their ungodliness, in the awful day of judgment, when the secrets of all hearts shall be revealed.

As this change of heart is called entering in at the strait gate, because it implies self-denial, mortification, self-renunciation, conviction and contrition for sin; and as all this is directly contrary to the dispositions of corrupt nature, it requires great and constant exertions, and mighty struggles of soul, under the influence of divine grace, to attain the blessing. For let none vainly imagine, that barely wiping their mouth will excuse them from damnation, or answer as a substitute for inward and outward holiness, in the great day of the wrath of God Almighty, when he shall come to judge the world in righteousness: therefore, "Seek ye the Lord while he may be found, call ye upon him while he is near: let the wicked forsake his way, and the unrighteous man his thoughts, and let him turn unto the Lord, who will have mercy upon him, and to our God, for he will abundantly pardon."[28]

And in this great and important work there is no time for delay; for life, the utmost extent of the day of grace, is uncertain; which is not only proved by the common occurrences of every day, but particularly by the instance of mortality which has occasioned our convention at this time; which speaks to you in the most pathetic language: "Be ye also ready, for in such an hour as ye think not the Son of man is risen up, and shut to the door, and ye begin to stand without, and to knock, saying, Lord, Lord, open unto us;" you will be only be answered with "depart from me all ye that work iniquity:"[29] therefore now return unto the Lord from whom you have departed, by sincere repentance, that your souls may live. Secure a supply of the oil of grace; trim your lamps, and prepare to meet the bridegroom at his coming, that ye may enter in to the marriage supper of the Lamb, before the door of mercy is forever shut.

I see before me a large number of mourners, whose showering tears bespeak the anguish of heart excited by the death of her, whose relics we have so recently followed to the house appointed for all the living. But hush the heaving sigh, and dry the briny tear, for your deceased relative, and our much-loved Christian sister, has, no doubt, found a safe passage through the strait and narrow gate to the blissful regions of eternal day; where she now joins the Church triumphant, around the dazzling throne of God, in songs of praise and shouts of victory.

And while you, with the rest of the congregation, have the offers of mercy yet held out to you in the name of Jesus Christ, who stands knocking at the door of your hearts for entrance; embrace it, and bid him welcome, that you may be prepared when death shall call you hence, to join the jubelant throng with our departed sister, and chant the wonders of redeeming grace forever.

But to you, especially, who are in the bloom of youth, this instance of mortality calls aloud to prepare for death; remember your all is at stake; death is at your door, and will shortly summon you to appear at the bar of God, who will assuredly bring you into judgement for living after the desires of your own wicked hearts. Reflect then for a moment, how awful it will be to die in your sins, strangers to God, and meet the awful Judge of quick and dead, to hear the sentence pronounced upon your guilty souls, "Depart ye cursed into everlasting fire, prepared for the devil and his angels."[30] To avert this dreadful doom delay no longer; but now, even now, embrace the offers of mercy tendered to you by the gospel of Jesus Christ, and experience his great salvation.

And finally, brethren, let us all consider our ways, turn to the Lord, and strive to enter in at the strait gate, that we may not be found among the number of those, who by seeking too late, shall not be able to enter in; that when we are called to lie upon our death bed, we may have the same ravishing views of heaven, our departed sister had two days before her death, who said, she "saw heaven opened, and heard the saints in glory sing:"[31] and like her, leave the world, crying glory! glory! glory! even so, Lord Jesus. Amen! and Amen!

I here subjoin the following elegy, composed on the death of our departed sister in Christ.

How wond'rous are thy ways, Almighty God!
Deep are thy councils; and severe thy rod!
Thy chast'ning hand, what mortal man can stay?
Or who can turn thy tenderness away?

Our friend is gone, but let us not repine:
The gem was ravish'd by the hand divine.
Call'd to adorn the dear Redeemer's crown,
And add new honours to Immanuel's throne.

Her virtue lives: and ever live it must;
Although her flesh lies slumb'ring in the dust.
Wipe off that tear, suppress the swelling sigh;
For she that lives in Christ can never die.

Grieve not, ye parents, give your sighing o'er:
The deep felt cause will soon be felt no more.
Your daughter lives in pleasures ever new,
On Zion's hill, where she looks out for you.

I shall now present the reader with the striking, but awful contrast with what I have just related, and which took place soon after. A very prophane (coloured) man, who was a great enemy to religion, living but a little distance from me, on his being taken sick, his wife, who was a serious woman, (but not allowed by her husband to attend religious meetings) sent for me to come and see him. I accordingly went, and continued to visit him every day while he lived; but found him, through his whole sickness, the most hardened obstinate sinner I ever met with. I conversed, prayed with, and exhorted him to no effect; for the most I could induce him to say of himself was, that he hoped or expected to recover. But the eighth day of his sickness, being Sabbath, and the day on which he died, I was sent for in the morning to go and see him. On coming to the house, I was informed by his wife, that, apprehending himself struck with death, he had that morning attempted to run away, asserting that he was flying from death, which he saw after him; but was apprehended and brought back by the neighbours. Upon hearing this, I concluded he was insane; but was soon convinced otherwise, and that his conduct was the effect of dread and terror: for on every other subject he appeared perfectly rational. I conversed with him about the sad condition his soul was in, and inquired of him the reason why he attempted to run away.—He replied, that death was after him. I told him that it was in vain to attempt to make his escape from death; but ought rather to seek a preparation for it. He observed, that in this respect it was a gone case with him: for, said he, "I am a damned wretch," and broke out in the most horrid oaths. After the morning service I visited him again, being accompanied by brother A.T. a local preacher, who asked him some questions concerning his condition; to which he answered, that it was a gone case with him, and began to curse and swear so horribly, that neither of us could find it in our hearts to pray with him. I called again, as did many others, towards evening, to see this wonder of depravity, and found him in the same frame of mind as before. He said the devils had come for him, and that he could see them all about the room. I asked him why he went on in the manner he did: he declared that he could not help it. I went to see him for the last time betwen ten and eleven o'clock at night, and left him about half an hour before his death belching out the most impious oaths and curses, which I was told he continued to do till death put a stop to it. Thus, living without the fear of God, he died in a state of mad despair, where we leave him, with the reader to reflect upon the awful contrast between such a death, and that of the young woman before mentioned; not doubting but his good sense will teach him which to prefer as his own. But withal remember, that if you would die the death of the righteous, in preference to that of the wicked, you must live their life also.

Before I close this little narrative, I will offer a few thoughts on the subject of true happiness, being the result of my own experience and observation, as well as suggested by the doctrines of the gospel of Jesus Christ.

Happiness is the grand object of the pursuit of every man. But alas:

how many fail of its attainment, by seeking for it where it is not be found.

But what is happiness? it may be asked, and where, and how is it to be obtained? To these inquiries none but the real christian, who lives in the light of the sanctuary, can give a decided and satisfactory answer.

God is the only source of true happiness;—and happiness therefore consists in the enjoyment of God only; and is in no other way to be obtained but by such a faith in Jesus Christ, as unites the soul to him, and possesses it of that "Righteousness, peace, and joy in the Holy Ghost," which the apostle Paul denominates the "Kingdom of God;" and is the well-spring of that joy and rejoicing, which he elsewhere recommends to the truly pious, by saying, "Rejoice in the Lord always, and again I say rejoice."[32]

The Divine perfections, attributes, and government, are a continual source of happiness and joy to the real Christian; for being united to God, he not only discovers their beauty and harmony, but rests in the fullest assurance, that they are all engaged to make him blessed, while he enjoys the witness of the amazing mercy of God, in the free pardon of all his sins.

He rejoices in the wisdom of God, as ordering all events, and as being engaged for his direction, in whatever station or condition of life, Divine Providence may have placed him, being fully persuaded that God will neither do, nor suffer to be done, what he would not do, or suffer to be done himself, could he but see the end of all things as perfectly as God does:—therefore he is contented and happy under all his dealings, knowing that adversity, pain and sickness, shall no less turn to his advantage, under the direction of infinite wisdom and goodness, than prosperity, ease, health and wealth; for whom the Lord loveth he chasteneth, and scourgeth every son whom he receiveth: and will make all things work together for good to them that love him.[33]

The power and omnipresence of God, are equally a source of the Christian's joy, for being every where at the same time, and able to accomplish all his purposes, can, not only purify his heart from sin, but give him victory over all his temporal and spiritual enemies, and afford support under every trial and burden.

So that the soul who trusts in the Lord Jesus, who has himself conquered all his enemies, rejoices in full assurance of being made more than conqueror, through Christ who has loved him. For he is a friend that sticketh closer than a brother.[34]

Our earthly friends may be absent when we want them most, and if present, would not in all cases know how to help us, if they would; nor have they it in their power in all cases to do it, and even the best of them may prove treacherous to our interest, and ruin us forever. But not so with our heavenly friend, who is infinitely wise, powerful, and good, whose veracity is pledged, that he will never leave nor forsake them who put their trust in him. Therefore, the true Christian must be happy.

The holy scriptures, which reveal the divine character and government, our duty to God and one another; and especially, as they assure the righteous of a glorious immortality, are an inexhaustable source of joy and rejoicing to the Christian, while every promise teems with the honey of everlasting love, and glares with the full blaze of future glory, upon the dazzled eyes of him who reads them by faith, as his own through grace.

In allusion to which, St. Austin says, "the word of God is like the starry heavens in a clear night:" "if," says he "you cast your eyes upon a given part of it, some stars immediately discover themselves to your view; but the more attention you give, the more stars will be breaking forth to the sight:" and so it is with the sacred scriptures, ever new, and ever unfolding new beauties, and increasing glories, to all the persevering followers of the Lord Jesus.[35]

The works of creation, which the mere philosopher views only as a series of natural causes and effects, unfold to the ravished sight of faith, the eternal power and God-head, beaming its own divine effulgence from every branch of the natural world; and the loving heart feels that he who made the stars is my Father and my God, under whose control are all the elements; these are the works of my great Redeemer, my Saviour, and my Friend, which all obey his sovereign will, and declare his matchless glory; from whose gracious hand, the most trifling benefit is received with the highest sensation of gratitude, and thus becomes a lasting blessing; while the greatest favours heaven can bestow upon the impenitent, through their unthankfulness, become but lasting curses, and serve to enhance their condemnation.

Indeed, nothing on earth can equal the Christian's happiness, and nothing else deserves that endearing name. For who can be so happy as he who knows his sins are all forgiven, that God is his reconciled Father and Friend; that he is entitled, through the merit of Jesus Christ, to the protection of the Almighty, and coheirship with his Son hereafter; for the security of which, the veracity of God himself is pledged, all whose promises in Christ Jesus are yea and amen. Who so happy as they that have an hope full of immortality beyond the grave, and are assured that all things shall work together for their good; so that their very sufferings shall only work out for them, a far more exceeding and eternal weight of glory. It was these things which the apostle John wrote to his brethren, that their joy might be full. It is by entering deep into the spirit of these things that the joy of Christ is fulfilled in the believer; and to be the helpers of their joys, has Jesus Christ sent his minsters with this commission, "Comfort ye, comfort ye my people, saith your God;"[36] and the more of this comfort the Christian enjoys, with the greater contempt does he look down upon all earthly pleasure, and crucifies himself the more to the world.

And as he partakes of the nature, as well as the enjoyment of God, it is his chief delight to diffuse happiness among his fellow-creatures, as far as is in his power, which only increases his joy, by the necessary happiness which arises from doing good to others, and making them happy; which returns to God in constant strains of adoration from every happy soul. May the God of grace and love, make the reader thus unspeakably happy in himself, and his service, and at last, bring both you and me to enjoy a state of consummate happiness, in the full enjoyment of his glory, in the world to come.

Finis

Notes

1. Matthew 3:10; Luke 3:9.
2. 2 Corinthians 12:9.
3. Revelation 21:8.
4. 1 Thessalonians 5:17.
5. Charles Wesley, "Lord of the Harvest, hear."
6. Psalms 107:8, 15, 21, 23.
7. 1 Corinthians 14:25.
8. Daniel Coker.
9. Isaiah 58:1.
10. Charles Wesley, "The Dying Christian."
11. Psalms 47:1.
12. Isaiah 12:6.
13. Hebrews 6:5.
14. Revelations 1:5–6.
15. 1 Thessalonians 4:14.
16. Matthew 18:11.
17. Luke 13:24.
18. John 4:16.
19. Luke 13:14.
20. John 10:9.
21. Luke 13:24.
22. Ephesians 2:8.
23. Luke 13:24.
24. *Ibid.*
25. John 6:37.
26. Luke 13:25.
27. Revelations 3:20.
28. Isaiah 55:6–7.
29. Luke 13:25–27.
30. Matthew 25:41.
31. Acts 10:11.
32. Phillipians 4:4.
33. Hebrews 12:6.
34. Proverbs 18:24.
35. Saint Austin is Augustine—not the bishop of Hippo (A.D. 354–430), but the first archbishop of Canterbury(d. A.D. 604).
36. Isaiah 40:1.

JOHN JEA.

African Preacher of the Gospel

THE

LIFE,

HISTORY,

AND

UNPARALLELED SUFFERINGS

OF

JOHN JEA,

THE AFRICAN PREACHER.

Compiled and Written by HIMSELF.

Printed for the Author.

John Jea

The Life, History, and Unparalleled Sufferings of John Jea, the African Preacher

I, John Jea, the subject of this narrative, was born in the town of Old Callabar, in Africa, in the year 1773. My father's name was Hambleton Robert Jea, my mother's name Margaret Jea; they were of poor, but industrious parents. At two years and a half old, I and my father, mother, brothers, and sisters, were stolen, and conveyed to North America, and sold for slaves; we were then sent to New York, the man who purchased us was very cruel, and used us in a manner, almost too shocking to relate; my master and mistress's names were Oliver and Angelika Triehuen, they had seven children—three sons and four daughters; he gave us a very little food or raiment, scarcely enough to satisfy us in any measure whatever; our food was what is called Indian corn pounded, or bruised and boiled with water, the same way burgo is made, and about a quart of sour butter-milk poured on it; for one person two quarts of this mixture, and about three ounces of dark bread, per day, the bread was darker than that usually allowed to convicts, and greased over with very indifferent hog's lard; at other times when he was better pleased, he would allow us about half-a-pound of beef for a week, and about half-a-gallon of potatoes; but that was very seldom the case, and yet we esteemed ourselves better used than many of our neighbors.

Our labour was extremely hard, being obliged to work in the summer from about two o'clock in the morning, till about ten or eleven o'clock at night, and in the winter from four in the morning, till ten at night. The horses usually rested about five hours in the day, while we were at work; thus did the beasts enjoy greater privileges than we did. We dared not murmur, for if we did we were corrected with a weapon an inch and-a-half thick, and that without mercy, striking us in the most tender parts, and if we complained of this usage, they then took four large poles, placed them in the ground, tied us up to them, and flogged us in a manner too dreadful to behold; and when taken down, if we offered to lift up our hand or foot against our master or mistress, they used us in a most cruel manner; and often they treated the slaves in such a manner as caused their death, shooting them with a gun, or beating their brains out with some weapon, in order to appease their wrath, and thought no more of it than if they had been brutes: this was the general treatment which slaves experienced. After our master had been treating us in this cruel manner, we were obliged to thank him for the punishment he had been inflicting on us, quoting that Scripture which saith, "Bless the rod, and him that hath appointed it." But, though he was a professor of religion, he forgot *that* passage which saith "God is love, and whoso dwelleth in love dwelleth in God, and God in him."[1] And, again, we are commanded to love our enemies; but it appeared evident that his wretched heart was hardened; which led us to look up unto him as our god, for we did not know him who is able to deliver and save all who call upon him in truth and sincerity. Conscience, that faithful monitor, (which either excuses or accuses) caused us to groan, cry, or sigh, in a manner which cannot be uttered.

We were often led away with the idea that our masters were our gods; and at other times we placed our ideas on the sun, moon, and stars, looking unto them, as if they could save us; at length we found, to our great disappointment, that these were nothing else but the works of the Supreme Being; this caused me to wonder how my master frequently expressed that all his houses, land, cattle, servants, and every thing which he possessed was his own; not considering that it was the Lord of Hosts,[2] who has said that the gold and the silver, the earth, and the fullness thereof,[3] belong to him.

Our master told us, that when we died, we should be like the beasts that perish; not informing us of God, heaven, or eternal punishments, and that God hath promised to bring the secrets of every heart into judgement, and to judge every man according to his works.[4]

From the following instances of the judgements of God, I was taught that he is God, and there is none besides him, neither in the heavens above, nor in the earth beneath, nor in the waters under the earth; for he doth with the armies of heaven and the inhabitants of the earth as seemeth him good; and there is none that can stay his hand, nor say unto him, with a prevailing voice, *what dost thou?*[5]

My master was often disappointed in his attempts to increase the produce of his lands; for oftentimes he would command us to carry out more seed into the field to insure a good crop, but when it sprang up and promised to yield plentifully, the Almighty caused the worms to eat it at the root, and destroyed nearly the whole produce; God thus showing him his own inability to preserve the fruits of the earth.

At another time he ordered the trees to be pruned, that they might have brought forth more fruit, to have increased his worldly riches, but God, who doth not as man pleaseth, sent the caterpiller, the canker-worm, and the locust, when the trees bore a promising appearance, and his fond hopes were blasted, by the fruits being all destroyed. Thus was he again disappointed, but still remained ignorant of the hand of God being in these judgements.

Notwithstanding he still went on in his wickedness until another calamity befell him; for when the harvest was full ripe, the corn cut down, and standing in shocks ready to be carried into the barn, it pleased God to send a dreadful storm of thunder and lightning, hail and rain, which compelled them to leave it out, till it rotted on the ground. Often were his cattle destroyed by distempers of various kinds; yet he hearkened not unto the voice of the Lord.

At one time, when his barns and storehouses were filled with all sorts of grain, and he rejoiced in the greatness of his harvest, it pleased the Almighty to send a very dreadful storm of thunder and lightning, which consumed a great part of his property; such scenes as these occurred several times, yet he regarded not the power of the Almighty, nor the strength of his arm; for when we poor slaves were visited by the hand of God, and he took us from time to eternity, he thought no more of our poor souls than if we had had none, but lamented greatly the loss of the body; which caused me very much to wonder at his actions, I being very young, not above eight or nine years of age, and seeing the hand of the Almighty, though I did not at that time know it was his works, in burning up the pastures, in permitting the cattle to die for want of water, and in causing the fruits of the earth to be blighted. At the same time a most violent storm of thunder and lightning was experienced, which, in the space of thirty or forty miles, consumed about thirteen houses, barns, and store-houses, which terrified us poor slaves in a terrible manner, not knowing what these things meant. Even my master and mistress were very much terrified, fearful of being destroyed by the violence of the weather.

About two or three days after this awful scene, a day of fasting, prayer, and thanksgiving, was commanded by General Washington, to pray to Almighty God to withdraw his anger from us; which day was observed by all, but us poor slaves, for we were obliged to fast, but were not exempted from work; our masters thinking us not worthy to go to a place of worship; which surprised me a great deal, being very ignorant, and I asked my parents what all this meant, but they could not tell me, but supposed, from what they had heard them say, they were worshipping their god; then I began to enquire how this could be, having heard my master often say, that all he possessed was his own, and he could do as he pleased with it; which, indeed, was the saying of all those who had slaves. My curiosity being thus raised, I made bold to speak to my master's sons, and asked them the reason they prayed and called upon God, and they told me because of the awful judgements that had happened on the land; then I asked what awful judgements they meant, and they said unto me, have you not seen how the Lord hath destroyed all things from off the face of the earth? and I answered yes; I then asked them who did this, and they told me God; then, said I, ought not God to be feared, seeing that he can build up and he can cast down,[6] he can create and he can destroy, and though we may cultivate our lands and sow our seed, we can never secure the crop without the favour of Him who, is the sovereign disposer of all things? They answered, yes. From this I observed that there were those who feared God when the weather was tempestuous, but feared him not when it was fine.

Seeing them act in such a wicked manner, I was encouraged to go on in my sins, being subject to all manner of iniquity that could be mentioned, not knowing there was a God, for they told us that we poor slaves had no God. As I grew up, my desire to know who their God was increased, but I did not know who to apply to, not being allowed to be taught by any one whatever, which caused me to watch their actions very closely; and in so doing, I, at one time, perceived that something was going forward which I could not comprehend, at last I found out that they were burying a slave master, who was very rich; they appeared to mourn and lament for his death, as though he had been a good man, and I asked them why they let him die; they said they could not help it, for God killed him: I said unto them, what, could you not have taken him away from God? They said, no, for he killed whomever he pleased. I then said he must be a dreadful God, and was led to fear least he should kill me also; although I had never seen death, but at a distance. But this fear did not last long, for seeing others full of mirth, I became so too.

A short time after this, there were great rejoicings on account of a great victory obtained by the Americans over the poor Indians, who had been so unfortunate as to lose their possessions, and they strove against the Americans, but they over-powered and killed thousands of them, and numbers were taken prisoners, and for this cause they greatly rejoiced. They expressed their joy by the ringing of bells, firing of guns, dancing and singing, while we poor slaves were hard at work. When I was informed of the cause of these rejoicings, I thought, *these* people made a great mourning when *God* killed one man, but they rejoice when *they* kill so many. I was thus taught that though they talked much about their God, they did not regard him as they ought. They had forgotten that sermon of our blessed Saviour's on the mount, which you find in St. Matthew's gospel, v. *chap* 43, 44, *v.*; and I had reason to think their hearts were disobedient, not obeying the truth, though it was read and preached to them; their hearts being carnal, as the Scriptures saith, were at enmity with God, not subject to the law of God, neither indeed could be; for they gave themselves up to the works of the flesh, to fulfil it in the lusts thereof.

My dear reader, consider the great obligations you are under to the Wise Disposer of all events, that you were not born in Africa, and sold for a slave, on whom the most cruel tortures are exercised, but that you were born in Britain, a land of freedom; and above all, be thankful for the opportunities you have of knowing the "true God, and Jesus Christ whom he has sent," and recollect that as you possess much, much will be required; and, unless you improve your advantages, you had better be a slave in any dark part of the world, than a neglecter of of the gospel in this highly favoured land; recollect also that even here you might be a slave of the most awful description:—a slave to your passions—a slave to the world—a slave to sin—a slave to satan—a slave of hell—and, unless you are made free by Christ, through the means of the gospel, you will remain in captivity, tied and bound in the chains of your sin, till at last you will be bound hand and foot, and cast into outer darkness, there shall be weeping and gnashing of teeth for ever.[7]

But, to return to myself, it was evident that our masters did not believe the report God gave of his Son, which the gospel holds forth to us, for if they had they would have instructed us poor slaves; but they did not think us, as have been before observed, worthy their notice. Frequently did they tell us we were made by, and like the devil, and commonly called us *black devils*; not considering what the Scriptures saith in the Song of Solomon, "I am black, but comely. Look not upon me, because I am black, because the sun hath looked upon me; my mother's children were angry with me; they made me keeper of the vineyards; but mine own vineyard have I not kept."[8] This latter sentence was verified in the case of us poor slaves, for our master would make us work, and neglect the concerns of our souls.

From my observations of the conduct and conversation of my master and his sons, I was led to hate those who professed themselves Christians, and to look upon them as devils; which made me neglect my work, and I told them what I thought of their ways. On this they did beat me in a most dreadful manner; but, instead of making me obedient, it made me the more stubborn, not caring whether I lived or died, thinking that after I was dead I should be at rest, and that I should go back again to my native country, Africa (an idea generally entertained by slaves); but when I told them this, they chastised me seven times the more, and kept me short of food. In addition to this punishment, they made me go to a place of worship, while the other slaves enjoyed a rest for an hour or two; I could not bear to be where the word of God was mentioned, for I had seen so much deception in the people that professed to know God, that I could not endure being where there were, nor yet to hear them call upon the name of the Lord; but I was still sent in order to punish me, for when I entered the place I had such malice against God and his people, as showed the depravity of my heart, and verified the Scripture which saith, "That the natural man understandeth not the things which are of God, for they are foolishness unto him; neither doth he know them, because he is not spiritually discerned."[9]

My rage and malice against every person that was religious was so very great that I would have destroyed them all, had it been in my power; my indignation was so increased on my entering the place of worship, that, "the form of my visage was changed," like Nebuchadnezzar's, when he ordered Shadrach, Mesbach, and Abednego, to be cast into the fiery furnace.[10] My fury was more particularly kindled against the minister, and I should have killed him, had I not feared the people, it not being in my power to kill him, grieved me very much; and I went home and told my master what the minister had said, and what lies he had told, as I imagined, in hopes that he would send me no more;

but he knowing this was a punishment to me, he made me go the more, for it was evident it was not for the good of my soul; this pained me exceedingly, so that I laid the blame to the minister, thinking that it was through his preaching so many lies, as I thought in my foolish opinion, that I was obliged to attend, not knowing that he spoke the truth, and I told the lies. The more I went to hear him preach, the more I wished to lay in wait to take away his life; but, as when the preaching was over, I was forced to return home to my master, and tell him what I had heard, I had no opportunity. At one time, the minister said that God was in the midst of them,[11] which astonished me very much, and I looked all about to see if I could see him, but I could not, and I thought I had as good eyes as any one; not having any idea that "God is a spirit, and they that worship him, must worship him in spirit and in truth," John iv. 24; and only to be seen by a spiritual mind in the exercise of faith.

I was thus sent every Sabbath-day, while the other slaves rested, for while the masters go to worship, the slaves are allowed to rest, but thinking that I deserved punishment I was compelled to go to the chapel; but instead of being benefitted by what I heard, I mocked and persecuted the people of God; and when I went home I told my master of the foolishness of preaching,[12] and that the people were mad, for they cried and beat their hands together. It amazed me very much to think they suffered such a noise in a place which they called *God's house*; on returning home I told my master what I had heard and seen, and what I thought of it, which pleased him very much. My hatred was so much against going to the chapel, that I would rather have received an hundred lashes.

Hearing the minister say that we must pray to God for his presence, I determined when I went away to do the same as I had seen the minister do; so when I got home, I retired into a secret place, and there began folding my hands together, shutting my eyes, and using many words which I had heard the minister say, not knowing whether they were right or wrong; and thinking for my much speaking, God would hear me, like the pharisees of old: little did I think that prayer was the sincerity of the heart, and such only is accepted of God; not being acquainted with his word; but I was obliged still to go and hear the minister, or else I should not have had my daily allowance, which was very small. So after thinking a short time, I consented to go one week more, and endeavour to find out "The Lamb of God, that taketh away the sins of the world,"[13] whom the minister pointed out; but all was in vain, for I was so tempted by Satan, that difficulties and troubles, whenever I attempted to pray, attended me. The temptations of the devil were so great, and my repeated attempts to pray so interrupted, that I resolved to go to the minister, and tell him my situation. I therefore went, and told him the state of my mind. He told me it was the works of the devil, to frustrate me in my endeavours to serve the Lord, but bid me go on praying in opposition to him. I thanked him for his kindness in telling me what to do, but believed him not; however, I still continued praying, in order to find out whether there was a God or not, being determined to take the minister's life away, if I could not find God.

Thus I endeavoured to pray, but such was my situation, that sometimes I could not utter a word; often when I began to pray, I fell asleep, which grieved me very much; conscience accusing me of neglect in my seeking after God. One day being sent as usual to the chapel, in order to punish me, the minister was preaching about prayer, my attention was immediately fixed on the minister to hear what he had to say on the subject, when he said that if any of us had been praying to God and found no benefit from it, we should pray again and again, and be more earnest, and the Lord would hear our prayers: for, "The effectual fervent prayer of a righteous man availeth much."[14] Not knowing the similarity of experience, I thought the minister was preaching about me, and exposing me to all the people, which so much vexed me, that I could not stay any longer, but left the place of worship, and returned home, crying and weeping all the way.

Having a very strong desire to know God, I often retired into some private place to pray, but did not receive any advantage for a long time, which grieved me very sorely. My own heart still suggested to me that there was no God, being so wicked and sinful; that I have since compared myself with those who were destroyed by the flood, Gen. viii. 21. But I have great reason to bless the Lord, that though my heart was deceitful above all things and desperately wicked, yet he did not destroy me, but that I might by his Spirit be converted to God.

From my being disappointed several times I began to despair of ever finding God, and I made a resolution if I did not find him in one more week, I would seek him no more, and would use all the means in my power to take away the minister's life. By earnest prayer and supplication,[15] before the week expired, I was led to see that I was a sinner; all my sins were brought to mind; and the vengeance of God hanging over my head, ready to crush me to pieces; which filled me with distress and anguish of mind, "The sorrows of death now seemed to compass me, and the pains of hell got hold upon me; I found trouble and sorrow."[16] My sins seemed like great mountains pressing on me, and I thought God would deal with me according to my sins, and punish me for my crimes. I knew not how to pacify the wrath of God, for when I looked round me I saw nothing but danger, for the threatenings of God against rebellious sinners, appeared to my view, some of which you will find in the 9th and 10th Psalms; and I had sinned against him with an high hand, and an outstretched arm; and had said in my heart, who is the Lord that I should serve him. But now the Lord shrewed me my sad state, and that I had spoken against him. I was in great distress and affliction, feeling the truth of what God says in his word, that he will send all the curses upon man for their disobedience; and this caused me to groan and cry in a most dreadful manner. The persecutions and threatenings which I had vowed against religious people, particularly the minister, now came to my mind, and filled me with bitter reflection. Sometimes, my terror of mind was so great, that I thought the earth would open, and swallow me up, as in the case of Korah, Dathan, and Abiram. Numbers xvi. 31–35.

My master and mistress, seeing my distress, asked me what was the matter; and I told them what a sinner I was, and what I feared on account of it: but they commanded me to go to work, for their was no fear of the earth's opening her mouth, and swallowing me up; that the minister had put the devil in me, and they would beat him out, and then they began beating me in a most dreadful manner, whilst I was in this distress of mind; and to add to my troubles, they would not permit me to attend the chapel, thus altering my punishment, though I felt the burden of my sins almost insupportable. In this state I was forced to go to work, with my flesh torn to pieces by their scourging, having large lumps raised on my back; and my soul was grieved and troubled within me. In this situation I went from one friend to another, crying "What shall I do to be saved?"[17] But they, instead of comforting, ridiculed me, and said I was mad.

In this miserable condition, I went to the minister, whom once I had so much despised, and enquired of *him*, what I must do to be saved; begging of him to read and pray for me, that God's anger might be turned away, and that he might be merciful unto me. After this I used to go to the minister every night, about ten or eleven o'clock, that he might read and pray to me; he told me I must pray for myself; but I said that

God would not hear my prayers, because I was so wicked: but he told me to go to God, and tell him what a wicked sinner I was, and beg him to have mercy on me. When I went home, I began calling upon God, but did not dare to look up unto heaven, where his honour dwelleth, being so exceedingly terrified, for I feared that God would send his thunder and lightning to destroy me, because of my sins and wickedness. And in my distress I called upon the Lord, and cried unto my God, which you read of in the 18th Psalm, though I could not believe him to be *my* God, I was so afraid of him.

My distress was so very great, that I could have exclaimed with one of old, that I could not give sleep to my eyes, nor slumber to my eye-lids; yea, my bed was watered with my tears:[18] seeing myself hanging over the brink of a burning hell, only by the brittle thread of life. My experiencing such hardships from my master and others led me to cry out, "O Lord, thou hast made me the off-scouring and the refuse in the midst of all the people; and all mine enemies have opened their mouths against me."[19] My enemies, my master and mistress, my mother, sisters, and brothers, chased me sorely without a cause, and increased my trouble by not permitting me to go to a place of worship; for now I began to see the need of a Saviour to save my soul, or else I must have perished for ever; and feeling that I was not prepared to die, and appear before the judgement seat of Christ, to give an account of the deeds done in the body. Having been led to see that they were very bad, it caused me to say, "Is it nothing to you all ye that pass by; behold and see if there be any sorrow like unto my sorrow, which is done unto me, wherewith the Lord, hath afflicted me, in the day of his fierce anger; from above he hath sent fire into my bones, and it prevaileth against them. He hath spread a net for my feet; he hath turned me back, he hath made me desolate, and faint all the day. The yoke of my transgressions is bound by his hand, they are wreathed, and come up upon my neck. He hath made my strength to fail; the Lord hath delivereth me into their hands from whom I am not able to rise up. For these things I weep, mine eyes runneth down with water; because the Comforter that should relieve my soul is far from me." Lament. of Jeremiah i. 12, 13, 14, 16.

In this distress I continued five or six weeks, and found no relief, being derided, persecuted, and tortured in the most cruel manner; every thing seemed to be against me; yea, even my victuals seemed like wormwood, and my drink like gaul. Thus I bowed my knees and my heart before the Lord, in great distress, begging the Lord to have mercy on my soul, that I might not perish; and in the bitterness of my soul, *"I set my face unto the Lord God, to seek by prayer and supplications, with fastings, and sackcloth, and ashes: And I prayed unto the Lord my God, and made my confession, and said, O Lord, the great and dreadful God, keeping the covenant and mercy to them that love him, and to them that keep his commandments; we have sinned and have committed iniquity, and have done wickedly, and have rebelled, even by departing from thy precepts, and from thy judgements: Neither have we hearkened unto thy servants the prophets, which spake in thy name to our kings, our princes, and our fathers, and to all the people of the land."* Daniel ix, 3, 4, 5, 6.

My troubles were so great, that I had nigh sunk into despair, the world, the flesh, and the devil, pressing on me solely. My enemies increased their persecutions, which led me to cry to the Lord to have mercy on my soul, and deliver me from my cruel enemies. Yea, I cried and mourned like a dove of the valley, upon the tops of the mountains; saying, *"Be merciful unto me, O God: for man would swallow me up; he fighting daily oppresseth me. Mine enemies would swallow me up: for they be many that fight against me, O thou Most High. What time I am afraid, I will trust in thee."* Psalm lvi. 1, 2, 3.

But the corruptions of my heart were so held forth to my view, that I exclaimed with David of old, *Psalm* li, to the 18th *verse.*

Such was my desire of being instructed in the way of salvation, that I wept at all times I possibly could, to hear the word of God, and seek instruction for my soul; while my master still continued to flog me, hoping to deter me from going; but all to no purpose, for I was determined, by the grace of God, to seek the Lord with all my heart, and with all my mind, and with all my strength, in spirit and in truth,[20] as you read in the Holy Bible. During five or six weeks of my distress, I did not sleep six hours in each week, neither did I care to eat any victuals, for I had no appetite, and thought myself unworthy of the least blessing that God had bestowed on me; that I exclaimed with the publican of old, *"God be merciful to me a miserable hell-deserving sinner."*[21] And while I was thus crying, and begging God to have mercy on me, and confessing my sins unto him, it pleased God to hear my supplications and cries, and came down in his Spirit's power and blessed my soul, and showed me the clear fountain of living water, which proceeded from the throne of God,[22] as you may read in the Revelations; yea, a fountain of water and blood, which flowed from Emanuel's side, to wash away my sins and iniquities, and he applied it unto my heart, and cleansed it from all iniquities, and said unto me, *"And when I passed by thee, and saw thee polluted in thine own blood, I said unto thee when thou wast in thy blood, Live; yea, I said unto thee when thou wast in thy blood, Live. I have caused thee to multiply as the bud of the field, and thou hast increased and waxen great, and thou art come to excellent ornaments: thy breasts are fashioned, and thine hair is grown, whereas thou wast naked and bare. Now when I passed by thee, and looked upon thee, behold, thy time was the time of love; and I spread my skirt over thee, and covered thy nakedness: yea, I sware unto thee, and entered into a covenant with thee, saith the Lord God, and thou becamest mine. Then washed I thee with water; yea, I thoroughly washed away thy blood from thee, and I anointed thee with oil. I clothed thee also with broidered work, and shod thee with badgers' skin, and I girded thee about with fine linen, and I covered thee with silk. I decked thee also with ornaments, and I put bracelets upon thy hands, and a chain on thy neck. And I put a jewel on thy forehead, and ear-rings in thine ears, and a beautiful crown upon thine head. Thus wast thou decked with gold and silver; and thy raiment was of fine linen, and silk, and broidered work; thou didst eat fine flour, and honey, and oil: and thou wast exceeding beautiful, and thou didst prosper abundantly. And thy renown went forth among the heathen for thy beauty: for it was perfect through my comeliness, which I had put upon thee, saith the Lord God."* Ezekiel xvi 6–14.

My dear reader, consider the state I was in, I was nearly naked, and had scarcely food to eat, and when I complained, I was tied up, both hands and feet, or put in chains, and flogged, so that the blood would run from my back to the ground; at one time he broke two of my ribs, by stamping and jumping upon me. Consider what a great deliverance I experienced, being released from the bondage of sin and satan, and delivered from the misery in which I was in, surely none else but the eternal God could effect so great a change.

I had sinned against God with an high hand and an out-stretched arm, and had said in my heart, who is God, or the Almighty, that I should fear him, and what profit is it that we have kept his ordinances, or that we have walked mournfully before the Lord of Hosts, Mal. iii. *chap.* part of the 14th *verse.* But for ever-blessed be the Lord God Almighty, who heareth the prayers and supplications of poor unworthy sinful creatures, for when I humbled myself, and walked mournfully before the Lord God Almighty, and kept his ordinances and his commandments, he sent his Spirit into my heart, which convinced me *"Of sin, of righteousness, and of judgement to come."* John xvi 8. This made me confess my sins and my wickedness, with shame and confusion of face;

and when I had confessed my sins and my wickedness to God, with grief and sorrow of heart, *"He was faithful and just to forgive me my sins, and to cleanse me from all unrighteousness."* 1 John i.13.

I was about fifteen years of age when the Lord was pleased to remove gross darkness, superstition, and idolatry, from my heart, and shined upon me with the glorious reconciliation and light of his countenance, and turned my darkness into day, and created a clean heart within me, and renewed a right spirit within me,[23] and said unto my soul, *"Let their be light,* (Gen. i. 3) *and their was light."* This *"was the true Light, which lighteth every man that cometh into the* [spiritual] *world."* John i.9. He was in my heart, and my heart was made by him a clean, new, and fleshy heart, and the heart of stone he took away, as says the prophet Ezekiel, and he renewed a right spirit within me, and gave me a broken spirit, and a humble and contrite heart, which God wilt not despise.[24] Jesus Christ now revealed himself to me, and appeared as, *"The altogether lovely, and the chiefest among ten thousands,"* [25] as he did to the church of old; and for my sorrow and sadness, he gave me joy and gladness in my heart: he also bound up my broken heart, and strengthened my feeble knees, and lifted up my hanging down hands, and comforted my mourning soul; as says the prophet Isaiah; yea, he also poured out the ointment of his grace, and to my sin-sick soul he made his strength perfect in my weakness; and found his grace sufficient for me, and caused me to exclaim in the language of the Psalmist, in the 103rd Psalm, *"Bless the Lord, O my soul: and all that is within me, bless his holy name, &c."*

This was the language of my heart, day and night, for his goodness and mercy, in delivering me from a wounded conscience, and from a broken spirit, and from all the enemies that rose up against me. Yea, he delivered me from the temptations of the world, the flesh, and the devil; and drew my feet out of the miry clay and horrible pit;[26] hewed me out of the rock of unbelief; and brought me through the waste howling wilderness of sin and iniquity, where my enemies laid in wait to destroy my soul, and watched to take away my life; doing every thing to prevent my rest; yea, they hooted, laughed, and scoffed at me; my master beating me to keep me from attending the house of God, but all this did not hinder me, for I blessed and praised his holy name that I was counted worthy to suffer with my blessed Jesus; and in all my sufferings I found the presence of God with me, and the Spirit of the Lord to comfort me. I found the hand of the Lord in every thing, for when I was beaten it seemed that the Spirit of the Lord was so great on me, that I did not regard the pain and trouble which I felt. At other times when kept without victuals, in order to punish me, I felt the love of God in me, that I did not regard the food; and all the language of my heart was—

> Wealth and honour I disdain,
> Earthly comforts all are vain;
> These can never satisfy,
> Give me Christ or else I die.

At other times when they gave me any refreshment, I acknowledged that it came from the immediate hand of God, and rendered unto him humble and hearty thanks in the best manner I could, as the Spirit gave me utterance, [27]which provoked my master greatly, for his desire was that I should render him thanks, and not God, for he said that he gave me the things, but I said, no, it all came from God, for all was his; that the Spirit of God taught me so; for I was led, guided, and directed by the Spirit, who taught me all things which are of God, and opened them unto my understanding.

Thus I could join with John in the Revelations, saying, "*Thou art worthy, O Lord, to receive glory, and honour, and power: for thou hast created all things, and for thy pleasure they are and were created.*" Rev. iv.9. For I then viewed all the things upon the earth as coming from God, and I asked my master where the earth came from; from God or man, and who had made it. He answered, that God made it. Then said I unto him, if God made the earth, he made the things on the earth, and the things in the earth, and the waters under the earth, Exodus xx.4. Yea, and besides this, he made the heaven also, and the things in heaven, and in the firmament of heaven, Gen. i. He also made hell for the devil and his angels; and when I took a survey of all these things, I thought "*I beheld, and I heard the voice of many angels round about the throne and the beasts and the elders: and the number of them was ten thousand times ten thousand, and thousands of thousands; Saying with a loud voice, Worthy is the Lamb that was slain to receive power, and riches, and wisdom, and strength, and honour, and glory, and blessing. And every creature which is in heaven, and on the earth, and under the earth, and such as are in the sea, and all that are in them, heard I saying , Blessing, and honour, and glory, and power, be unto him that sitteth upon the throne, and unto the Lamb for ever and ever. And the four beasts said, Amen. And the four and twenty elders fell down and worshipped him that liveth for ever and ever.*" Rev. v.12, to the end.

When I took a view of the smallest insect, it showed me, that none but the Almighty could make them, I therefore asked my master who made the insects. He answered, that they came forth out of the ground, but I said unto him, that if God made the ground, surely he made the insects also; for *"All things were made by him; and without him was not any thing made that was made."* John i.4.[28] From this passage it is evident that every thing which our eyes behold, God made it, and he hath put life into every living, moving, and creeping thing;[29] and that he hath made all the dust of the earth, the sand of the coast of the sea, the rocks and the hills, the forests, the sea, and the fountains of water; yea, every thing that can be mentioned.

Seeing then the greatness, power, and goodness, of God, how thankful ought we to be for every mercy and blessing he so richly bestows on us, and what favours we enjoy above many of our fellow-creatures; but, on the contrary, how many do we see walking contrary to God's will and commands; swearing, cursing, and abusing the holy name of God; treating with disdain and contempt the mercies of God; who made all things good for his own glory, and for the good of our souls and bodies; and has left upon record that we should have dominion over all things.

How often do we hear our fellow-creatures swear in a most dreadful manner; should the reader be of this class, attend to the words of our Lord and Savior, in that ever-memorable sermon on the mount; *"Ye have heard that it hath been said by them of old time, Thou shalt not forswear thyself, but shall perform unto the Lord thine oaths: But I say unto you, Swear not at all: neither by heaven; for it is God's throne: Nor by the earth; for it is his footstool: neither by Jerusalem; for it is the city of the great King. Neither shalt thou swear by thy head, because thou canst not make one hair white or black: But let your communication be, Yea, yea; Nay, nay: for whatsoever is more than these cometh of evil."* Matthew v. 33–37. Seeing this to be the case, *"What manner of persons ought ye to be in all holy conversation and godliness."* [30]

The time is drawing nigh when we must all appear at the bar of God, to give an account of the deeds done in the body. *"But, beloved, be not ignorant of this one thing, that one day is with the Lord as a thousand years, and a thousand years as one day. The Lord is not slack concerning his promise, as some men count slackness; but is long-suffering to us-ward, not willing that any should perish, but that all should come to repentance."* 2 Peter iii. 8, 9.

O impenitent sinner! consider the uncertainty of time, and that *"Now is the accepted time, now is the day of salvation."*[31] Consider the many exhortations and admonitions the Scriptures holds out to your view: *"Have I any pleasure at all that the wicked should die? saith the Lord God; and not that he should return from his ways, and live?"* Ezekiel xviii. 23. *"Who will have all men to be saved, and to come unto the knowledge of the truth."* 1 Timothy ii.4. *"For yourselves know perfectly that the day of the Lord so cometh as a thief in the night."* 1 Thess. v.2. *"But know this, that if the good man of the house had known in what watch the thief would come, he would have watched, and would not have suffered his house to be broken up. Therefore, be ye also ready: for in such hour as ye think not, the Son of man cometh."* Matthew xxiv. 43, 44. See Luke xii.39. Revelations xiv.15. Revelations iii. 3. 2 Peter iii. 10.

My dear reader, though the word of God informs us that it will be in the night, consider that you may not be permitted to live to that night, for you know not when this night will come; and if God should summon thee to appear before his tribunal this day, or this night, how dost thou think to appear before him in thy wickedness? If thou had not been led to Christ for salvation, how awful will the sentence be unto thee, "Depart, ye cursed, into everlasting punishment, prepared for the Devil, and his angels."[32] O! what a dreadful sentence! But should you be holy and righteous what a joyful sound will it be unto you to hear the welcome salutation of "Come, ye blessed of my father, inherit the kingdom prepared for you from the foundation of the world."[33] O! what cheering words!

I would therefore advise you, my dear reader, to endeavour, if you have not, to seek the Lord, to attain this blessing, and to shun that dreadful place of punishment which you have heard of. Consider the multitude of sins which thou hast committed, and remember, that "One leak will sink a ship," and one single sin will sink thy soul into everlasting perdition; or, in plainer terms, into that lake which burneth with fire and brimstone, where the worm dieth not, and the fire is not quenched. Read the ixth chapter of the gospel by St. Mark. Matthew xvi. 28. xvii. 1, 22. xviii. 1. Luke xi. 49. 1 Cor. xii. 3 Matthew x.42. xviii. 6. v. 29. xviii. 8. Isaiah lxvi. 24. Leviticus ii. 13. Matthew v.13.

There are many, it is to be lamented, in our day, that profess religion, but by their life and conduct they betray themselves, and crucify their Lord and Master, by putting him to an open shame; but a true christian is merciful to all, endeavouring always to do good. But this was not the case with me, for before I knew God, it was always my delight to do evil in persecuting the people of God, and committing all manner of sin and wickedness, to my own shame and confusion; "*Wherefore I give you to understand, that no man speaking by the Spirit of God calleth Jesus accursed: and that no man can say that Jesus is the Lord, but by the Holy Ghost.*" 1 Cor. xii.3. "*And whosoever shall give to drink unto one of these little ones a cup of cold water, only in the name of a disciple, verily I say unto you, He shall in no wise lose his reward.*" Matthew x.42. "*But whoso shall offend one of these little ones which believe in me, it were better for him that a millstone were hanged about his neck, and that he were drowned in the depth of the sea.*" Matthew xviii. 6. But I did not think while I was persecuting the people of God, that he was able to cast me, both soul and body, into hell, where the worm dieth not, and the fire is not quenched. My dear reader, if you cannot do the followers of Jesus any good, do not injure them; consider what a solemn assertion is made in their behalf.

The least darling lust will prevent thy entering into the heavenly and blessed paradise; "*Wherefore if thy hand or foot offend thee: cut them off, and cast them from thee: it is better for thee to enter into life halt or maimed, rather than having two hands or two feet to be cast into everlasting fire.*" Matthew xviii. 8. But I thought nothing of this, and was living in the indulgence of my heart, and fulfilling my carnal desires; but blessed and praised be the God of my salvation, for he has turned my darkness into his glorious and marvellous light. May it please the Lord to turn every sinner's heart, as he was pleased to turn mine; and translate them out of the kingdom of Satan into the kingdom of his dear Son; and stop them from going down to the place of eternal punishment.

But, to resume my narrative, when my heart was changed by divine grace, and I became regenerated and born again of the water and of the Spirit, and became as a little child, I began to speak the language of Canaan to my master and mistress, and to my own friends, but it seemed to them as if I was mad, or like one that was mocking them, when I bid them leave off their sins and wickedness, by the aid of God's divine Spirit, and be saved by grace, through faith in the Lord Jesus Christ,[34] and said that they must be regenerated and born again of the water and of the Spirit, or else they could not enter into the kingdom of heaven; showing them the necessity of that important doctrine by the conversation of Jesus Christ with Nicodemus, John iii. But, though they professed christianity, they knew nothing of what it meant; which surprised me exceedingly, and I exclaimed, "Are ye Christians, and know not these things?" And when I had thus exclaimed unto them, they thought I had lost my reason; yea, my dear mother and sisters, my master and his family, in particular, thought so of me; thus, *"My foes were those of my own house."* [35]

But being taught and directed by the Spirit of God, I told my master, mistress, my mother, sisters, and brothers, that there was nothing too hard for the Almighty God to do, for he would deliver me from their hands, and from their tyrannical power; for he had began the work of grace in my heart, and he would not leave it unfinished, for whatsoever grace had begun, glory would end. He gave me to see the first approach of evil; and he gave me power over my besetting sins, to cast them from me, and to despise them as deadly poison. He armed me with the whole armour of divine grace, whereby I quenched all the fiery darts of the wicked, and compelled Satan to retreat; and put him to flight by faithful and fervent prayer.

In addition to these he gave me power over the last enemy, which is death;[36] that is, I could look at it without any fear or dread; though it is the most terrible of all other things. There is nothing in the world that we can imagine, so dreadful and frightful as death. It is possible to escape the edge of the sword—to close the lions' mouths—to quench the fiery darts;—but when death shoots its poisoned arrows—when it opens its infernal pit—and when it sends forth its devouring flames—it is altogether impossible to secure ourselves, to guard ourselves from its merciless fury. There is an infinite number of warlike inventions, by which we defeat the evil designs of the most powerful and dreadful enemies; but there is no stratagem of the most renowned general, no fortification, ever so regular or artificial, no army, ever so victorious, that can but for a moment retard the approaches of death; this last enemy, in the twinkling of an eye, flies through the strongest bulwarks, the thickest walls, the most prodigious towers, the highest castles, and the most inaccessible rocks; makes its way through the strongest barricadoes, passes over trenches, pierces the impenetrable armour, and through the best-tempered breastplates it strikes the proudest hearts, it enters the darkest dungeon, and snatches the prisoners out of the hands of the most trusty and watchful guards. Nature and art can furnish us with nothing able to protect us from death's cruel and insatiable hands. There are none so barbarous, but they are sometimes overcome by the prayers and tears of such as implore their mercy; nay, such as have lost all sense of humanity and goodness, commonly spare in their rage, the weakest age and sex; but unmerciful death hath no more regard to such as are humble, than to those those that resist and defy it; it takes no notice of infants' tears and cries, it plucks them from the breasts of their tender-hearted mothers; it stops its ears to the requests of trembling old age, and casts to the ground the grey heads as so many withered oaks. At a battle, when princes and generals of the enemy's are taken prisoners, they are not treated as common soldiers; but unmerciful death treds under feet as audaciously the prince as the subject, the master as the servant, the noble as the vassal, the rich Dives and the begging Lazarus;[37] together it blows out with the same blast, the most glorious luminaries and the most loathsome lamps. It hath no more respect for the crowns of kings, the pope's mitre, and the cardinal's cap, than for the shepherd's crook, or the poor slave's chains; it heaps them all together, and shuts them in the same dungeon. There is no war, though ever so furious and bloody, but it is interrupted with some days, or at least some hours, of cessation or truce; nay, the most inhuman minds are at last tired with bloody conquests; but insatiable death never saith it is enough, at every hour and moment it cuts down multitudes of the human race; the flesh of all the animals that have died since the creation of the world, has not been able to glut this devouring monster. All warfare is doubtful, he that gains the victory to day, may soon after be put to flight; he that at present is in a triumphant chariot may become the footstool of his enemy; but death is always victorious, it triumphs with an insufferable insolence over all the kings and nations of the earth; it never returns to its den, but when loaded with spoils, and glutted with blood, the strongest Samson and the most victorious David, who have torn in pieces, and have overcome lions and bears, and have cut off the heads of giants, have at last yielded themselves, and been cut off by death. The great Alexanders and the triumphing Caesars, who have made all the world to tremble before them, and conquered the most part of the habitable earth, could never find any thing that might protect them from death's power; when magnificent statues and stately trophies were raised to their honour, death laughed at their vanity, and made sport with their rich marbles, where so many proud titles are engraved, which cover nothing but a little rotten flesh and a few bones, which death has broken and reduced to ashes.

We read in the prophecies of Daniel, that King Nebuchadnezzar saw in a dream a large image of gold, both glorious and terrible: its head was of pure gold, its breasts and arms were of silver, its belly and thighs of brass, its legs of iron, and its feet partly of clay and partly of iron. As the king was beholding it with astonishment, a little stone, cut out of a mountain, without hands, was rolled against the feet of this prodigious image, and broke it all to pieces; not only the clay and iron were broken, but also the gold, the silver, and the brass, all became as the chaff which the wind bloweth to and fro. This great image represented the four universal monarchies of the world, *viz.,* that of Babylon, of the Persians and Medes, of the Greeks, and of the Romans; it represented also the vanity and inconstancy of all things under the sun, for what is the pomp, the glory, the strength, and the dignities of this world, but as smoke driven with the wind, a vapour that soon vanishes away, a shadow that flies from us, or a dream that disappears in an instant. Man, created in the image of God, at his first appearance seems to be very glorious, for a while, and become terrible, but as soon as death strikes at the earthly part, and begins to break his flesh and bones, all the glory, pomp, power, and magnificence of the richest, the most terrible, and victorious monarchs, are changed into loathsome smells, into contemptible dust, and reduced to nothing.[38] *"Vanity of vanities; all is vanity."*[39]

Since, therefore, death is so impartial as to spare none, and its power so great, that none can escape or resist it, it is no wonder if it appears so terrible, and fill with fear, grief and despair, the minds of all mortals who have not settled their faith and assurance on God; for there is no condemned prisoner but trembles when he beholds the scaffold erecting, upon which he is designed to be broken on the wheel, or sees in the fire, irons with which he is to be pinched to death.

In the midst of an impious feast, King Belshazzar saw the fingers of a man's hand, writing these words upon the wall of his palace: *Mene, Mene, Tekel, Upharsin*; which the prophet Daniel thus interpreted: *Mene*; God hath numbered thy kingdom, and finished it. *Tekel*; thou art weighed in the balances, and art found wanting. *Peres; or, Upharsin*; thy kingdom is divided, and given to the Medes and Persians.[40] As soon as this great monarch had cast his eyes upon this miraculous writing, it is said, that his countenance was changed, and his thoughts troubled him, so that the joints of his loins were loosed, and his knees smote one against another.[41] Certainly the proud worldling has a greater cause to be dismayed in the midst of his glory and pleasure, when he may perceive death writing upon every wall of his house, in visible characters, and printing upon his forehead, that God hath numbered his days, and these in which he now breathes, shall be soon followed by an eternal night; that God hath weighed him in the balance of his justice, and found him as light as the wind; and that the Almighty Creator, unto whom vengeance belongs, will soon divest him of all his glory and riches, to clothe therewith his enemies.

What comforts can be found for wretched sinners, who do not only understand their final sentence, but also hear the thundering voice of the great Judge of the world, exasperated by their impieties? They now perceive hell prepared to swallow them up, and the fiery chains of that doleful prison ready to embrace them; they may at present feel the hands of the executioner of divine justice, that seize upon them already, and see themselves stretched and tortured in that place where there shall be weeping, and wailing, and gnashing of teeth;[42] they may feel the fierce approaches of that fire and brimstone, which is the second death, for it may be justly said of these wretched varlets, that hell comes to them before they go to it, and that in this life they partly feel the grievous pangs of their future torments: therefore some of them offer violence to themselves, and commit horrid murder upon their own persons, as if they were not afraid to die by a hand wicked enough; the *expectation of death* to them, is more sufferable than *death itself*, and they would rather cast themselves into the bottomless pit of hell, than endure the apprehensions and fears of hell in their guilty consciences; and to be delivered from the flashes of hell fire, they cast themselves in a brutish manner into that unquenchable burning.

But that which is most terrible is, that the horrid and insufferable fears that seize upon the wicked, are not short and transitory; for, as a criminal that knows there is sentence of death pronounced against him, continually thinks upon the torments that are preparing for him; as soon as he hears the doors unlocking, he imagines that some are entering to drag him from his prison to execution; in some sense he desires what he apprehends, and hastens the approach of that which he wishes, but cannot avoid. Thus desperate sinners, that know there is a sentence of eternal death proclaimed against them in the court of the king of kings, and that from this sentence there is no appeal nor escape, must needs be in continual fears, such foresee the fearful image of death that disturbs their quiet, and St. Paul expresses himself, "*Through fear of death were all their lifetime subject to bondage*." Heb. ii.15. That is, they are like so many wretched slaves, that tremble under the inhuman power of a merciless tyrant.

There are some atheists who talk of death with contempt and scorn, and who make an open profession of braving death, without the least fear; nevertheless, they feel in them some secret thorns with which death often galls them, some fears and apprehensions with which it tortures and disquiets them, when they dream least of it; it is true they for the most part boast of not fearing the approaches of death, and laugh at it when they imagine that it is a distance from them, but these are they who are most apt to tremble at the near approach of the grim countenance of death, and soonest discover their weakness and despair. There are many that seem to laugh at death, while their laughter is only an appearance upon the lips; they are like a child newly-born, who seems to smile when it is inwardly tormented in the bowels; or like those that eat of a herb, which causes a pleasant laughter to appear upon the lips of those who partake of it, but into whose noble parts it conveys a mortal poison.

There are some, I confess, that die without any concern, but these are either brutish or senseless persons, much like unto a sleeping drunkard, who may be cast down a precipice, without any knowledge or foresight of the danger; or, they are pleasant mockers, like the foolish criminals who go merrily to the gallows; or, such as are full of rage and fury, who may well be compared to an enraged wild boar, that runs himself into the huntsman's snare. Such monsters of men as these, deserve not to be reckoned among rational and understanding creatures.

From the fear of death it pleased the Lord to deliver me by his blessed Spirit; and gave me the witness of his Spirit to bear witness with my spirit, that I was passed from death unto life, and caused me to love the brethren. At this time I received this full evidence and witness within me, I was about seventeen years of age, then I began to love all men, women, and children, and began to speak boldly in the name of the living God, and to preach as the oracles of God, as the Spirit and love of God constrained me; as the poet says,

> The Love of God doth constrain,
> To seek the wandering souls of men.[43]

For I beheld them wandering away from God, like lost sheep, which caused me to exhort them to turn unto the shepherd and bishop of their souls, from whom they had so greatly revolted, and to fly from the wrath to come. When they reviled me, I told them of Christ's example: "*Who did no sin, neither was guile found in his mouth: Who, when he was reviled, reviled not again; when he suffered, he threatened not; but committed himself to him that judgeth righteously.*" 1 Peter ii. 22, 23. And I endeavoured to follow his steps, by exhorting and praying for them to turn from their evil ways, although they were so inveterated against me, and strove to the utmost of their power to make me suffer as an evil-doer. But, blessed be God, that I counted it all joy that I was worthy to suffer for the glory of God, and for the good of my soul. For the word of God saith, *"But and if ye suffer for righteousness' sake, happy are ye; and be not afraid of their terror, neither be troubled; But sanctify the Lord God in your heart: and be ready always to give an answer to every man that asketh you a reason of the hope that is in you with meekness and fear: Having a good conscience: that whereas they speak evil of you, as of evil doers, they may be ashamed that falsely accuse your good conversation in Christ. For it is better if the will of God be so, that ye suffer for well doing, than for evil doing."* 1 Peter iii. 14–17.

I was sold to three masters, all of whom spoke ill of me, and said that I should spoil the rest of the slaves, by my talking and preaching. The last master I was sold to, I ran from to the house of God, and was baptized unknown to him; and when the minister made it known to him, he was like a man that had lost his reason, and swore that I should not belong to any society; but the minister informed him it was too late, for the work was already finished, and according to the spiritual law of liberty, I was considered a worthy member of society. My master then beat me most cruelly, and threatened to beat the minister over the head with a cane. He then took me before the magistrates, who examined me, and inquired what I knew about God and the Lord Jesus Christ. Upon this I made a public acknowledgement before the magistrates, that God, for Christ's sake, had pardoned my sins and blotted out all mine iniquities, through our Lord Jesus Christ, whereby he was become my defence and deliverer; and that there is no other name under heaven, given to man, whereby he shall be saved, but only in the name of our Lord Jesus Christ. On hearing this, the magistrates told me I was free from my master, and at liberty to leave him; but my cruel master was very unwilling to part with me, because he was of the world. *"They are of the world: therefore speak they of the world, and the world heareth them."* 1 John iv. 5. This was evident, for if my master had been of God he would have instructed me in the Scriptures, as God had given him ability, and according to the oracles of the living God; for we have all one father, and if any man teach let him do it as God gives him ability; so saith the Scriptures. But my master strove to baffle me, and to prevent me from understanding the Scriptures: so he used to tell me that there was a time to every purpose under the sun, to do all manner of work, that slaves were in duty bound to do whatever their masters commanded them, whether it was right or wrong; so that they must be obedient to a hard spiteful master as to a good one. He then took the bible and showed it to me, and said that the book talked with him. Thus he talked with me endeavouring to convince me that I ought not to leave him, although I had received my full liberty from the magistrates, and was fully determined, by the grace of God, to leave him; yet he strove to the uttermost to prevent me; but thanks be to God, his strivings were all in vain.

My master's sons also endeavoured to convince me, by their reading in the behalf of their father; but I could not comprehend their dark sayings, for it surprised me much, how they could take that blessed book into their hands, and to be so superstitious as to want to make me believe that the book did talk with them; so that every opportunity when they were out of the way, I took the book, and held it up to my ears, to try whether the book would talk with me or not, but it proved to be all in vain, for I could not hear it speak one word, which caused me to grieve and lament, that after God had done so much for me as he had, in pardoning my sins, and blotting out my iniquities and transgressions, and making me a new creature, the book would not talk with me; but the Spirit of the Lord brought this passage of Scripture to my mind, where Jesus Christ says, "*Whatsoever ye shall ask the Father in my name, ye shall receive. Ask in faith nothing doubting: for according unto your faith it shall be unto you.*[44] *For unto him that believeth, all things are possible.*"[45] Then I began to ask God in faithful and fervent prayer, as the Spirit of the Lord gave me utterance,[46] begging earnestly of the Lord to give me the knowledge of his word, that I might be enabled to understand it in its pure light, and be able to speak it in the Dutch and English languages, that I might convince my master that he and his sons had not spoken to me as they ought, when I was their slave.

Thus I wrestled with God by faithful and fervent prayer, for five or six weeks, like Jacob of old, Gen. xxxii. 24. Hosea xii. 4. My master and mistress, and all people, laughed me to scorn, for being such a fool, to think that God would hear my prayer and grant unto me my request. But I gave God no rest day nor night, and I was so earnest, that I can truly say, I shed as many tears for this blessing, as I did when I was begging God to grant me the pardon and forgiveness of my sins. During the time I was pouring out my supplications and prayers unto the Lord, my hands were employed, labouring for the bread that perisheth, and my heart within me still famishing for the word of God; as spoken of in the Scriptures, *"There shall be a famine in the land; not a famine of bread, nor of water, but of the word of God."*[47] And thus blessed be the Lord, that he sent a famine into my heart, and caused me to call upon him by his Spirit's assistance, in the time of my trouble.

The Lord heard my groans and cries at the end of six weeks, and sent the blessed angel of the covenant to my heart and soul, to release me from all my distress and troubles, and delivered me from all mine enemies,[48] which were ready to destroy me; thus the Lord was pleased in his infinite mercy, to send an angel, in a vision, in shining raiment, and his countenance shining as the sun, with a large bible in his hands, and brought it unto me, and said, " *I am come to bless thee, and to grant thee thy request,"*[49] as you read in the Scriptures. Thus my eyes were opened at the end of six weeks, while I was praying, in the place where I slept; although the place was as dark as a dungeon, I awoke, as the Scripture saith, and found it illuminated with the light of the glory of God, and the angel standing by me, with the large book open, which was the Holy Bible, and said unto me, *"Thou hast desired to read and understand this book, and to speak the language of it both in English and in Dutch; I will therefore teach thee, and now read;"* and then he taught me to read the first chapter of the gospel according to St. John; and when I had read the whole chapter, the angel and the book were both gone in the twinkling of an eye, which astonished me very much, for the place was dark immediately; being about four o'clock in the morning in the winter season. After my astonishment had a little subsided, I began to think whether it was a fact that an angel had taught me to read, or only a dream; for I was in such a strait, like Peter was in prison, when the angel smote him on the side, and said unto Peter, *"Arise, Peter, and take thy garment, and spread it around thee, and follow me."* And Peter knew not whether it was a dream or not; and when the Angel touched him the second time, Peter arose, took his garment, folded it around him,and followed the angel, and the gates opened unto him of their own accord. So it was with me when the room was darkened again, that I wondered within myself whether I could read or not, but the Spirit of the Lord convinced me that I could; I then went out of the house to a secret place, and there rendered thanksgivings and praises unto God's holy name, for his goodness in showing me to read his holy word, to understand it, and to speak it, both in the English and Dutch languages.

I tarried at a distance from the house, blessing and praising God, until the dawning of the day, and by that time the rest of the slaves were called to their labour; they were all very much surprised to see me there so early in the morning, rejoicing as if I had found a pearl of great price, for they used to see me very sad and grieved on other mornings, but now rejoicing, and they asked me what was the reason of my rejoicing more now than at other times, but I answered I would not tell them. After I had finished my day's work I went to the minister's house, and told him that I could read, but he doubted greatly of it, and said unto me, "How is it possible that you can read? For when you were a slave your master would not suffer any one, whatever, to come near you to teach you, nor any of the slaves, to read; and it is not long since you had your liberty, not long enough to learn to read." But I told him, that the Lord had learnt me to read last night. He said it was impossible. I said, "Nothing is impossible with God, for all things are possible with him; but the thing impossible with man is possible with God,[50] for all things are possible with him; but the thing impossible with man is possible with God: for he doth with the host of heaven, and with the inhabitants of the earth, as he pleaseth, and there is none that can withstay his hand, nor dare to say what dost thou? And so did the Lord with me as it pleased him, in shewing me to read his word, and to speak it, and if you have a large bible, as the Lord showed me last night, I can read it." But he said, "No, it is not possible that you can read." This grieved me greatly, which caused me to cry. His wife then spoke in my behalf, and said unto him, "You have a large bible, fetch it, and let him try and see whether he can read it or not, and you will then be convinced." The minister then brought the bible to me, in order that I should read; and as he opened the bible for me to read, it appeared unto me, that a person said, "That is the place, read it." Which was the first chapter of the gospel of St. John, the same the Lord had taught me to read. So I read to the minister; and he said to me, "You read very well and very distinct;" and asked me who had learnt me. I said that the Lord had learnt me last night. He said that it was impossible; but, if it were so, he should find it out. On saying this he went and got other books, to see whether I could read *them*; I tried, but could not. He then brought a spelling book, to see if I could spell; but he found to his great astonishment, that I could not. This convinced him and his wife that it was the Lord's work, and it was marvellous in their eyes.

This caused them to spread a rumour all over the city of New York, saying, that the Lord had worked great miracles on a poor black man. The people flocked from all parts to know whether it was true or not;

and some of them took me before the magistrates, and had me examined concerning the rumour that was spread abroad, to prevent me, if possible, from saying the Lord had taught me to read in one night, in about fifteen minutes; for they were afraid that I should teach the other slaves to call upon the name of the Lord, as I did aforetime, and that they should come to the knowledge of the truth.

The magistrates examined me strictly, to see if I could read, as the report stated; they brought a bible for me to read in, and I read unto them the same chapter the Lord had taught me, as before-mentioned, and they said I read very well and distinct, and asked me who had taught me to read. I still replied, that the Lord had taught me. They said it was impossible; but brought forth spelling and other books, to see if I could read them, or whether I could spell, but they found to their great surprise, that I could not read the other books, neither could I spell a word; then they said, it was the work of the Lord, and a very great miracle indeed; whilst others exclaimed and said that it was not right that I should have my liberty. The magistrates said that it was right and just that I should have my liberty, for they believed that I was of God, for they were persuaded that no man could read in such a manner, unless he was taught of God.

From that hour, in which the Lord taught me to read, until the present, I have not been able to read in any book, nor any reading whatever, but such as contain the word of God.

Through the report of the minister (whose name was the REVEREND PETER LOWE, a pastor of the Presbyterian church) and the magistrates, I was permitted to go on in the strength of the Lord, and to proclaim the glad tidings of salvation by Jesus Christ, unto every one, both great small, saying unto those that were christians, *"Rejoice with me, for the Lord hath liberated my soul from all my enemies."* I was so over-joyed that I cried out, *"Make a joyful noise unto God, all ye lands: Sing forth the honour of his name: make his praise glorious, &c."* as in the lxvith Psalm.

I was now enabled, by the assistance of the Holy Spirit, to go from house to house, and from plantation to plantation, warning sinners, in the name of Jesus, to flee from the wrath to come; teaching and admonishing them to turn from their evil course in life; whilst some mocked and others scoffed at me, many said that I was mad, others pointed at me, and said there goes *"the preacher,"* in a mocking and jeering manner. Sometimes after I had been preaching in a house, and was leaving it, some of the people, who were assembled together, without the door, would beat and use me in a very cruel manner, saying, as the Jews of old did to Jesus Christ, when they smote him with the palms of their hands, "*Prophesy unto us it was that smote thee*?"[51]

But, for ever blessed be the Lord, he was pleased to give me one soul for my hire, and one seal to my ministry; which caused me to bless the Lord, and ascribe all the honour and glory to his name, for not having let my labours been in vain. This poor soul to whom the Lord was pleased to bless my feeble endeavours, was a poor black slave, the same as I had been; the Lord in infinite mercy, was pleased to liberate his soul from the bondage of sin and Satan, and afterwards from his cruel master.

It was a law of the state of the city of New York, that if any slave could give a satisfactorily account of what he knew of the work of the Lord on his soul, he was free from slavery, by the Act of Congress, that was governed by the good people the Quakers, who were made the happy instruments, in the hands of God, of releasing some thousands of us poor black slaves from the galling chains of slavery.

After this poor man had received his liberty from slavery, he joined me in hand and heart, willing "*To follow the Lamb of God whithersoever he goeth*."[52] His employment while with his master, was sweeping chimneys; but now his master, who was God, had given him his labour to endeavour to sweep the evils out of the hearts of poor slaves. He and I used to go from house to house, and in barns and under hedges, preaching the gospel of Christ, as the Spirit of God gave us utterance;[53] and God added unto our number such as should be saved. In the course of about nineteen months, it pleased the Lord to add to our number about five hundred souls; and when we could not find room enough in the houses, we used to preach out of doors in the fields and woods, which we used to call our large chapel, and there we assembled together on Saturday evenings about eleven o'clock, after the slaves had done their masters' work, and continued until Sunday evening about ten or eleven o'clock. The other black man and myself used to go fourteen miles of a night to preach, and to instruct our poor fellow brethren, and thought ourselves well paid for our trouble in having a congregation together in the name of the Lord.

I knew it was a hard task for the poor slaves to get out, because when I was a slave I had gone fifteen miles to hear preaching, and was obliged to get back before sun rising, to go to my work, and then, if my master knew I had been to hear preaching, he would beat me most unmercifully, so that I encouraged the other poor slaves to seek the Lord, and to be earnest in prayer and supplication, for well I knew that the Lord would hear and deliver them, if they sought him in sincerity and in truth, as the Lord delivered me; for they did not suffer for evil doing, but for doing the will of God. Being under that promise which says, *"But and if ye suffer for righteousness' sake, happy are ye:"*[54] Yea, this was the encouragement that I gave them—*"Forasmuch then as Christ hath suffered for us in the flesh, arm yourselves likewise with the same mind: for he that hath suffered in the flesh hath ceased from sin; That he no longer should live the rest of his time in the flesh to the lusts of men, but to the will of God. For the time past of our life may suffice us to have wrought the will of Gentiles, when we walked in lasciviousness, lusts, excess of wine, revellings, banquetings, and abominable idolatries: Wherein they think it strange that ye run not with them to the same excess of riot, speaking evil of you: Who shall give account to him that is ready to judge the quick and the dead. For for this cause was the gospel preached also to them that are dead, that they might be judged according to men in the flesh, but live according to God in the spirit. But the end of all things is at hand: be ye therefore sober, and watch unto prayer."* 1 Peter iv. 1–7.

We informed them that they must cease to do evil,[55] and learn to do well, for the end of all their troubles was near at hand. We told them that they should not desire nor covet the dainties of this world, for it was the deceitfulness of man's evil and wicked heart, which made him desire to partake of those things, which is not for his benefit, but will tend to destroy him; as the lying prophet caused the man of God to be destroyed, enticing him to go back to his house, to eat and drink with him, although the man of God was forbidden to go back, nor to eat bread, nor to drink water, in the place, nor to go back by the way as he came; but the lying prophet persuaded the man of God to return back, for an angel had sent him, and that he was to return back, and to eat and drink, and afterwards he should proceed on his journey. Being over-persuaded by the lying prophet, he returned back, but he lost his life, for not truly believing and keeping the commandments of God, which he had so strictly commanded him. 1 Kings xiii.

My dear reader, take care what company you keep, and take care whom you eat and drink with; for many would almost persuade you that they were saints, but by their gluttonous way of living, their hearts are like a knife to your throat. *"When thou sittest to eat with a ruler, consider diligently what is before thee: And put a knife to thy throat, if thou be a man given to appetite. Be not desirous of his dainties: for they are deceitful meat. Labour not to be rich: cease from thine own wisdom. Wilt thou set thine eyes upon that which is not? for riches certainly make themselves wings; they fly away as an eagle toward heaven. Eat thou not the bread of him that hath an evil eye, neither desire thou his dainty meats: For as he thinketh in his heart, so it he: Eat and drink, saith he to thee; but his heart is not with thee. The morsel which thou hast eaten shalt thou vomit up, and lose thy sweet words. Speak not in the ears of a fool: for he will despise the wisdom of thy words. Remove not the old landmark; and enter not into the fields of the fatherless: For their redeemer is mighty; he shall plead their cause with thee.*" Proverbs xxiii. 1–12.

We told the poor slaves that God had promised to deliver them that call upon him in time of trouble, out of all their distress; for "*He would be with them in six troubles, and in the seventh he would not forsake them.*"[56] We encouraged them to be angry with, and not to commit, sin, as the Scripture saith, "*Be ye angry, and sin not;*"[57] For sin brought all their punishment upon them, whatever they suffered; therefore, I exhorted them to hate sin, and to fly from it as from the face of a serpent; and to remember that our blessed Lord had said, that we should have persecution in the world, but in him we should have peace; for the world hated him and the world knew him not, and therefore they would hate us, because they hated him first; for they knew him not, neither do they know us, because he has chosen us out of the world: therefore our Lord has said, "*It is through many tribulations that you shall enter the kingdom of heaven: for he shall be hated of all men for my name's sake, and they shall cast out your name as evil, and they that kill you will think that they do God service; and they shall say all manner of evil against you falsely, for my sake. Rejoice: and be exceeding glad: for great is your reward in heaven: for persecuted they the prophets and apostles that were before you:*"[58] We encouraged them in the Christian life, and said to them "*Finally, be ye all of one mind, having compassion one of another, love as brethren, be pitiful, be courteous: Not rendering evil for evil, or railing for railing: but contrariwise blessing; knowing that ye are thereunto called, that ye should inherit a blessing. For he that will love life, and see good days, let him refrain his tongue from evil, and his lips that they speak no guile: Let him eschew evil, and do good; let him seek peace, and ensue it. For the eyes of the Lord are over the righteous, and his ears are open unto their prayers: but the face of the Lord is against them that do evil.*" 1 Peter iii. 8–12.

Thus we went on preaching in the name of the Lord, and it pleased God to bless our feeble efforts, by adding unto our number such as should be saved.

At this time the Lord was pleased to raise up some white friends, who were benevolent and kind to us, when they saw our simpleness, and that God prospered us in our manner and way of worship; who joined their mites with our's, and purchased a piece of ground, and built upon it a meeting-house, in the city of New York, for us poor black Africans to worship in, which held about *fifteen hundred people!* They also procured white preachers twice a week to preach, to assist the other black man and myself.

Being thus highly favored, we now had preaching three times on the Sabbath-day, and every night in the week; and the number of them that were added unto the society, was about *nine hundred and fifty souls!*

I continued at this place four years after that, preaching with the other preachers; for we were appointed to preach in rotation. The word of the Lord grew and multiplied exceedingly, for it pleased the Lord, sometimes at one service, to add to our number *fifteen souls!* and, sometimes *more!* At our watch nights and camp meetings, I have known one hundred and fifty, or two hundred, awakened at one time; by which it was evident that the time was like the day of Pentecost; which you have an account of in the second chapter of Acts.

Thus, when we assembled together with one accord, the Lord was pleased to send down his convincing and converting spirit, to convince and convert the congregation, and they were filled with the spirit of prayer, which caused them to groan and cry unto God, begging him to have mercy upon their never-dying souls, to such a degree, that it caused some to say, that the people were drunk, others said they were possessed with devils,[59] many said they were mad, and others laughing, mocking, and scoffing at them; while the people came running in out of the streets and houses to see what was the matter; and many of *them* were convinced of sin, and of righteousness, and of judgement to come; crying out with the jailor of old, "*What shall we do to be saved?*"[60] We still continued speaking as the Spirit gave us utterance.

It was our heart's desire, and prayer to God, that every sinner might be saved; so we went on in the strength of God, by the aid of his Spirit, warning sinners every where to repent and believe the gospel, that their souls might be saved through grace, by faith in the Lord Jesus Christ. When the congregation grew numerous, and there were enough preachers besides myself, I was then constrained by the Spirit, and the love of God, to go about four hundred miles from thence, to preach the everlasting gospel to the people there, at a place called Boston, in North America. I continued preaching there about three years and a half, and the Lord crowned my feeble endeavours with great success, and gave me souls for my hire, and seals to my ministry.

After being at Boston three years and a half, I returned to New York, to see my mother, sisters, brothers, and friends, and after arriving there, I thought it necessary to enter into the state of matrimony, and we lived very comfortably together about two years, being of one heart and one mind, both of us belonging to the Methodist society in New York. My wife was of the Indian colour. To add to our comfort the Lord was pleased to give us a daughter.

But a circumstance transpired which interrupted our felicity, and made me very unhappy: My wife's mistress had been trying to persuade her not to be so religious, for she would make herself melancholy to be so much at the house of God, and she did not like it; she told her she thought it was no harm to sing songs, and to do as the rest of the people of the world did, and said there was a time for every purpose under the sun: a time to be born, and a time to die; a time to plant, and a time to pluck up that which is planted; a time to kill, and a time to heal; a time to break down, and a time to build up; a time to weep, and a time to laugh; a time to mourn, and a time to dance; a time to cast away stones, and a time to gather stones together; a time to embrace, and a time to refrain from embracing; a time to get, and a time to lose; a time to keep, and a time to cast away; a time to rend, and a time to sew; a time to keep silence, and a time to speak; a time to love, and a time to hate; a time of war, and a time of peace.[61] Thus her mistress spoke, not thinking that these were spiritual times, nor considering that the Scriptures were wrote by inspiration and that they must be understood by the Spirit; *"For what man knoweth the things of a man, save the spirit of man which is in him? even so the things of God knoweth no man, but the Spirit of God Now we have received, not the spirit of the world, but the spirit which is of God; that we might know the things that are freely given to us of God. Which things also we speak, not in the words which man's wisdom teacheth, but which the Holy Ghost teacheth; comparing spiritual things with spiritual. But the natural man receiveth not the things of the Spirit of God: for they are foolishness unto him: neither can he know of them, because they are spiritually discerned."* 1 Cor. ii. 12, 13, 14.

From this it appeared that her mistress did not understand the things which were of God, although she was a professor of religion; for she was continually attempting to persuade her, to turn to the ways of the world, and said that so much religion was not required. By these persuasions, my wife began to listen to the advice of her mistress, and to the temptations of the Devil's cunning arts, and began neither to fear God, nor regard man; and wanted me to turn to the beggarly elements of the world; but I told her I was determined by the grace of God, to live and die for God, so that whether I lived or died I should be the Lord's; begging and beseeching her to turn unto God, with full purpose of heart, that he might have mercy on her poor heart; informing her, that "Thus saith the Lord, turn ye even to me with all your heart, and with fasting, and with weeping, and with mourning; And rend your heart, and not your garments, and turn unto the Lord your God: for he is gracious and merciful, slow to anger, and of great kindness, and repenteth him of the evil. Who knoweth if he will return and repent, and leave a blessing behind him; even a meat offering and a drink offering unto the Lord your God?" Joel, ii. 12, 13,14. But she would not hearken unto me, for she was led away by the advice of her mistress, and the temptations of Satan. She now used her poor little innocent and harmless infant very cruel, in order to prevent me from going to the house of God: during my absence from home, she used to try every method in her power to make the poor little babe suffer; her mother always took the child's part, and endeavoured as much as possible to hinder her from using it ill, and when I returned home she would acquaint me of my wife's transactions. On account of this she beat her mother in such a manner, that it caused her death, being pregnant at the time, so that she was not able to resist her wicked undertakings. Thus if she had been dealt with according to the law of God, she would have been put to death, for the Scriptures saith, "He that smiteth his father or mother, shall be surely put to death." Exod. xxi.15.

Thus, my wife treated her mother, that she died by her cruel usage. Her mistress on this took her to task, and beat her very much, for using her mother in such a manner, particularly in her situation; and told her that she was become a hardened sinner, desiring her to turn unto the Lord, that he might have mercy upon her, or else she would certainly perish; but she was so hardened in her heart, that she could not bear to hear the name of the Lord mentioned; for she would curse and swear, and break and destroy every thing she could get at. It now seemed as if the devil had taken full possession of her heart, and now her master and mistress persuaded me to intreat her to go to the house of God, but she would not, the more I entreated her, the worse she was, and abused and ill-used me as she did the poor infant.

One day when I was gone to my mother's house, which was about nine miles from home, she was so overpowered by the temptation of the Devil, that she *murdered the poor little infant!* by squeezing it between her hands. When I returned home, I was greatly surprised to see a number of people assembled together at the door of my house; and on enquiring what was the matter, they told me that my wife had killed the child. I said unto her, "What hast thou been doing?" She replied, "I have killed the child, and I mean to kill you, if I possibly can." I then said to her, "My dear wife, what is the reason of your doing this horrid deed? what do you think will become of your never-dying soul?" She said, that she expected to go to eternal misery; and therefore she was determined to do all the mischief she could.

She was taken before the judge, and found guilty of the crime laid to her charge, that murdering of her infant. She acknowledged that she had committed the horrid deed; and therefore suffered according to the law. Before her punishment took place, I frequently visited her, to endeavour to convince her of the state of her soul, and begged her to pray unto God to have mercy upon her soul, and to strengthen her in her dying moments; but her heart was so hardened by sin, that it was all in vain.

This, my dear reader, you must think, was a fiery trial for me to endure; it almost cast me down to the ground, and to make shipwreck of faith and a good conscience: indeed, my state of mind was such, that it caused me to go to a river, several times, in order to make away with myself; thus the old lion would have devoured me; but, thanks be to God, he gave me grace to withstand the temptations of the Devil at last; and enabled me to say, "Blessed be the God and Father of our Lord Jesus Christ, which according to his abundant mercy hath begotten us again unto a lively hope by the resurrection of Jesus Christ from the dead. To an inheritance incorruptible, and undefiled, and that fadeth not away, reserved in heaven for you, Who are kept by the power of God through faith unto salvation ready to be revealed in the last time. Wherein ye greatly rejoice, through now, for a season, if need be, ye are in heaviness through manifold temptations: That the trial of your faith, being much more precious that of gold that perisheth, though it be tried with *fiery trials*, might be found unto praise and honour and glory at the appearing of Jesus Christ." 1 Peter i. 3–7. Thus the Lord gave me encouragement by his blessed Spirit, saying "Think it not strange concerning the fiery trial which is to try you, as though some strange thing happened unto you: But rejoice, inasmuch as ye are partakers of Christ's sufferings; that, when his glory shall be revealed, ye may be glad also with exceeding joy. If ye be reproached for the name of Christ, happy are ye; for the spirit of glory and of God resteth on you; on their part he is evil spoken of, but on your part he is glorified. But let none of you suffer as a murderer, or as a thief, or as an evil doer, or as a busy body in other men's matters. Yet if any man suffer as a Christian, let him not be ashamed: but let him glorify God on this behalf." 1 Peter iv. 12–16.

The cause of my wife's destroying her child was attributed, by many, to my being so religious, and through religion; but they had forgotten the language of the Scripture which saith, "Can a woman forget her sucking child, that she should not have compassion on the son of her womb? yea, they may forget, yet will I not forget thee." Isaiah xlvix. 15. Thus was this passage exemplified, in my wife forgetting the child of her own womb, but blessed be God, he delivered *me* out of all my distress,[62] and endued me with a double portion of his divine grace, and lifted me up upon my feet again, to travel on to Zion; and gave me strength

To bear my cross from day to day,
And learn to watch as well as pray,
And gave me his blessed Union.

I continued two years after this in New York, preaching the everlasting gospel, both to saints and sinners, and the Lord was pleased to bless my weak efforts. After this the love of God constrained me to travel into other parts to preach the gospel, when I again visited Boston, in North America, where I tarried about twelve months, and the Lord blessed my ministry, and owned by labours, to the conversion of many.

From thence I travelled to a place called Salisbury, about forty miles from Boston, where I met with great success; for God, by his Spirit, was pleased to convince and convert *five or six souls of a night!* I tarried at this place between nine and ten months.

After that time, it pleased God to put it into my mind to cross the Atlantic main; and I embarked on board of a ship for that purpose. The name of the ship was *The Superb of Boston*, and the captain's name was Able Stovey, with whom I agreed to sail with for seventeen dollars per month. I was quite unacquainted with the sea, and was very much pleased in going on board the vessel; but the case was soon altered, for the first day I went on board to work, and the captain and the men asked me if I came on board to work. I told them yes. They asked me where my clothes were. I said I had them on my back. They asked me if that was all I had. I told them I thought I had sufficient, for I was not certain of staying longer than one day; for if I did not like it I would not stay out the month; for I thought that a person going to sea, could go one day, and return the next.

After they had told me what to do, which was to clean the coppers, I went and looked all about the ship, but could not find them, not knowing what they were; at last I asked one of the sailors where the coppers were, for the captain had ordered me to clean them, so he shewed me where they were. Those which they called coppers, were a couple of black iron things; and they told me I must make them very clean, and that I was to cook the victuals, being cook of the ship. The coppers were very large, for the ship was about four hundred tons burden. I then began to rub the coppers as I was ordered, and the more I rubbed them, the more the rust came off, and the blacker they looked. After two hours after I began cleaning them, the captain asked me if I had cleaned the coppers; I told him I could not get them clean; but he told me I must be sure to clean them well.

During this time the vessel had got under weigh, and was sailing through the river, which was very pleasant, until we got outside of the light-house, when the ship began to roll about very much, which greatly terrified me. The captain coming to me, said, "How do you come on?" I told him that I was tired, and that I wanted to get home. He told me that I should soon get home; and asked me how the sailors' suppers got on. I said, "I cannot get these black things clean; they are certainly not copper." The captain said, "Never mind, let them alone, and have another trial tomorrow." But I said within myself, "You shall not catch me here to-morrow, if I can get on shore." The captain seeing how I was, bade me go below, for the men had some cold beef for supper, and that I should rest myself. When I was going below, I looked at the man at the helm with an evil eye, thinking he made the ship to go on one side on purpose to frighten me the more; but before I got down to the hold I fell down, by the vessel rolling, and all the men sung out, "Hollo, there is a horse down:" and they laughing at me so, made me the more afraid and terrified, and after I had got down into the hold, I was afraid the ship would fall, and I strove to keep her up by pushing, and holding fast by different parts of the ship, and when the waves came dashing against the sides of the ship, I thought they were sea lions, and was afraid they would beat a hole through the ship's side, and would come in and devour me; when day-light appeared, I was very much tired and fatigued, for I had been holding and trying to keep the ship upright all the night; in the morning I asked the sailors why they did not keep the ship upright, and one of the men said, pointing to another, "That is the man that makes the ship go on one side." This they said in their scoffing way, to deride me. Having been about eight or ten days at sea, I found out what it was, in some measure. The weather was very boisterous, the sea running very high, and thundering and lightning very much; the reason of which was, I believe, because they so ill-used and abused me, and swore they would throw me overboard, or beat me so that I should jump overboard. When they saw me praying to God, they called me by way of dersion, a Jonah, because I prayed to God to calm the tempestuous weather. On the contrary, they were making game of the works of the Lord,[63] and said that the old man had fine fire works, for it gave them light to go up on the yards to furl the sails; but to their great terror, after they had furled the sails, it pleased the Lord to send his lightning and thunder directly, which killed two men on the spot. One of them was burnt like a cinder, his clothes were totally consumed, not so much as a bit of a handkerchief nor any thing else being left. His name was George Begann, about thirty-six years of age. The other's name was James Cash, about twenty-five years of age: his body was entirely burnt up, not a single bit of it was to be seen, nothing but the cinders of his clothes, one of his shoes, his knife, his gold ring, and his key.

Seven more were wounded, some in their backs, and others in different parts of their bodies: and appeared to be dead for about ten or fifteen minutes.

At the time this dreadful carnage happened, I was standing about seven or eight feet from them; my eye-sight was taken from me for four or five minutes, but my soul gave glory to God for what was done. When I recovered my sight I saw the captain standing in the cabin gangway, and the cabin-boy and three passengers behind them, lamenting greatly, ringing their hands, and plucking their hair; the captain crying out—"O! my men, we are all lost!" I then took the boldness to speak unto him, and said, "Why do you cry and lament? You see that your ship is not hurt, and that the Lord has been pleased to spare your life; and what the Lord has done is right."[64]

A short time after we had survived this awful scene, the captain exclaimed, "O! my men, my men, the ship is on fire!" On hearing this, the men that were able to move, were roused to take off the hatches, to see where the fire was. But, blessed be God, the ship was not on fire, for it was part of the men's clothes who were consumed, which had got down into the hold, and was burning, which caused a very great smoke; for the sailors stood round the main-mast (excepting four who were at the helm) which was the most materially injured; that part of the cargo which was near the main-mast, consisting of tobacco and staves for casks, was nearly all consumed, but the ship sustained no damage whatever.

The captain and ship's crew were very much terrified when they saw the power of God in killing and wounding the men, and destroying the cargo; which judgements were sent on them, "*Because they rebelled against the words of God, and contemned the counsel of the Most High: Therefore he brought down their heart with labour; they fell down, and there was none to help. Then they cried unto the Lord in their trouble, and he saved them out of their distresses. He brought them out of darkness and the shadow of death, and brake their hands in sunder. Oh that men would praise the Lord for his goodness, and for his wonderful works to the children of men!*" Psalm cvii. 11–15.

Should the reader of this be like those, against whom the judgements of God were so remarkably displayed, for their sins and rebellion against him, particularly in making sport with his awful warnings, let me intreat of him to consider the cases above recorded; and let him ask himself, "Am I able to stand before the power of that God who '*Is greatly to be feared;*' whose arm in mighty, and whose hand is strong; and who is called '*The God of the Whole Earth?*'"[65]

We had not been more than a fortnight at sea, after the first deliverance from the thunder and lightning, when we were visited by most dreadful whirlwinds and hurricanes, which dismasted the ship, and made her almost a wreck. We were forty-two days in the Gulph of Mexico, without receiving any assistance whatever; during three weeks of which we had not any dry clothes to put on, not one of us, and we were obliged to eat our victuals raw, for the weather was so very boisterous, that we could not light a fire; we were also put on short allowance, both of victuals and water, for we did not know how long it would be before we should meet with any deliverance. The quantity of provisions and water we were allowed was—half a pound of raw beef or pork, a biscuit and a half, and half a pint of water, for four and twenty hours. During this dreadful tempest, the snow and rain descended rapidly, which we caught, and put into casks , and of this we were only allowed the same quantity as of the good water.

My dear reader, consider what great distress we must have been in at this time, when the ship was tossed and rolled about in such a dreadful manner, and expecting every moment that the ship would be staved in pieces, by the furiousness of the raging sea. Yea, this also terrified me, as well as the rest of the men, when it first began, and I entreated the Lord God Almighty to have mercy on us, that we might once more, by his grace and by the aid of his Spirit, arrive at our desired port; for our hearts were faint within us, and our spirits within us were famishing, that it caused every man on board to be earnestly inclined to call upon the Lord for deliverance; for they now believed that the Lord had sent this distress upon them, that they might earnestly desire the word of God, for the Scriptures saith, "*Behold, the days come, saith the Lord God, that I will send a famine in the land, not a famine of bread, nor a thirst for water, but of hearing the words of the Lord: And they shall wander from sea to sea, and from the north even to the east, they shall run to and fro to seek the word of the Lord, and shall not find it. In that day shall the fair virgins and young men faint for thirst.*" Amos viii, 11–13. Thus was our hearts faint within us, and we sought for the words of God's promise, unto us wretched miserable sinners, that "*In the time of trouble he would deliver us;*"[66] and I have every reason to believe that the Lord did hear our feeble breathings, for we perished not, but at the end of forty-two days, we saw a sail making towards us, and afterwards another, which both came to our assistance.

Thus, blessed be God, our feeble breathings were heard, when we cried unto God with a sincere heart, he delivered us out of this distress,[67] for these two vessels supplied us with provisions and water, and spars, whereby we were able to make jury-masts, so that we were enabled to gain the state of Merelian, in Virginia, which is not far from Baltimore, there we remained until our ship was repaired, and after that, we set sail for England, our destined port being London. When we arrived at the Downs, we were commanded to go to Amsterdam, in Holland; we tarried there about three weeks for further orders, and then we were ordered to go to Liverpool, in England.

When we arrived at Liverpool, I enquired for the people that were followers of the Lord Jesus Christ, seeing that the place was large and populous, I believed in my heart, that God had a people there, and I began to tell the people there of the goodness of God towards me on the sea, and to the ship's company; declaring of his wonderful works on the sea, and rendering God humble and hearty thanks for our safe arrival in port. The love of God constrained me[68] to preach to the people at Liverpool, as I had done to those in North America.

Thus, dear reader, I have informed you, how God had brought me safe into Liverpool, and did not destroy me when I was on the sea, but brought me safe into Liverpool, to preach the everlasting gospel; although I was very ill of a pleurisy, which was occasioned by the ill-treatment I had received on board of ship, for they used to flog, beat, and kick me about, the same as if I had been a dog; they also rubbed grease and dirt over my face and eyes; oftentimes they swore they would beat me till they made me jump overboard, but I never did; and sometimes they would call me a Jonah. This was the treatment I experienced from the officers and men of the ship, until it pleased the Lord to send the thunder and lightning, and the whirlwinds and hurricanes, which was the cause of softening their hearts a little, seeing the Lord pouring down his anger, and destroying some of the men by which they began to be terrified and alarmed, and I had peace even until I came to Liverpool.

While I was at Liverpool I told the people what the Lord had done for me on the seas, and how he had delivered me from the hands of my enemies, and by the grace of God I gave them to understand, that these officers and men were not sinners above all the people in the world; but, unless *they* repented, that they should all likewise perish; as the Scripture saith: *"And Jesus answering said unto them, Suppose ye that these Galileans were sinners above all the Galileans, because they suffered such things? I tell you, nay: but except ye repent, ye shall all likewise perish. Or those eighteen, upon whom the tower in Siloam fell, and slew them, think ye that they were sinners above all men that dwelt in Jerusalem? I tell you, nay: but except ye repent, ye shall all likewise perish."* Luke xiii. 2–5.

Thus I preached unto the people in Liverpool, faith, repentance, and remission of sin by Jesus Christ, and the glad tidings of salvation. By these means the people inclined their ears, and believed the report which I gave concerning the Lord Jesus Christ, our blessed Savior, for many were alarmed by the Spirit of God, turned from the evil of their ways, repented, and were converted to God; *"Forasmuch as I saw that my labour was not in vain in the Lord;"*[69] for the Almighty blessed and owned my feeble endeavours; although I was very ill and desired to go to the infirmary; but the good friends that God had raised up unto me, Christian brethren and sisters, would not suffer me to go, but kept me still with them, in order that I should recover my health.

During the time I stayed with them, I still continued preaching and exhorting them in the name of Jesus; so that the report of my preaching and exhorting spread all through Liverpool, and in the country. I had not preached more than a month at Liverpool, before they sent for me into the country, then

> The love of God did me constrain,
> To seek the wandering souls of men;
> With cries, intreaties, tears, to save,
> To snatch them from the burning blaze.
>
> For this let man revile my name
> No cross I shun, I fear no shame;
> All hail reproach and welcome shame
> Only thy terrors Lord restrain.
>
> My life, my blood, I here present
> If for the truth they may be spent
> Fulfil thy sovereign counsel Lord,
> Thy will be done, thy name ador'd.
>
> Welcome thy strength, I God of Pow'r
> Then let winds blow or thunders roar
> Thy faithful witness will I be
> They're fixed, I can-do all through thee.[70]

This was the language of my heart, while I paused upon the words which the people had spoken unto me, about my going into the country; for I was not rightly settled in my mind, whether I should stay in Liverpool, go to America, or go into the country; but I saw that the Lord had hitherto blessed and owned my feeble endeavours, and the love of Christ constraining me, I determined to go into the country.

The first place I arrived at was Baudley Mores, about fourteen miles from Liverpool, where I met with Mr. Christopher Hooper, who had travelled in the time of Mr. Wesley. I also met with Mr. Cooper, a Methodist preacher. These were the first brothers in Christ that gave me liberty to preach in the country. Here much good was done in the name of the holy child Jesus, for many were convinced and converted to God, whenever there was preaching.

At Baudley Mores, I was sent for to go to Manchester, and great success attended my preaching there. While at Manchester, I was sent for from Lancashire to preach, and there the Lord gave me many seals to my ministry, and souls for my hire. In this place I was blessed by the

Spirit of God, to preach in every chapel and preaching house that was in the place, except it was the Church of England, and there was no place that was sufficient to hold the congregation.

During my stay at Lancashire, I was sent for to go into Yorkshire, and when I arrived there, I preached there also, and had greater success than at any place I ever had preached in before; for I was permitted to preach in every place of worship, in the Methodist, Baptist, Calvinist, Presbyterian, and every other place, excepting the Church of England; and the Spirit of the Lord filled my heart, and the glory of God filled my soul, and the Lord was pleased to send his blessed Spirit with his word, to convince and convert the people, for sinners were convinced and converted to God, transgressors were taught the ways of the Lord, believing children of God were edified, and God was glorified. Some nights I think there were *fourteen* or *fifteen souls converted!* sometimes more and sometimes less. Thus the Lord blessed and prospered my ways, even until I got to Sunderland, and there I preached, and had great success. The Lord owning and blessing my ministry in this manner, caused great hatred to spring up among the brethren, so that they desired the people not to follow me, for they said that they could not get a congregation to preach unto, worth speaking of. This was the case with one of the preachers with whom I travelled; while the other was my friend, and desired me to continued preaching in the name of the Lord. His name was Mr. John Booth, about forty years of age. The other's name, who was my enemy, was Mr. Chittle; he was of rich parents, and for the sake of his father he was offended with me: for I and his father preached together in one meeting-house, his father first, and I afterwards. His father being an old man he did not preach very often, only on particular occasions; for this reason he was to preach the same evening as I did, for he wished to convince the people that they should not follow after a man, but after Christ. He compared me to poor Lazarus; because wherever I went to preach the meeting-houses could not hold the people, but wherever the other preachers went to preach, they had plenty of room, having scarcely any congregation; which caused him to preach on this part of the gospel: "*Now a certain man was sick, named Lazarus, of Bethany, the town of Mary and her sister Martha. (It was that Mary which appointed the Lord with ointment, and wiped his feet with her hair, whose brother Lazarus was sick.) Therefore his sisters sent unto him, saying, Lord, behold, he whom thou lovest is sick. When Jesus heard that, he said, This sickness is not unto death, but for the glory of God, that the Son of God might be glorified thereby. Now Jesus loved Martha, and her sister, and Lazarus. When he had heard therefore that he was sick, he abode two days still in the same place where he was. Then after that saith he to his disciples, Let us go into Judea again. His disciples said unto him, Master, the Jews of late sought to stone thee; and goest thou thither again? Jesus answered, Are there not twelve hours in the day? If any man walk in the day he stumbleth not, because he seeth the light of this world. But if a man walk in the night, he stumbleth, because there is no light in him. These things said he: and after that he saith unto them, Our friend Lazarus sleepeth; but I go that I may awake him out of sleep;* that is to say, that he would raise him from the dead." John xi. 1–11. "*Then when Jesus came, he found that he had lain in the grave four days already. Now Bethany was nigh unto Jerusalem, about fifteen furlongs off: And many of the Jews came to Martha and Mary, to comfort them concerning their brother. Then Martha, as soon as she heard that Jesus was coming, went and met him: but Mary sat still in the house. Then said Martha unto Jesus, Lord, if thou hadst been here, my brother had not died. But I know, that even now, whatsoever thou wilt ask of God, God will give it thee. Jesus saith unto her, Thy brother shall rise again. Martha saith unto him, I know that he shall rise again in the resurrection at the last day. Jesus said unto her, I am the resurrection, and the life: he that believeth in me, though he were dead, yet shall he live.*" 17–25. Now Jesus would convince them, that whosoever believeth in him should never die, for they seemed to be doubtful of his words, although he had said unto them that he was the resurrection and the life, yet it seemed to be a doubtful matter for them to believe, for "*When Mary was come where Jesus was, and saw him, she fell down at his feet, saying unto him, Lord, if thou hadst been here, my brother had not died.*" 32. Which showed that they believed Jesus was able to keep him alive while living, but not to raise him when stinking in the grave; for they said unto him, *by this time he stinketh. "When Jesus therefore saw her weeping, and the Jews also weeping which came with her, he groaned in the spirit, and was troubled.*" 33. Now we have reason to believe that Jesus was concerned because of their unbelief which caused him to groan in the spirit, and be troubled. "*And said, Where have ye laid him? They said unto him, Lord, come and see. Jesus wept.*" 34, 35. It is evident that he wept because they could not yet believe; as he wept over Jerusalem for their sin and unbelief, and had told them he would save them, but they would not be saved. This showed that he loved them, as he did Lazarus, and all other sinners; and as he raised Lazarus from the grave, so he would raise every sinner from the grave of sin and wickedness, if they would but hearken and listen to the calls, invitations, and preaching of the everlasting gospel, and by his blessed Spirit convince and convert them to God. For "*God is love.*"[71] This the Jews acknowledged, and said, "*Behold how he loved him! And some of them said, Could not this man, which opened the eyes of the blind, have caused that even this man should not have died? Jesus therefore again groaning in himself cometh to the grave. It was a cave, and a stone lay upon it. Jesus said, Take ye away the stone. Martha, the sister of him that was dead, saith unto him, Lord, by this time he stinketh: for he hath been dead four days. Jesus saith unto her, Said I not unto thee, that if thou wouldest believe, thou shouldest see the glory of God? Then they took away the stone from the place where the dead was laid. And Jesus lifted up his eyes, and said, Father, I thank thee that thou hast heard me. And I knew that thou hearest me always: but because of the people which stand by I said it, that they may believe that thou hast sent me. And when he thus had spoken, he cried with a loud voice, Lazarus, come forth. And he that was dead came forth, bound hand and foot with grave-clothes: and his face was bound about with a napkin. Jesus saith unto them, Loose him, and let him go. Then many of the Jews which came to Mary, and had seen the things which Jesus did, believed on him. But some of them went their ways to the Pharisees, and told them what things Jesus had done.*" 36–46.

Now at this time the Jews' passover was near at hand,[72] so that they were in full expectation that Jesus would come to the feast, they they might have an opportunity of laying hands upon him, to destroy him. "Much people of the Jews therefore knew that he was there: and they came not for Jesus' sake only, but that they might see Lazarus also, whom he had raised from the dead. But the chief priests consulted that they might put Lazarus also to death; Because that by reason of him many of the Jews went away, and believed on Jesus." Luke xii. 9, 10, 11.

Thus did this preacher, who I took to be my friend, but was my enemy, for he strove to kill me, as the Scripture saith, "He that hateth his brother without a cause is a murderer." 1 John iii. 15. And whosoever hateth his brother whom he seeth daily, how can he say that he loves God. "We love him because he first loved us. If a man say, I love God, and hateth his brother, he is a liar: for he that loveth not his brother whom he hath seen, how can he love God whom he hath not seen? And this commandment have we from him, That he who loveth God love his brother also." 1 John iv. 19, 20, 21. It was evident that he hated me without a cause, therefore as the Scriptures inform us, he was a murderer, " And ye know that no murderer hath eternal life abiding in him."

Had he been led by the Spirit of God[73] he would not have hated me.

Slaves were most attracted to religions which taught human equality before God and the importance of the sacrifice of Jesus Christ.

"Now the works of the flesh are manifest, which are these; adultery, fornication, uncleanness, lasciviousness, idolatry, witchcraft, hatred, variance, emulations, wrath, strife, seditions, envyings, murders, drunkeness, revellings, and such like: of the which I tell you before, as I have also told you in time past, that they which do such things shall not inherit the kingdom of God. But the fruit of the Spirit is love, joy, peace, long-suffering, gentleness, goodness, faith, meekness, temperance: against such there is no law." Galatians iv. 18–24. Now it is evident, that if he had walked in the Spirit, and lived in the Spirit, he would not have desired vain glory, or envied others: for he and his father strove to the uttermost to prevent my usefulness, and hinder me from spreading the gospel of Jesus Christ; for his father was to preach against me, as has been before mentioned, in order that the people should not go to hear me preach. During which time I was sitting in the pulpit behind him, for I was to preach after him. He then began to explain who Lazarus was, and said that he was a poor man, a porter, of no reputation, and making out that scarcely any notice was taken of him, because he was a poor stinking man. He then exclaimed to the people, that they were all running after a poor dead Lazarus, and that they did not come to see Jesus; and told the people that they might as well throw their bibles and books away, as to be always running after a poor dead man, nothing but a poor wounded Lazarus.

Thus he preached to the people, and told them he was sorry to say, that they had been running to see and hear a poor dead Lazarus, that was risen from the dead, and that they were not then come to see Jesus, but Lazarus. This was his discourse to the congregation, and then he closed the subject; and said, "Our friend, our black brother, will speak a few words unto you."

I then stood up and addressed the congregation, saying, "Men and brethren, I shall not take a text, but only make a few remarks, by God's assistance, on what our brother has spoken unto you concerning poor Lazarus." I then stated unto them the particulars of that transaction, which has been noticed. I then said unto the congregation, "Spiritually speaking, who is this Lazarus? Yea," said I, "every sinner is as Lazarus; for we were all born in sin, and brought forth in iniquity, dead in trespasses and sins, laying in the grave of sin and wickedness, and stinking in the nostrils of the Almighty God."

My dear reader, are you laying in the grave of sin and wickedness? For many have been laying in that state ten, twenty, thirty, yea, and some fifty years, stinking in the nostrils of the Almighty God; and indeed, so are all sinners, who sin against God, and disbelieve his blessed word; if therefore becomes you to enquire and examine whether you have been raised from this awful state or not.

The Jews did not only come to see Lazarus, because of the miracle which was wrought by Jesus Christ on him, but that they might be enabled to lay hands upon him, and kill him, even as they wanted to kill Jesus Christ; for, they said, if they let him alone, his life and conduct, wherever he went, would shew that he was that dead stinking Lazarus, whom Jesus had raised from the grave. So it is with everyone, whether they be men or women, that confesses Jesus Christ before man on earth, being an evident proof that they are rise from the grave of sin and wickedness by the resurrection of the Lord Jesus Christ from the dead, even as Jesus Christ himself confesseth.

I told them, our brother that had preached against me, had not always been a preacher, but was once like other men, for he was born in sin, and brought forth in iniquity, and going astray from the womb, telling lies, and was laying in the grave of sin and wickedness, and stinking in the nostrils of the Almighty. But God, in his infinite goodness and mercy, was pleased to send his only begotten Son into the world,[74] to save all such as should not perish, who lay in the grave of sin and wickedness: Jesus Christ being troubled in the spirit for poor sinners, wept over him as he did over Jerusalem, and rolled the stone of unbelief from his heart, and cried with a loud voice, and said unto him, "Awake, thou that sleepest, and arise from the dead, and Christ shall give thee light."[75] Thus the grave of sin and wickedness opened, and the dead sinner arose from it, by the Spirit of God, bound with the grave clothes of lust, and his face bound up with a napkin[76] of speechlessness, but God said unto the Spirit, Loose him and let him go.

Thus I said God had done to our brother that preached against me, and that he had opened his grave in which he had once lain stinking in the nostrils of God; and that Jesus had risen him from the grave, and had loosened him by his Spirit, to let him go to the gospel feast, to shew himself unto all men, that he was the stinking sinner Christ had risen by his Spirit, to preach the gospel to every creature.

On hearing this the congregation clapt their hands and shouted.

These pretended friends, the father and son, were now more inveterated against me than ever, because I followed the commission of our blessed Lord and Savior Jesus Christ. They wrote many letters against me, and sent them abroad in every direction, to prevent my preaching the gospel of Christ: but, blessed be God, they were not able to prevent me, for the Lord prospered me and blessed my undertakings, which caused a great division amongst the people, and some of them wished me to tarry with them, but I thought it best to go away, and not stay to hurt any of their feelings; because God hath commanded us to live in peace one with another, and hat pronounced his blessing upon them, saying, "Blessed are the peace-makers, for they shall be called the children of God." Matthew v. 9.

I did not tarry at Sunderland above three or four months after this, but took a journey to Liverpool; and from thence I went to New York, where I stayed about nine months, preaching, and visiting my relations, and my brothers and sisters in Christ. During the time I was at New York, I had the happiness to know that my mother and elder brother were converted to God, but they were afraid to apply to the magistrates for their liberty. I daily exhorted them to hold on until the end, and at last they should receive the crown that fadeth not away. While I was with my brethren and sisters in Christ, the Lord blessed and owned my feeble endeavours, and crowned them with the success of his Spirit.

I was now well acquainted with travelling, both by sea and land, so that I knew what it was to suffer and do well: for you must think that I suffered very much by travelling to and fro; but I counted it all joy that I was worthy to suffer for the glory of God; for our trials and tribulations which are but for a moment, are not worthy to be compared with the glory that shall be given us hereafter. For I did not suffer as an evil-doer, nor as a busy-body in other men's matter, nor as a murderer.

After staying at home about nine or ten months, I was constrained to travel abroad again; so I took shipping at New York for Boston. When I arrived there, I began preaching the everlasting gospel, and found the Lord blessed and owned my feeble endeavours. But I was not contented to stay here above three or four months, being still constrained to go farther, to see how the people lived in the other parts of the world, and to preach the gospel unto them. I accordingly embarked at Boston for Amsterdam, in Holland; and there I preached the gospel for one year, which was the whole time I stayed there; and I preached the gospel unto them, in their own language; and the Lord crowned my feeble endeavours, and blessed them by his Spirit.

From Amsterdam I went to Rotterdam, and tarried about two months and a half, preaching the gospel, and I thank God that my labours were not in vain, for I saw some of the fruit of my labour, and the people treated me very kindly.

From thence I took shipping, and went to Helder, about a hundred miles from Hamburgh, and stayed there about two months; here I also found prosperity.

At Helder I embarked for Boston, in North America, and arrived there in safety. I continued two years and a half at Boston preaching the word of life, which was crowned with abundant success and prosperity, many of the people there being convinced, and converted to God.

After that I was constrained by the love of God to take another journey abroad, and I went from Boston to New Orleans, and remained there three months, striving by all possible means, with God's assistance, to do good, but all was in vain, for the people were like those of Sodom and Gomorrah,[77] for it appeared that they neither feared God, nor regarded man. Sunday was their greatest holiday; for they were singing, dancing, playing at billiards, cards, and dice, and every evil thing that could be mentioned, was committed on the Sabbath-day. There were very few persons that had any religion whatever, only here and there one that was a little more serious, which grieved me so much, that I could not content myself to stay at New Orleans any longer, because of the unbelief of the people. Jesus himself declares that when he went into a certain place, he did not many mighty works there, because of their unbelief; and he departed and went into another country.[78] He also gave commission to his disciples that whatsoever country or house they went into, they should say, "Peace be unto this house."[79] And the son of peace was in the house, their peace would abide them; but if not, their peace would return to them again. And, whatsoever house would not receive them, they should shake off the dust of their feet, as a testimony against the people.[80] And thus it was with me, for I did not abide at New Orleans; but by the assistance of God, I took a ship, and sailed for Liverpool, and we had a pleasant voyage thither. But, on the passage, one evening, the captain had forgotten to order his officers to take in a single reef in the top-sails of the ship, as had been done every night, though the weather was ever so fine; so the captain asked me, as I was going upon deck, to tell the mate to go down into the cabin. I accordingly told the mate, and he went done to the captain, who asked him if he had ordered the sailors to take in a single reef into the top-sails, as usual. The mate told him no, for as the weather appeared so fine, he thought it not necessary. But the captain said it did not signify how fine the weather was, he desired it might be done, for he did not know what the weather might be before the morning. This was about the dusk of the evening, when the sailors were in their beds; the mate therefore called them to turn out, to take in a single reef in the top-sails; the sailors grumbled very much, and said there was not wind enough to carry the ship two knots an hour, but they were obliged to do it, whether they liked it or not, which made some of them curse and swear bitterly. Particularly one young man, about nineteen or twenty years of age, for he wished that the vessel might sink, that we might all go to hell together. I could not then help speaking unto him, and asked him if he were not ashamed to talk in such a manner, and what he thought would become of himself. He said unto me, "I do not want any of your preaching, for I am willing to go to hell for my part." One of the sailors said unto him in a jesting manner, "Why, then, you do not care if *we* all go to hell." The young man said no, for he was willing to go. He put on his jacket, and went upon deck, in order to go up on the main top-sail yard-arm, and was the first there; but no sooner had he got on the yard-arm, than he was struck with the DART OF DEATH, and fell into the water without a groan or a struggle, and sunk as if he had been a stone. not having enough time to say, The Lord have mercy upon me; for we were all eye-witnesses of it, and could not say any otherwise, but that he had his desire fulfilled.

I engaged myself at New Orleans as steward and cook of this ship, in order to get to Liverpool: and I thanked the Lord that we all arrived in safety at Liverpool, except the young man above-mentioned.

When I arrived at Liverpool, I could not forget God's promises to his people if they were obedient, that he would send blessings upon them, that there should not be room enough to receive them; as the Scriptures saith, "Bring ye all the tithes into the storehouse, that there may be meat in mine house, and prove me now herewith, saith the LORD of hosts, If I will not open you the windows of heaven, and pour you out a blessing, that there shall not be room enough to receive it. And I will rebuke the devourer for your sakes, and he shall not destroy the fruits of your ground: neither shall your vine cast her fruit before the time in the field, saith the Lord of hosts. And all nations shall call you blessed." Malachi iii. 10, 11, 12.

But, on the contrary, if they were disobedient, God hath said, "But if ye will not hearken unto me, and will not do all these commandments; And if ye shall despise my statutes, or if your soul abhor my judgements, so that ye break my covenant; I also will do this unto you; I will even appoint over you terror, consumption, and the burning ague, that shall consume the eyes, and cause sorrow of heart: and ye shall sow your seed in vain, for your enemies shall eat it. And I will set my face against you, and ye shall be slain before your enemies: they that hate you shall reign over you; and ye shall flee when none persueth you. And if ye will not yet for all this hearken unto me, then I will punish you seven times more for your sins. And I will break the pride of your power; and I will make your heaven as iron, and your earth as brass; And your strength shall be spent in vain: for your land shall not yield her increase, neither shall the trees of the land yield their fruits. And if ye walk contrary unto me, and will not hearken unto me; I will bring seven times more plagues upon you, according to your sins. I will also send wild beasts among you, which shall rob you of your children, and destroy your cattle, and make you few in number; and your high-ways shall be desolate. And if ye will not be reformed by me by these things, but will walk contrary unto me; Then will I also walk contrary unto you, and will punish you yet seven times for your sins. And I will bring a sword upon you, that shall avenge the quarrel of my convenant: and when ye are gathered together within your cities, I will send the pestilence among you; and ye shall be delivered into the hand of your enemy. And when I have broken the staff of your bread, ten women shall bake your bread in one oven, and they shall deliver you your bread again by weight: and ye shall eat, and not be satisfied. And if ye will not for all this hearken unto me, but walk contrary unto me; Then I will walk contrary unto you also in fury; and I, even I, will chastise you seven times for your sins. And ye shall eat the flesh of your sons, and the flesh of your daughters shall ye eat. And I will destroy your high places, and cut down your images, and cast your carcases upon the carcases of your idols, and my soul shall abhor you. And I will make your cities waste, and bring your sanctuaries unto desolation, and I will not smell the savour of your sweet odours. And I will bring the land into desolation: and your enemies which dwell therein shall be astonished at it. And I will scatter you among the heathen, and will draw out a sword after you: and your land shall be desolate, and your cities waste. Then shall the land enjoy her sabbaths' as long as it lieth desolate, and ye be in your enemies land; even then shall the land rest, and enjoy her sabbaths. As long as it lieth desolate it shall rest; because it did not rest in your sabbaths, when ye dwelt upon it. And upon them that are left alive of you I will send a faintness into their hearts in the land of their enemies; and the sound of a shaken leaf shall chase them; and they shall fall when none persueth. And they shall fall one upon another, as it were before a sword, when none persueth: and ye shall have no power to stand before your enemies. And ye shall perish among the heathen, and the lands of your enemies shall eat you up. And they that are left of you shall pine away in their iniquity in your enemies' lands; and also in the iniquities of their fathers shall they pine away with them. If they shall confess their iniquity, and the iniquity of their fathers, with their trespass which they trespassed against me' and that also they have walked contrary unto me; And that I have also walked contrary unto them, and have brought them into the land of their enemies; if then their uncircumcised hearts be humbled, and they then accept of the punishment of their iniquity: Then will I remember my covenant with Jacob, and also my convenant with Isaac, and also my convenant with Abraham will I remember; and I will remember the land. The land also shall be left of them, and enjoy her sabbaths, while she lieth desolate without them: and they shall accept of the punishment of their iniquity: because, even because they despised my judgements, and because their soul abhorred my statutes. And yet for all that, when they be in the land of their enemies, I will not cast them away, neither will I abhor them, to destroy them utterly, and to break my covenant with them: for I am the Lord their God. But I will for their sakes remember the covenant of their ancestors, whom I brought forth out of the land of Egypt in the sight of the heathen, that I might be their God: I am the Lord." Leviticus xxvi. 14–45.

Dear reader, how well would it be for us, and all mankind, to confess unto God our sins and our wickedness, and return and repent of our iniquities, that God may have mercy upon us, and forgive us our sins, and cleanse us from all unrighteousness;[81] that we might not be cut off from the land of the living; as that young man was on board of the ship in which I went to Liverpool. That was for our example, that we should not follow his wicked ways, either by life or conversation, but that we should repent and believe the gospel, that our souls might be saved through the grace of our Lord Jesus Christ, and by faith in his precious blood; that we might be holy in all conversation, while we are tabernacling in this vale of tears, and that our speech might be seasoned with divine grace.

This is the way I spoke to the people when I arrived at Liverpool, and they gladly received me as a brother in Christ, and believed the exhortation which I gave them.

During my stay at Liverpool, they provided me a place to preach in, which was in Byram Street. I was as plain with them as God was pleased to give me ability, by his blessed Spirit, preaching the everlasting gospel of our Lord and Saviour Jesus Christ; for "I would not have them to be ignorant, how that all our fathers were under the cloud, and all passed through the sea; And were all baptized unto Moses in the cloud and in the sea; And did all eat the same spiritual meat; And did all drink the same spiritual drink: for they drank of that spiritual Rock that followed them: and that Rock was Christ. But with many of them God was not well pleased: for they were overthrown in the wilderness. Now these things were our examples, to the intent we should not lust after evil things, as they also lusted. Neither be ye idolaters, as were some of them; as it is written, The people sat down to eat and drink, and rose up to play. Neither let us commit fornication, as some of them committed, and fell in one day three and twenty thousand. Neither let us tempt Christ, as some of them also tempted, and were destroyed of serpents. Neither murmur ye, as some of them also murmured, and were destroyed of the destroyer. Now all these things happened unto them for ensamples: and they are written for our admonition, upon whom the ends of the world are come. Wherefore let him that thinketh he standeth take heed lest he fall. There hath no temptation taken you but such as is common to man: but God is faithful, who will not suffer you to be tempted above that ye are able; but will with the temptation also make a way to escape, that ye may be able to bear it. Wherefore, my dearly beloved, flee from idolatry. I speak as to wise men; judge ye what I say." 1 Cor. x. 1–15.

Thus I endeavoured, by the grace of God, to shew the people, that most men and women were baptized in different churches and in different manners, under a great cloud of witnesses;[82] and have passed through seas of troubles and difficulties; and did not eat of that spiritual bread of life, which is the word of God; and did all drink of that spiritual drink, the waters which cometh from the throne of God. But with many of *them* God was not well pleased; but overthrew them in this world: for some of them were mockers, scoffers, drunkards, whoremongers, idolaters, swearers, backbiting their neighbours, and some their own brothers and sisters, yea even their fathers and mothers. But to speak plain, and be candid with you, I would ask, if it is not so now-a-day, amongst us? You hear the husband abusing his wife for seeming to take a little of this spiritual drink, which is *faith in the blood of our blessed Redeemer.* On the other hand, you will see the woman mocking and scoffing at her husband, if he appears rather inclined to be baptized in the blood of the Savior, to be purged from dead works, and from sin and wickedness.

My dear reader might be one of these characters, but I hope not, for unless you repent and become baptized in Jesus's favour, and be, by him, washed and cleansed from dead works, which is sin and wickedness, before another day appears to your eyes, you might be cut down as cumberers of God's holy ground, and be added unto the number of the three-and-twenty thousand, who fell in one day for their sins and abominations. But if you should be baptized with the baptism of Christ, by his Spirit resting and abiding in the altar of your heart, it will convince you that no other baptism will avail you any thing, but the blood of Jesus Christ, which cleanseth from all sin.

My young friends, I would intreat of you, by the grace of God,[83] to examine yourselves, and search the bottom of your heart, to know if you are one of those rebellious children. Dost thou love thy father and mother? or dost thou curse and hate them? If thou curse and hate them, consider thou art cursing and hating thy maker; for before thou wast made, God made thy parents; and, did he not make thee? Yea, he did, for He is the maker of us all; and there is nothing made, but what was made by the immediate hand of God;[84] and as he is able to make alive, is he not also able to kill? Yea, my dear reader, consider but for a moment, that if the Lord was able to kill three-and-twenty thousand in one day, he will not be one moment in taking thy life. For, in the twinkling of an eye, the breath which we now breathe, is taken from us; and, if we are not baptized with the Holy Ghost and with fire, we cannot enter the kingdom of God.

Perhaps some of you may be enquiring what you should do; I would answer you in the words of our Savior, where it is said, "*And the people asked him, saying, What shall we do then? He answereth and saith unto them, He that hath two coats, let him impart to him that hath none; and he that hath meat, let him do likewise. Then came also publicans to be baptized, and said unto him, Master, what shall we do? And he said unto them, Exact no more than that which is appointed you. And the soldiers likewise demanded of him, saying, And what shall we do? And he said unto them, Do violence to no man, neither accuse any falsely; and be content with your wages.*" Luke iii. 10–14.

It pleased God to sent the Spirit of his Son into my heart, to bear witness with my spirit that I was a child of God, and that he had chosen me out of the world; therefore the world hated me, because I was not of the world; but they who were of God loved me, because that God had loved them first, and had shed abroad in their hearts the love of his Son, that they should love one another, even as God hath given us commandment.[85] Thus did the people of Liverpool, for they showed me great kindness beyond measure, by God's assisting of them by his blessed Spirit: he that had two coats gave me one, and he that had meat did the same; and God crowned my feeble endeavours with great success, and gave me many seals to my ministry, and souls for my hire.

On taking my farewell of the people at Liverpool, after I had been there about five months, preaching the everlasting gospel, and ministering the ordinances of our blessed Lord and Savior, which was the third time I had been to Liverpool, I said unto them, "Now, my dear and beloved friends in Christ, I am about to leave you in body, but I hope not in spirit; for I trust we shall see each other (who are followers of Christ) and that we shall meet in heaven around his throne: where parting shall be no more,[86] where all trials and troubles shall have an end, where sorrow and sighing shall flee away, where the tears shall be for ever wiped from our eyes,[87] where our wearied souls shall be at rest, where the wicked shall cease troubling us, and where our souls shall rejoice with joy unspeakable and full of glory, and join with all the host of heaven, in singing the song of Moses and the Lamb, hallelujahs, and praises unto God for ever and ever."[88]

I then embarked at Liverpool for Newberry Port, in North America, and, thank God, we arrived in safety. I did not tarry at Newberry Port because I had some business to transact at Boston; where I arrived in safety, and settled my affairs, by God's assistance. I also met with many brothers and sisters in Christ, who were glad for my arrival. I stayed at Boston about three months, preaching the gospel of our blessed Jesus, and him crucified; and blessed and praised be God, my labours were not in vain, for many were alarmed and awaked out of their sleep of carnal security, turned from the evil of their ways, and walked in Christ the good old way to eternal joy, many souls were edified, and God glorified.

It appeared that God had greater work for me to do, and to go through many trials and tribulations, for it is through them that we are to enter the kingdom of God. After I had been at Boston three months and a half, I was constrained by the Spirit of God, to take a journey into a foreign country; so I took my leave from the people at Boston, who were sorry to part with me, so we parted with each other in body, but not in mind; and sung the following hymn:

We part in body, not in mind;
  Our minds continue one;
And each to each in Jesus join'd,
  We hand in hand go on.

Subsists as in us all one soul,
  No power can make us twain;
And mountains rise and oceans roll,
  To sever us in vain.

Present we still in spirit are,
  And intimately nigh;
While on the wings of faith and prayer,
  We each to other fly.

In Jesus Christ together we
  In heavenly places sit:
Cloth'd with the sun, we smile to see
  The moon beneath our feet.

Our life is hid with Christ in God:
  Our life shall soon appear,
And shed his glory all abroad,
  In all his members here.

The heavenly treasure now we have
  In a vile house of clay:
But he shall to the utmost save,
  And keep us to that day.

Our souls are in his mighty hand,
  And he shall keep them still;
And you and I shall surely stand
  With him on Sion's hill!

Him eye to eye we there shall see;
  Our face like his shall shine:
O what a glorious company,
  When saints and angels join!

O what a joyful meeting there!
  In robes of white array'd,
Psalms in our hands we all shall bear
  And crowns upon our head.

Then let us lawfully contend,
  And fight our passage through;

Bear in our faithful minds the end,
    And keep the prize in view.

Then let us hasten to the day,
    When all shall be brought home!
Come, O Redeemer, come away!
    O Jesus, quickly come!

God of all consolation, take
    Thy glory of thy grace!
Thy gifts to thee we render back,
    In ceaseless songs of praise.

Thro' thee we now together came,
    In singleness of heart;
We met, O Jesus, in thy name,
    And in thy name we part.

By the assistance of God, I took ship at Boston for Venneliea, in the East Indies; not to please myself, but for the glory of God, and the good of souls; as the Scriptures saith, "*Let no man seek his own, but every man another's wealth. Whatsoever is sold in the shambles, that eat, asking no question for conscience sake: For the earth is the Lord's and the fullness thereof. If any of them that believe not bid you to a feast, and ye be disposed to go; whatsoever is set before you, eat, asking no question for conscience sake. But if any man say unto you, This is offered in sacrifice unto idols, eat not for his sake that shewed it, and for conscience sake: for the earth is the Lord's, and the fullness thereof: Conscience, I say, not thine own, but of the other: for why is my liberty judged of another man's conscience? For if I by grace be a partaker, why am I evil spoken of for that which I give thanks? Whether therefore ye eat, or drink, or whatsoever ye do, do all to the glory of God. Give none offence, neither to the Jews, nor to the Gentles, nor to the church of God: Even as I please all men in all things, not seeking mine own profit, but the profit of many, that they may be saved.*" 1 Cor. x. 24, to the end.

This was my motive in going to the East Indies, that whatsoever I did, to do it for the honour and glory of God; not to seek mine own interest, but the interest of my Lord and Master Jesus Christ; not for the honour and riches of this world, but the riches and honours of that which is to come: I say, not for the riches of this world, which fadeth away; neither for the glory of man; not for golden treasure; but my motive and great concern was for the sake of my Lord and Master, who went about doing good, in order to save poor wicked and sinful creatures.

We had a good passage to Venneliea, but were not permitted to land, although the ship remained there a fortnight. We then received orders to sail to Buones Ayres, where we arrived all safe and well, excepting me, for I was ill a fortnight with pains in my legs. We laid at Buones Ayres about eight months, but I had not the pleasure of preaching the gospel there, on account of the war between the Spainiards and the English; it was the period that General Achmet[89] took Monte Video, and General Whitelock[90] came to assist him with his army. So I continued preaching on board of our own ship, by God's assistance.

During the time we laid there, one of the sailors, a young man about eighteen or nineteen years of age, having considerable property on board of the ship, which he wanted to smuggle on shore, (which indeed was the traffic of the whole ship's crew, both officers and men) was boasting of his money, and that he would go on shore, and get intoxicated, and when we got to our destined port, he would visit every place of riot and vice. So I said unto him, "You had better think about a dying hour; for though you are young you must die, and you do not know how soon; for there is nothing more certain than death, and nothing more uncertain than life." But he said, that he did not want any of my preaching, and that he should live till we arrived at our destined port, and enjoy his pleasure; but to his great surprise he never lived to see it, for that same day he went to go on shore, and from our ship he went alongside of another, when he fell out of the boat, and sunk immediately, not having time to say one word; the whole of the ship's company being eye-witnesses of it. That ship's name was *The Arrow of Boston, in North America*; and the ship to which he and I belonged, was *The Prince of Boston, in North America*. We remained at Buones Ayres eight months, and when all the vessels that were there, were ordered to the different ports to which they belonged: we accordingly made for Boston, where we all safely arrived, except the young man who was drowned.

I had engaged myself on board of the above ship, as cook, for seventeen Spanish dollars per month, in order that I should not be burdensome to the church of God; and this was the way I acted whenever I travelled; for, as St. Paul saith, "*I would rather labour with my hands than be burdensome to the church.*"[91]

When we arrived at Boston I was involved in trouble by the captain wanting to wrong me out of my wages, for he entered a law-suit against me in order to cast me into prison; but thank God it was not in his power, for "*There is no condemnation to them which are in Christ Jesus, who walk not after the flesh, but after the Spirit;*"[92] and this the captain found to his sorrow, for God, by his blessed Spirit, delivered me out of his hands and from the power of the law; the captain and mates having to pay all costs and charges of the court, for injuring my character, which amounted to two thousand dollars for the captain; eight hundred for the chief mate; and eight hundred for the second mate. The amount of which, a man, whom I took for my friend, received for me, and went away with, and I never saw him any more, which distressed me greatly.

The remainder of my troubles and distresses during my stay in the West Indies, in the different islands, and also in the State of Virginia and Baltimore, where I was put in prison, and they strove to make me a slave, (for it was a slave country) were very severe; but God delivered me by his grace, for he has promised to be with us in six troubles, and in the seventh he will not leave us nor forsake us; and that there shall be nothing to harm or hurt us, if we are followers of that which is good. By these promises I was encouraged not to repine at the losses and crosses I had met with.

I staid at Boston about four months, and preached the gospel there with great success, by the aid and assistance of God's Spirit. After that time I had a desire to go to Ireland to preach the gospel; so I parted with the dear people at Boston in body, but not in mind, our minds continuing one, for it grieved them a great deal that I would go from them, but I was constrained by the Spirit of God, although I had not forgotten the troubles and difficulties that God had brought me through; for I was ready to join with the poet, and say,

Come all ye weary travellers,
And let us join and sing,
They everlasting praises
Of Jesus Christ our King;
We've had a tedious journey,
And tiresome, it is true;
But see how many dangers
The Lord has brought us through.

At first when Jesus found us,
He call'd us unto him,
And pointed out the dangers
Of falling into sin;
The world, the flesh, and Satan,
Will prove to us a snare,

Except we do reject them,
By faith and humble prayer.

But by our disobedience,
With sorrow we confess,
We long have had to wander
In a dark wilderness;
Where we might soon have fainted,
In that enchanted ground
But now and then a cluster
Of pleasant grapes we found.

The pleasant road to Canaan
Brings life, and joy, and peace,
Revives our drooping spirits,
And faith and love increase.
We own our Lord and Master,
And run at his command,
And hasten on our journey
Unto the promis'd land.

In faith, in hope, in patience,
We now are going on,
The pleasant road to Canaan,
Where Jesus Christ is gone:
In peace and consolation,
We're going to rejoice,
And Jesus and his people
Shall ever be our choice.

Sinners! why stand ye idle,
While we do march along?
Has conscience never told you
That your are going wrong?
Down the broad road to ruin,
To hear an endless curse;—
Forsake your ways of sinning,
And go along with us.

But if you do refuse us,
We'll bid you now farewell,
We're on the road to Canaan,
And you the way to hell;
We're sorry thus to leave you,
And rather you would go;

Come, try a bleeding Savior,
And feel salvation flow.

Oh! sinners be alarmed,
To see your dismal state;
Repent and be converted,
Before it is too late;
Turn to the Lord by praying,
And daily search his word,
And never rest contented
Until you find the Lord.

Now to the King immortal
Be everlasting praise,
For in his holy service,
We mean to spend our days;
Till we arrive at Canaan,
That heav'nly world above,
With celestial praises,
Sing his redeeming love.

Farewell to sin and sorrow,
I bid you all adieu;
And you my friends prove faithful,
And on your ways pursue:
And if you meet with troubles,
And trials in your way;
Then cast your care on Jesus,
And do not forget to pray.

He never will upbraid you,
Tho' often you request;
Will give you grace to conquer
And take you home to rest.

I therefore embarked at Boston for Ireland, and arrived safe at Limerick, where the brethren and sisters in Christ gladly received me. The prosperity of the work of the Lord in this place, was a memorial, like unto the day of Pentecost; for God showered down righteousness into the hearts of the people in copious showers, so that many of the people thought that miracles were wrought, by the weak instrumentality of my preaching the everlasting gospel. By this means the fame of my preaching spread through the country, even from Limerick to Cork. I preached in Limerick and in the country villages round, and by the Spirit of God, many people were convinced and converted. I also preached to the regiment, at the request of the commanding officer and the mayor of Limerick. The mayor was so kind as to go with me to protect me from the Romans; for they were very much inveterated against me, and said they would have my life. And when the mayor did not go with me, a guard of soldiers was sent. By the command of the mayor and the commanding officer, five of the Roman priests were brought before them, and ordered to give a reason why they were so malicious against me. They could only say, that I would not believe their doctrine, neither would they believe mine; and one of the head priests said, that I was going to hell. The mayor and commanding officer then said, that they would defy any person in Limerick to dispute my doctrine. Then three of the priests said unto them, "We cannot deny or dispute his doctrine." They then went out full of rage and fury, and determined in lay in wait for my life. After this I had greater success than ever, although running greater hazard of losing my life, but I said,

> I am not ashamed to own my Lord,
> Nor to defend his cause;
> Maintain the honour of his word,
> The glory of his cross.
>
> Jesus, my God, I know his name,
> His name is all my trust;
> Nor will he put my soul to shame,
> Nor let my hope be lost.
>
> Firm as his throne his promise stands,
> And he can well secure,
> What I have committed to his hands,
> Till the decisive hour.

Thus I spoke in the name of Jesus. After having preached a month, three Protestant ministers came to visit me, and to discourse on the doctrines of election and reprobation, at the house of Mr. Wawy, not far from the custom-house, in Limerick, where I was staying. They came three days following, with their bibles, and as many as fifteen people with them, to hear them discourse with me on the subject. They asked me what my opinion was of election and reprobation. I told them what my opinion was, that every person might be elected by the grace of God, through the Spirit of the Lord: for "*By grace are ye saved; and that not of yourselves, for it is the gift of God.*" And that my opinion of reprobation was, that they who believed not, should be damned; Mark xvi. 16. They then said unto me, "Do you not know that God hath a chosen and peculiar people, whom he hath foreknown, elected, and predestinated? and that they are his peculiar people and his royal priesthood?"[93] I answered, "Yes; I have heard and read it." Then said they, "Do not you recollect that God hath made some vessels to honour, and some to dishonour; some to be saved, and some to be damned? and that we were all in the hands of God as clay in the hands of the potter?" I then said unto them, "I perceive that you are of a cavilling principle, but I will not argue or cavil on the principles of religion; for where argument and strife is there is confusion and every evil work, which is not of God, but the devil; for as the Scriptures saith, "*Who is a wise man, and endued with knowledge? Let him shew out of a good conversation, his works with meekness of wisdom. But if ye have bitter envying and strife in your hearts; glory not, and lie not against the truth. This wisdom descendeth not from above, but is earthly, sensual, devilish: for where envying and strife is there is confusion and every evil work. But the wisdom that is from above, is first pure, then peaceable, gentle, and easy to be intreated; full of mercy and good fruits; without partiality and without hypocrisy; and the fruit of righteousness is sown in peace of them that make peace.*"[94] Therefore I said unto them "I will not argue with you at all; will you make out God to be the author of sin and wickedness, as you are yourselves? Do you not recollect that God made all things, made them good, and blessed them? and that God made man after his own lovely image and likeness, crowned him with honour and glory, made him but a little lower than the angels, gave him power over the whole creation, and over every thing that liveth, creepeth, and groweth on the face of the earth, and the earth and the fullness thereof?[95] And how is it you say, that there is a certain number to be saved, and a certain number to be lost? Are you so ignorant that you do not know your own bibles? to know what God saith in the first chapter of Genesis, from the twenty-sixth verse to the end? "*And God said, Let us make man in our image, after our likeness: and let them have dominion over the fish of the sea, and over the fowl of the air, and over the cattle, and over all the earth, and over every creeping thing that creepeth upon the earth. So God created man in his own image, in the image of God created he him; male and female created he them. And God blessed them, and God said unto them, Be fruitful, and multiply, and replenish the earth, and subdue it: and have dominion over the fish of the sea, and over the fowl of the air, and over every living thing that moveth upon the earth. And God said, Behold, I have given you every herb bearing seed, which is upon the face of all the earth, and every tree, in the which is the fruit of a tree yielding seed; to you it shall be for meat. And to every beast of the earth, and to every fowl of the air, and to every thing that creepeth upon the earth, wherein there is life, I have given green herb for meat: and it was so. And God saw every thing that he had made, and, behold, it was very good. And the evening and the morning were the sixth day."*

But should any of my readers be ready to say, How then is man deprived of this great happiness? I answer, By believing the Devil rather than God; for which he was driven out of Paradise: For God had given man a strict charge, and made a covenant with him, that if he broke this covenant by eating of the forbidden fruit, he should lose the happiness of his soul. But, "*The serpent said unto the woman, Ye shall not surely die: For God doth know that in the day ye eat thereof, then your eyes shall be opened, and ye shall be as gods, knowing good and evil. And when the woman saw that the tree was good for food, and that it was pleasant to the eyes, and a tree to be desired to make one wise, she took of the fruit thereof, and did eat; and gave also unto her husband with her, and he did eat.*" Genesis iii. 4, 5, 6. Hereby they disobeyed God, and lost the happiness of their souls, which was their life: for they had no more union and communication with God, being driven out of paradise.

This was the case with the man of God that disobeyed God by eating and drinking in the place where God had forbidden him.

This was also the case with the Jews, who were the chosen and elect people of God; for he hath declared because of their unbelief, they should not enter into his rest, although it was appointed for them from the foundation of the world; as the Scriptures saith, "Let us therefore fear, lest, a promise being left us of entering into his rest, any of you should seem to come short of it. For unto us was the gospel preached, as well as unto them: but the word preached did not profit them, not being mixed with faith in them that heard it. For we which have believed do enter into rest, as he said, As I have sworn in my wrath, if they shall enter into my rest: although the works were finished from the foundation of the world. For he spake in a certain place of the seventh day on this wise, And God did rest the seventh day from all his works. And in this place again, If they shall enter into my rest. Seeing therefore it remaineth that some must enter therein, and they to whom it was first preached entered not in because of unbelief. Let us labour therefore to enter into that rest, lest any man may fail after the same example of unbelief. "Hebrews iv. 1–6, 11. By which it is evident, if we believe we shall enter in, and if we believe not we shall not enter into that rest which remaineth for the people of God.

This was likewise the case with the Israelites, whom the Lord saved and brought safe out of the land of Egypt, but afterwards destroyed them that believed not; as the Scriptures saith, "I will therefore put you in remembrance, though ye once knew this, how that the Lord, having saved the people out of the land of Egypt, afterward destroyed them that believed not. And the angels which kept not their first estate, but left their own habitation, he hath reserved in everlasting chains under darkness unto the judgement of the great day. Even as Sodom and Gomorraha, and the cities about them[96] in like manner, giving themselves over to fornication, and going after strange flesh, are set forth for an example, suffering the vengeance of eternal fire. Likewise also these filthy dreamers defile the flesh, despise dominion, and speak evil of dignities. Yet Micheal the archangel, when contending with the devil he disputed about the body of Moses, durst not bring against him a railing accusation, but said, The Lord rebuke thee. But these speak evil of those things which they know not: but what they know naturally, as brute beasts, in those things they corrupt themselves." Jude 5–10.

Thus I spoke unto the ministers, and said, "May the Lord change your hearts, your minds, and your thoughts; and give you a better understanding of his blessed word." Now they were contending with me three days, at the end of which time they were convinced by the word of God, and his Holy Spirit, that they were wrong and I was right. They then gave me the right-hand of fellowship, we joined in prayer with each other, shook hands, and parted in love and friendship. I remained two years in Ireland, preaching the gospel, until the year 1805; when I was constrained by the love of God to leave these beloved people, who were very sorry to part with me.

Before my departure from Ireland, I took to me a partner in life, who is still alive and with me. Her name is Mary Jea, a native of Ireland. This was my third time of marriage. My second wife died a natural death, while I was at Holland; she was a Malteese woman; and her name was Charity Jea. My first wife's name was Elizabeth Jea, of whom mention has been made before. I have had several children, none of whom are alive, but I hope they are all in heaven, where I expect to see them, by the grace of God, and spend an endless day of praise around his dazzling throne, where parting shall be no more for ever.

I and my wife accordingly took ship at the Cove Cork for St. John's in Hallifax; but after we were on board, we found we were obliged to come to England, to take convoy from Portsmouth. When we arrived at Portsmouth, my wife was taken ill; and the friends in Christ thought it necessary that she should remain until her health was restored, and then to follow me, or else for me to return for her. But to our sad disappointment we set sail from Portsmouth in the evening with a breeze of wind, which lasted till near the morning, when about eight or nine o'clock we were becalmed; and as we were laying to becalmed off Torbay, about five or six miles from the land of Torbay. and striving to get up with the convoy, we were taken by a French privateer, who carried us into Pampoole[97] in France. Our vessel was the brig *Iscet of Liverpool*, Henry Patterson, Master.

After we landed at Pampoole, we were marched to Cambria, which was seven hundred miles from Pampoole. After a long march we arrived safe at Cambria, after many severe troubles and trials. Here I remained five years in the prison at that place; and was constrained by the love of God to preach to the people there, the unsearchable riches of Jesus Christ, and God was pleased to crown my feeble endeavours with great success; and, in eighteen months, the Lord was pleased to add to my number two hundred souls; the number of the people in the prison was about three thousand: and I had liberty from the commissary general of the Depot, to preach to all of them.

After I had been there eighteen months, orders came from the minister of Paris, that all who were called Americans, were to go away; we were accordingly marched away to Brest, seven hundred miles from Cambria; and all the dear prisoners in the depot were very sorry to part with me, the same as if I had been their own father; but I was forced to go. This was the Lord's doings and it was marvellous in our eyes. I told them that God had promised me in his word that he would deliver me from all my enemies, both temporal and spiritual, by his blessed Spirit; but they would not believe me, until they saw me going away; they then were exceedingly sorrowful,[98] and made a subscription for me, which amounted to about nine crowns. On the morning before I went away, I preached my farewell sermon, which was from the 2 Cor. xiii. 11. "Finally, brethren, farewell. Be perfect, be of good comfort, be of one mind, live in peace, and the God of love and peace shall be with you." We arrived safe at Brest, thanks be to God, but we had great trials and difficulties on our march thither, being obliged to walk without shoes, and having no more provisions than what we could buy by our scanty allowance, which was a half-penney per mile; and when our feet were so sore that we could not march, we were not allowed any thing. Some of us had no clothes to cover our nakedness; and our lodgings at nights were in barns and cow-houses, and we were obliged to lay down the same as beasts, and indeed not so comfortable, for we were not allowed straw nor any thing else to lay on.

As soon as we arrived at Brest we were sent on board of a French corvette, under American colours, to go and fight against the English, but twenty, out of two hundred that were sent on board, would not enlist under the banner of the tyrants of this world; for far be it from *me* ever to fight against Old England, unless it be with the sword of the gospel, under the captain of our salvation, Jesus Christ. Those of us who would not fight against the English, were sent on board of a French man of war, that they should punish us, but they would not, but sent us to Morlaix, about thirty miles from Brest, where they put us in prison, and kept us upon bread and water for a fortnight, then all the rest consented to go back on board of the corvette, rather than to be sent again to the depot, for we were to be sent back loaded with chains, and under joint arms. I was the only one that stood out; and I told them I was determined not to fight against any one and that I would rather suffer any thing than do it. They said they would send me back to Cambria, and they would keep me upon bread and water, until the wars were over. I said I was willing to suffer any thing, rather than fight. They then took me before the council and the head minister of the Americans, to examine me. They asked me which I liked to do, to go back to the ship, or to be marched to Cambria. I told them they might send me on board of the vessel, if they liked; but if they did I was determined not to do any work, for I would rather suffer any thing than fight or kill any one. They then consulted together what they should do with me; and made up their minds to turn me out of the prison. The head minister then asked me what I was at, that I would not fight for my country. I told him that I was not an American, but that I was a poor black African, *a preacher of the gospel*. He said, "Cannot you go on board, and preach the gospel there?"—"No, Sir," said I, "it is a floating hell, and therefore I cannot preach there." The said the council, "We will cool your Negro temper, and will not suffer any of your insolence in our office." So they turned me out of their office; and said that I had liberty to go any where in the town, but not out of the town; that they would not give me any work, provisions, or lodgings, but that I should provide it myself. Thus was I left upon the mercy of God, but was enabled to cast my care and dependance on the Lord Jesus; for he has promised to deliver those who call upon him in the time of trouble; and I did call upon him in the time of my trouble and distress, and he delivered me.

I was two days without food, walking about without any home, and I went into the hospitals, gaols, and open streets, preaching the gospel unto every creature, as Christ hath commanded us.

Thus I went about preaching the gospel of our Lord and Savior Jesus Christ. Often, at the conclusion of my sermons, many of the nobility and gentry came to me, and said, "We are much edified by your preaching; when do you preach again?" I told them, in the mornings at nine o'clock, and in the afternoons at three, by God's assistance. Thus I did both Sundays and other days, when the weather would permit, during the time I was at Morlaix.

It pleased God to raise up a friend unto me on the second day of my distress, after I was turned out of Morlaix prison into the streets, by order of the American counsellor Mr. Dyeott, and Mr. Veal the American minister of France. The French commissary-general gave me liberty to preach every where God would permit me; so I went on in the name of the Lord, preaching and exhorting the people to put their trust in the Lord, and serve him truly with fear, reverence, and godly sincerity. This dear friend, whom God was pleased to raise up unto me, was so alarmed by my preaching, that he was constrained by the love of God to come and speak unto me, and asked me where I lived. I told him no where. He asked me if I had any place to stay at. I told him no; for I had been turned out of prison two days, and was not suffered to work, and was not allowed to go farther than the bounds of the town; that I might humble myself to the order of the American counsellor, to go on board of the corvette, to fight against the English. Thus they strove to punish me; but it was utterly in vain, for this friend took me to his house and family; his family consisted of a wife and four children; who received me into their house as an angel of God, and gave me food, raiment, and lodging, for fourteen months, and charged me nothing for it, but said, that the Lord would repay them seven-fold for what they had done. Thus they gladly received me into their house, as Lot did the angels, Genesis xix.

But Mr. Dyeott, the American counsellor, told the people that received me into their house, that they should turn me out of doors, in order that I should go on board of the corvette, to fight against England; and if they would not order me out of their house, they should not have any satisfaction for what they were doing for me; for they were preventing me from going on board the corvette. Thus he endeavoured to lay every obstacle in my way, by trying to prevent those people from doing for me; but the dear man and woman said, that if no person satisfied them for their doings, God would, and as for me I should not perish, for as long as they had a mouthful of victuals, I should have part of it, and such as they had I should be welcome to, the same as their own children. Some said that I was imposing on these people, for Mr. Tangey had only one shilling and three-pence per day, which he earned by hard labour, and said it would be far better for me to go on board of the corvette, for thereby I should be enabled to obtain a great sum of prize-money. But I told them, as I had Mr. Dyeott, that I would not go on board if they would give me a guinea for every breath I drew, and that I would sooner starve and die first, than I would go on board; and that if they carried me on board in irons I would lay there and die before I would do the least work. I had been on board four weeks before, laying upon the bare deck, without bed or blankets; and I counted it a floating hell, for the evil language of the officers and sailors, continually cursing and swearing; and my humble supplications and petitions were unto God that he would deliver me from this vessel; and God did deliver me.

Some persons said unto those of the house where I was staying, that they were wrong in keeping me, but they would not hearken unto them, and kept me, until peace was proclaimed between France and Great Britain, and all the soldiers were out of France. I then made application to Mr. Dyeott for a passport to England, but he denied me, and said that he would keep me in France until he could send me to America, for he said that I was an American, that I lied in saying I was married in England, and that I was no African. I told him with a broken heart, and crying, that I was an African, and that I was married in England. But he contradicted me three times. When I told the people where I lived, they said that he was rich, and that it was impossible for me to get clear, and asked me if I thought I should. I told them yes, for all things were possible with God, and to him that believed all things were possible, and according to our faith it should be unto us;[99] and my faith was such, that I believed God would deliver me.

A captain of an English ship of war, laying at Morlaix, advised me to go to the French commissary, to get a passport to England, and that if I succeeded, he would take me in his ship. Accordingly I went to the French commissary, who sent me to the mayor, and I asked him if his honour would have the goodness to grant me a passport to England, to see my wife. The mayor answered and said unto me; "You must go to Mr. Dyeott, the American counsellor, to get a passport." I said unto him, "Sir, it is no use; I have been to him three times, and he pushed me out of doors, and would not suffer me to speak to him." Then the mayor said, "Stop a moment, and I will send a letter to him;" he then wrote a letter, and gave it to me, saying, "Take this to Mr. Dyeott." I accordingly carried the letter to Mr. Dyeott, who opened the letter and read it; after he had so done, he said unto me, "Had you the impudence to go to the mayor?" I said, "Yes, sir, for I was compelled to do it." He then took me by the shoulders, and pushed me out of doors, and said that he would keep me as long as he possibly could. I then returned to the house where I lived, crying and mourning, and my spirit within me was troubled; and the people asked me what made me cry. I told them that I had been to the counsellor, and he would not let me go, and said that he would keep me as long as he could. They said it was what they expected. I said that God had told me to call upon him in the time of trouble, and he would deliver me.[100] So I passed that night in fasting and prayer unto God, and wrestled with him as Jacob did with the angel; and blessed be God, I *did* prevail. I went to the mayor in the morning, and asked him if Mr. Dyeott had said any thing to him concerning me. He said no; and asked me what Mr. Dyeott said unto me. I said that he would not give me any thing, for he would not suffer me to work, or to go to England; but said he would keep me perishing in France, until he could send me to America. The mayor said, "Stop awhile, and I will send a gentleman with you to Mr. Dyeott." The gentleman accordingly went with me to him, and asked him what he meant to do with me. He said that he meant to keep me, and send me to America, for I was an American. The gentleman then said, "You must not keep this poor black man in this manner; you have kept him already fourteen months without food or employment; and if he be an American, why do you not give him American support?" He said, "Because he will not go on board the vessel I have provided for him." At that moment the mayor came in, and said, "What do you mean to do with this man?" He said, "I mean to keep him in France until I can send him to America." The mayor said, "You cannot keep him in this manner, you must give him a passport to England." But he said he would not. The mayor said if he would not, he would; and told me to come with him to his office: I went with him, and he gave me a passport to embark at St. Maloes on board of any vessel that was going to England.

As I was going to St. Maloes I met with an English captain, whose brig was laying at Morlaix, and he said that he was going to Guernsey, in three hours time; and as he had heard me preach at Morlaix, he would give me my passage for nothing.

Then I told the dear people at the house where I had lived, who were exceedingly glad, and thankful to God for my deliverance. I also was thankful to God our blessed Lord and Savior Jesus Christ, that brotherly love had continued.

I arrived safe at Guernsey, and brotherly love did not withdraw itself from me there, for the brethren in Christ gladly received me, and gave me the right-hand of fellowship,[101] treated me as a brother, and gave me liberty to preach in the different chapels; and I can say with truth, there was no chapel large enough to hold the congregations. I remained there fifteen days, and during that time there were many souls convinced and converted to God. After that I departed from them in the Guernsey packet, for Southampton, and they furnished me with every thing convenient for me; and thank God, I arrived there in safety, and was cordially received by the brethren, who gave me the use of their chapels to preach in, and much good was done during my stay. They kindly furnished me with every thing that was necessary. But I did not stay there any more than four days, because I wanted to come to Portsmouth. I arrived safe at Portsmouth, and found my wife well, which I bless God for; I was gladly received by the brethren in Christ, and preached for several of them; and I can say with truth, that all those who have received me in the name of Christ, are brethren unto me, and I pray that the Lord will bless them, and give them all a happy admittance into his kingdom, there to sing the song of Moses and the Lamb, for ever and ever.

My dear reader, I would now inform you, that I have stated this in the best manner I am able, for I cannot write, therefore it is not so correct as if I have been able to have written it myself; not being able to notice the time and date when I left several places, in my travels from time to time, as many do when they are travelling; nor would I allow alterations to be made by the person whom I employed to print this narrative.

Now, dear reader, I trust by the grace of God, that the small house in Hawk Street, which the Lord hath been pleased to open unto me, for the public worship of his great and glorious name, will be filled with converts, and that my feeble labours will be crowned with abundant success.

A Hymn.

Come, O thou Traveller unknown,
Whom still I hold , but cannot see!
My company before is gone,
And I am left alone with thee:
With thee all night I mean to stay,
And wrestle till the break of day.

I need not tell thee who I am;
My misery and sin declare:
Thyself hast call'd me by my name;
Look on thy hands, and read it there:
But who, I ask of thee, who art thou?
Tell me thy Name, and tell me now.

Lo vain thou strugglest to get free,
I never will unloose my hold,
Art thou the Man who died for me?
The secret of thy love unfold:
Wrestling I will not let thee go,
Till I thy Name, they Nature know.

Wilt thou not yet to me reveal
Thy new, unutterable Name?
Tell me, I still beseech thee, tell;
To know it now, resolv'd I am:
Wrestling I will not let thee go,
Till I thy Name, thy Nature know.

What though my shrinking flesh complain,
And murmur to contend so long?
I rise superior to my pain:
When I am weak, then I am strong:
And when my all of strength shall fail,
I shall with the God-man prevail.

Finis

Notes

1. John 4:16.
2. 1 Samuel 1:11.
3. Psalms 96:11, 98:7.
4. Ezekiel 4:3.
5. Daniel 4:35.
6. Psalms 102:10.
7. Matthew 8:12.
8. Song of Solomon 1:5–6.
9. 1 Corinthians 2:14.
10. Daniel 3:19.
11. Psalms 46:5.
12. 1 Corinthians 1:21.
13. John 1:29, 36.
14. James 5:16.
15. Acts 1:14; 2 Chronicles 6:39.
16. Psalms 116:3; 2 Samuel 22:6.
17. Acts 16:30.
18. Psalms 6:6.
19. Lamentations 3:45–46.
20. Deuteronomy 6:5; 11:3; Matthew 22:37.
21. Luke 18:13.
22. Revelations 7:15–17.
23. Ezekiel 18:31.
24. Ezekiel 11:20.
25. Song of Solomon 5:10.
26. Psalms 40:2.
27. Acts 2:4.
28. Actually John 1:3.
29. Genesis 1:25–26; Acts 10:12; 11:6.
30. 2 Peter 3:11.
31. 2 Corinthians 6:2.
32. Matthew 25:31.
33. Matthew 25:34.
34. Ephesians 2:8.
35. Matthew 10:36.
36. 1 Corinthians 15:16.
37. Luke 16:19–20.
38. Daniel 2:35–49.
39. Ezekiel 1:2, 14; 13:19.
40. Daniel 5:25–29.
41. Daniel 5:6.
42. Matthew 8:12; 13:42, 50; Luke 13:28.
43. Charles Wesley, "The Minister's prayer; Christ's constraining love." Jea replaced Christ with God in the first line of the second stanza.

44. John 15:16.
45. Mark 9:23.
46. Acts 2:4.
47. Amos 8:11.
48. Psalms 18:17.
49. John 12:46; Psalm 20:4.
50. Luke 1:37, 18:27.
51. Matthew 26:67.
52. Revelations 14:4.
53. Acts 2:4.
54. 1 Peter 3:14.
55. Isaiah 1:16.
56. Job 5:19.
57. Ephesians 4:26.
58. Acts 14:22.
59. Acts 2:13.
60. Acts 16:30.
61. Ecclesiastes 3:1–8.
62. from Psalms 107:6.
63. Acts 27:14.
64. Acts 27:24–28.
65. Isaiah 54:5.
66. Nehemiah 9:24.
67. Obadiah 14.
68. 2 Corinthians 5:14.
69. 1 Corinthians 15:58.
70. See note 43.
71. John 4:16.
72. John 6:4.
73. Romans 8:14.
74. John 3:16.
75. Ephesians 5:14.
76. John 11:14.
77. Jude 7.
78. Mark 6:6.
79. Luke 10:5.
80. Matthew 10:14.
81. Jeremiah 33:8.
82. Hebrews 12:1.
83. 1 Corinthians 11:28.
84. Eccesiastes 2:24.
85. John 3:23.
86. Revelations 7:17.
87. Revelations 21:4.
88. Revelations 15:3.
89. Samuel Achmuty, Jr. (1756–1822) was a distinguished English general and son

of Samuel Auchmuty, Anglican rector and head of the school for slaves at Trinity Church in New York City. Auchmuty served with distinction in the American Revolution and in India in the 1790s. After service in Montevideo, he eventually became commander-in-chief in Ireland, but died shortly after taking post. (Sidney Lee, ed., *Dictionary of National Biography* 62 vols. (London, 1885–1900), 2:246–48.

90. General John Whitelocke (1757–1833) who commanded a disasterous march against the Spanish in Montevideo in 1806, at which the British were forced to sue for peace after heavy losses. Whitelocke received blame while Auchmuty was marked for promotion. After his return to England, Whitelock was court martialed. *Dictionary of National Biography*, 61:119–21.

91. 2 Corinthians 11:9.

92. Romans 8:1.

93. Deuteronomy 14:2; 1 Peter 2:9.

94. James 3:13–18.

95. Genesis 1:25–28.

96. Jude 7.

98. Paimpol, a small Breton fishing village.

99. Matthew 26:22; Luke 18:23, 24.

100. Matthew 19:26.

101. Psalms 27:15, 41:4; 1 Samuel 24:15.

102. Galatians 2:9.

103. Charles Wesley, "Wrestling Jacob: I will not let thee go." parts 1 and 2.

A

COLLECTION

OF

HYMNS.

Compiled and Selected

By JOHN JEA,

AFRICAN PREACHER OF THE GOSPEL.

PORTSEA:

Printed by J. Williams.

1816.

Appendix 1

The Hymns of John Jea

In 1816, soon after publishing his autobiography, John Jea compiled over three hundred hymns in a songbook. The book included approximately twenty-nine of his own hymns, twenty-eight hymns identified as Charles Wesley's, and eighteen by Isaac Watts's. The purpose of this book was clear. Itinerants carried handy pocket-books of verse in their travels and sang well-known hymns at their extemporaneous services.[1] Methodism relied heavily on hymns in services and ministers wrote and published vast numbers of songs. Charles Wesley wrote over six thousand alone. African-American Methodists quickly adopted the form. In 1801 Richard Allen published his own hymns in collections of Methodist songs. In the years after the close of the slave trade in 1808, Peter Williams, Jr., William Hamilton, and Robert Y. Sydney all wrote commemorative hymns and anthems. These efforts were usually single hymns. Jea's compositions are one of the most significant collections of early African-American autobiographical poetry.[2]

My decision to ascribe these twenty-nine poems to Jea was based on two factors. Several poems are clearly autobiographical and deal with themes of Africa, slavery, and freedom. Others are grouped with the autobiographical hymns, work closely with Jea's spirited theological method, and are unknown outside of this collection. I have checked all the hymns against other Methodist hymnals of the period, and collections of Wesley and Watts cited in the bibliography.

In his massive study of African-American spirituals, John Lovell proved that hymns cannot be understood outside of their social and political context. Examining antebellum black spirituals, Lovell argued that African-Americans articulated communal resistance to slavery and a desire for freedom through the folk idiom of hymns.[3] Other African-American hymns of this era celebrated victories over slavery or admonished listeners to bear life's burdens. Jea does this in at least four poems, which are among the earliest published manifestations of this tradition.

The Dutch Reformed church of his youth used "lining out" in which the precentor sang the psalm for the congregation one or two lines at a time, ending on a definite pitch. The congregation repeated the line, with slight elaborations of the tune. Worshippers learned the songs by rote and often altered the tunes a little each time they sang. A significant advantage of this was that it used popular airs and tunes. Itinerants could be certain their new congregations knew a specific melody. It was a language they held in common.

This practice dovetailed with African ways and became principal features of black religious services. Jea often relied upon African musical formats for his hymns. He would improvise using the methods by which African songsters alternated improvised lines and fixed refrains. Jea's hymns are chants, best suited to African-American "hush harbor," or secret ceremonies, which Jea led during his years in America.[4]

As Nathan O. Hatch has argued, spiritual songs were a primary means by which people wrested spiritual control from the churches and ministers. Music was a "spontaneous, moving medium capable of capturing the identity of plain people." Early gospel music ranged from deeply personal renditions of individual religious experiences to rousing march songs of collective enterprise. Blacks, often forbidden to invoke their own theology by paternalist white congregations, used hymns as a distinctive music, "a treasure that external restraints could not take away."[5] Part of the significance of Jea's hymns is that, like his narrative, they fused individual salvation and collective solidarity with fierce, politicized antislavery. He is among the first of the African-American ministers to combine the sacred and the political in sermons and song.[6]

Jea sang to camp meetings and congregations the saga of his enslavement and liberation through Christianity. His exhortations, biblical usage, and songs, fit best within the radical Methodist or evangelical tradition. The various sects known as Ranters used hymns extensively. While they included favorites by the Wesleys or Isaac Watts, they preferred popular tunes by Lorenzo Dow or borrowed melodies from lewd and ribald tavern songs. Hymns were often written in the first person plural, or in dialogue emphasizing the sense of community.

Jea's hymns individualize many of the most common themes. His most autobiographical hymns describe his confrontations with God and, later, invoke God against his enemies. In topic and treatment, hymns 280–283, and 296 seem the most autobiographical. Other hymns address particularly African concerns. For example, hymns 252, 285–288, and 296 proclaim what James Cone has described as the unity of all African peoples through God. Hymn 284 articulates Jea's acceptance of Christ as precondition to liberation.

The origins and themes of Jea's poems display the interactions of African and European-American theology and are unique among early African-American hymnists. In his accounts of battles with the slave masters and spiritual salvation, Jea's songs reveal the making of an African-American identity composed of Christian morality realized by the crusade against slavery. Although that abolitionism had clear and sympathetic meaning to his English listeners, it meant the most in black camp meetings in America. That underlying antislavery message is what gives Jea's hymns their greatest power and importance.

Notes

1. [John Jea], *A Collection of Hymns Compiled and Selected by John Jea, African Preacher of the Gospel* (Portsea, 1816). The only known copy of this book is at the Bodleian Library, Oxford University.

2. George Osborn, ed., *The Poetical Works of John and Charles Wesley,* 13 vols. (London, 1868–1872); John R. Tyson, *Charles Wesley, A Reader* (New York, 1989); John Wesley, *A Collection of Hymns for the Use of the People Called Methodists* (London, 1779 with many subsequent editions).

3. Dorothy Porter included hymns by Allen, Sidney, Williams and Hamilton in her *Early Negro Writing, 1760–1837* (Boston, 1971), 559–71. Shortly after Jea's publication, Peter Spencer published the *African Union Hymn Book, Designed as a Companion for the Pious, and All Friends of All Denominations. . . .* (Wilmington, Del., 1822).

4. John Lovell, *Black Song: The Forge and the Flame: The Story of How the Afro-American Spiritual was Hammered Out* (New York, 1970), 14–17, 123–26.

5. Eileen Southern, *The Music of Black Americans: A History* (New York, 1971), 30–31.

6. Nathan O. Hatch, *The Democratization of American Christianity* (New Haven, 1989), 153-58; Lawrence W. Levine, *Black Culture and Black Consciousness: Afro-American Folk Thought from Slavery to Freedom* (New York, 1977), 17–55, 162–68.

7. For discussion of this fusion see Graham Hodges, "Root and Branch, African-Americans in New York and eastern New Jersey, 1613-1863," ch. 11, forthcoming.

8. Julia Stewart Werner, *The Primitive Methodist Connexion: Its Background and Early History* (Madison, Wis., 1984), 151–52.

9. James H. Cone, *The Spirituals and the Blues: An Interpretation* (Westport Conn., 1972), 34–36.

The Hymns of John Jea

252. Works of Creation (C. M.)*

AFRICA nations, great and small,
Upon this earthly ball,
Give glory to the God above,
And crown him Lord of all.

'Tis God above, who did in love
Your souls and bodies free,
By British men with life in hand,
The gospel did decree.

By God's free grace they run the race,
And did his glory see,
To preach the gospel to our race,
The gospel Liberty.

His wisdom did their souls inspire,
His heavenly riches spread;
And by the Spirit of the Lord,
They in his footsteps tread.

280. Confession (C. M.)

WHEN I from Africa did come,
I was both small and young;
I did not know where I did go,
Because I was so young.

My father and my mother too,
We all were stole away;
My sisters and my brothers too.
Were took by the ship's crew.

We were took on board, and there we laid,
And knew not what to do;
The God above to us in love,
Did his kind aid afford.

When we were carried 'cross the main,
To great America,
There we were sold, and then were told
That we had not a soul.

Thanks be to God who did in love
To us his mercy show,
Did to my soul his gospel show,
By grace, almighty power.

281. Confession of Master and Mistress (C. M.)

OUR master and our mistress too,
To us they did confess,
That we were theirs, and not our own,
They bought us with a price.

The price of silver and of gold,
Which they did call their own,
The sons and daughters did the same,
As their grandfathers did.

They did not think that God well knew
All they did think and say
Against us poor African slaves,
As they do every day.

But God who did poor Joseph save,
Who was in Egypt sold,
So did he unto us poor slaves,
And he'll redeem the whole.

* Jea consecutively numbered the hymns in his book for easier reference during his services. After each hymn's title Jea included a standard notation of text meter. This was not an indication of tune but of the hymn's syllable length. C. M. stands for common meter; S. M. for short meter; L. M. for long meter; and P M. for peculiar meter.

Then shall we give him all the praise,
And glory to his name;
Redeeming love shall be our song,
And end with endless days.

282. Confessing Christ (C. M.)

WHEN I was fifteen years of age,
God did his grace bestow;
Convicting and converting grace
Did fill my heart with love.

When first I saw my wretched case,
I broke my heart with grief;
I groan'd with inward groans, and said,
O Christ give me relief.

Thus did the Saviour then appear,
With love and pity too,
Did give his life that I may live,
And be for ever new.

A new-born babe in Christ my God,
My soul and spirit too,
Be born of water and of blood,
And wash'd as white as snow.

I thank God for his blessed Son,
For me he did atone;
I own him for my father God,
And my eternal home.

283. Taking My Leave (C. M.)

AFTER I preach'd in America,
I bid my friends adieu,
That I must go and preach God's word
To others as well as you.

'Tis God's command, and I must go,
And leave all other things below:
Leave mother, sister, here below;
And all I see and know.

My life, my thoughts, my evil ways,
They all must stay behind;
And bid farewell to every fear,
Christ wipes my weeping eye.

He fills my heart with love divine,
And kisses me with a smile,
And says to me that I am his,
The darling of his soul.

I give God thanks for his great gift,
The saviour of my soul,
He redeem'd my soul from slavery,
And made me all his own.

284. Trusting in Christ (S. M.)

I thank God, that did set
My soul at liberty;
My body freed from men below,
By his almighty grace.

I will be slave no more,
Since Christ has set me free,
He nail'd my tyrants to his cross,
And bought my liberty.

I bless the Lord that he
Has made my spirit whole,
Therefore to him my heart I'll give,
And all I have and hold.

The world's glittering wealth,
I bid it all farewell;
The gold, the silver, and all things
That is upon this land.

Dear Saviour, O how long,
Shall this bright hour delay?
Fly swifter round, ye wheels of time,
And bring the welcome day.

285. God's Goodness
(S. M.)

I BLESS my God and King,
For all I do on earth;
I feel his Spirit and his love
Draws my poor soul above.

My tongue shall now arise
To praise his holy name;
Whilst I am trav'lling here below,
With all his blessed saints.

Tho' once I naked was,
And scarce had any robe,
Now I am cloth'd with righteousness,
The mantle of my God.

'Tis he adorn'd my soul,
And made salvation mine;
Upon a poor polluted worm
He made his grace to shine.

And lest the shadow of a spot
Should on my soul be found;
He took the glorious Saviour's robe
And cast it all around.

286. God's Goodness
(C. M.)

MY gracious ever-loving God,
To thee what shall I say?
I humbly thank thee for thy grace,
And all thou'st done for me.

Thy heavenly robe of grace exceeds
What earthly princes wear;
These ornaments, how bright they shine!
How white thy garments are!

The spirit, wrought my faith and love,
And hope, and every grace;
But Jesus spent his life to work
The robe of righteousness.

Strangely, my soul, art thou array'd
By the great sacred Three!
Give all the glory to his name,
Let all thy powers agree.

Tis Christ that wash'd thee in his blood,
And purified thy soul!
Now you are pure and spotless too,
And wash'd as white as snow.

287. Vision of Christ's Kingdom
(C. M.)

GOD doth his glorious kingdom show
To every sincere soul;
They who have given up their hearts,
His Spirit makes them whole.

Lo what a glorious sight appears
To our believing eyes;
The earth and sea is past away,
With the old rolling skies.

The sea of trouble it is gone, Of danger and despair,
Th' deceitful heart the lying tongue,
And all that mock and swear.

From the third heavens where God resides,
That holy happy place;
The new Jerusalem comes down,
Adorn'd with shining grace.

Attending angels shout for joy,
And the bright armies sing,—
"Glory to God above the skies.
"The everlasting King."

288. Remembrance of God (C. M.)

REMEMBER this, poor mortal slave,
What I shall to thee say,
Thy mortal body is the Lord's,
Give glory to his name.

The God of glory doth come down,
To save thy soul and body;
Poor mortal slaves receive the crown,
Which God in Christ had won.

His own soft hand shall wipe the tears
From all your weeping eyes;
Your pains and griefs, and groans and fears,
And death itself shall die.

How long, dear Saviour, oh how long
Shall this bright hour delay?
Fly swifter round ye wheels of time,
And bring the welcome day.

I thank my God, my Advocate,
That undertook my cause;
Made slaves the partners of his throne,
Although they were all lost.

289. Encouragement (P. M.)

HARK! poor slave, it is the Lord,
It is the Saviour, hear his word;
Jesus speaks and speaks to thee,—
"Say, poor sinner, lovest thou me?"

Thou dost say "I'm not a slave,
"I was born on British ground;"
O remember when thou wast
In chains of sin and mis'ry bound.

I, the Lord, did thee deliver,
And when wounded heal'd thy wounds,
Sought thee wandering, set thee right,
Turn'd thy darkness into light.

Can a man so hardened be,
As not to remember me?
Yes, he may forgetful be,
Yet will I remember thee.

Thou shalt see my glory soon,
When the work of grace is done;
Partners of my throne shall be,—
"Say, poor sinner, lovest thou me?"

290. A Desire to Know Our Characters (P. M.)

LORD, I desire for to know
How to serve my God below?
How to serve thee with my heart?
How to choose the better part?

Tis a point I long to know,
Oft it causes anxious thought—
Do I love the Lord or no?
Am I his, or am I not?

If I love, why am I thus?
Why this dull and lifeless frame?
Hardly, sure, can they be worse
Who have never heard his name.

Could my heart so hard remain;
Never to cry to God within;
Every trifle give me pain;
If I knew a Saviour's name?

When I turn my eyes within,
All is dark, and vain, and wild,
Fill'd with unbelief and sin;—
Can I deem myself a child?

O my God to thee I cry,
Save my soul from sin and hell!
Send thy Spirit in my heart,
Bid my unbelief depart.

291. Confessing of Sin (P. M.)

IF I pray, or hear, or read,
Sin is mix'd with all I do;
You that love the Lord indeed,
Tell me, is it thus with you?

Yet I mourn my stubborn will,—
Find my heart is full of sin;
You that love the Lord indeed,
Tell me is it thus with you?

Could I joy his saints to meet;
Sit with Mary at thy feet;
Find thy promise to me sweet;
Love the Lord and kiss his feet?

Lord, remove my doubts and fears,
That which hide thy people's eyes;
Shine upon thy work of grace,
Show in Christ thy smiling face?

Let me love thee and adore;
Let me love thee evermore;
If I lov'd thee e'er before,
Let me love thee more and more.

Let me love thee above all;
Let me ever on thee call;
Wait for ever at thy feet,
Till thy glory is complete.

[292.] 72. Giving God the Heart (C. M.)

O GOD, may I for ever be,
    Fill'd with joy and with thee;
Thy glory in me now complete,
    Let me set at thy feet.

Take now my heart and let it be
    Clos'd to all things but thee;
Seal now my breast and let me wear
    Thy gracious pledge of love.

Complete thy work, and crown thy grace,
    That I may faithful prove;
And listen to that small-still voice,
    Which only whispers love.

Which teaches me what is thy will,
    And tells me what to do;
Which covers me with shame when I
    Do not thy will pursue.

Take my poor heart just as it is,
    Set up there in thy throne;
So shall I love thee above all,
    And live to thee alone.

Thus shall I show to all below,
    What thou hast done for me;
That thou didst die for all mankind,
    And shed thy blood so free.

293. For the Morning (C. M.)

I HEAR thy voice, O God of grace,
    That loudly calls for me;
That I may rise and feel thy face,
    Before the dawning day.

While others still lie in their beds,
    And have no thought to pray,
Their sleep doth still keep them secure,
    Like death, upon the frame.

But, O my God, 'tis thou that hears
    My morning feeble cries;
I cry for grace, thy Spirit's aid,
    Before the sun do rise.

That like the sun I may fulfil,
    My bus'ness of the day;
To give the life that Jesus did,
    To go and preach to-day.

O like the sun I would fulfil,

My duties and obey;
Thy Spirit's voice that speaks within,
And tells me keep the day.

294. A Warning to the Young (S. M.)

YOUNG men and women, hear
What God Almighty says;
"Delight not in your evil ways,
"But seek eternal rest."

If you delight to please
Your carnal appetites,
With wanton songs, and mirth, and wine,
Remember judgment is not far.

Its not a day from thee,
God knows your secret hearts;
They're all recorded in his book
Which surely shall be brought.

But, O, the Almighty God,
When here he shall appear
In flaming fire from heav'n above,
Thou shalt his thunders hear.

But oh! thou says "Not yet,
"This dreadful day delays;
"We still may dance, and sport, and play,
"As we did yesterday."

My dear young friends, O hear,
Whate'er the gospel says,
You may be full of joy to-day,
E'er night you may be dead.

295. Advice to Youth (L. M.)

GOD, from on high beholds your thoughts,
His book records your secret thoughts!
The works of darkness you have done,
Must all appear before God's Son.

Ye men and women, old and young,
Who cheer'd your hearts with wine and rum,
Enjoy'd the days of mirth, and said
The day of judgment never comes.

The vengeance of your holy due
Shall strike your heart with terror through;
While twice ten thousand thunders roar,
Shall shake the globe from pole to pole.

Where will you find a hiding place
To answer for his injured grace?
The fiery flames shall burn thy face,
And thou shalt find no hiding place.

Now in the heat of youthful blood,
Remember thy Creator God;
Behold the aged sinners goes,
Strait down to hell, with endless woes.

296. God's Dominion Over the Sea (L. M.)

WHEN I from America did come,
I ran at God's command;
According as he gave his grace,
I told to every one.

Some did me mock, and some deride,
And thus to me did say,
They'd take and throw me overboard,
Before the end of day.

Not thinking that there was a God
Who heard what they did say;
But God who sees and knows their thoughts
Did his own grace display.

By sending down his mighty rod
Of lightning on that day;
Seven were wounded, two destroy'd,
By God's almighty power.

Then, O they saw the mighty power
Of God's almighty hand,
Who sent the lightning to devour
The mortal feeble men.

297. Its God That Rules the Sea (C. M.)

I THANK my God that he did hear
My mortal feeble voice,
When I did cry with heart sincere,
He made my soul rejoice.

In the said ship from whence I came
From North America,
The cruel men and boist'rous sea,
Did make me sore afraid.

Which made me cry unto my God,
For mercy and for aid;
My God he heard my mournful cries,
And did with thunders roar.
He did all my enemies confound,
And made their hearts to ach;
His mighty thunders then did roar,
His lightnings then did flash.

Caus'd every soul on board to cry—
"Lord save me, or I die?"
The Lord of Hosts did hear their cries,
Did on us mercy show.

298. God Rules both Earth and Sea (L. M.)

GOD of the sea, whose thundering voice
Makes all the roaring waves rejoice;
And one soft word of thy command,
Can sink them silent in the sand.

If but our Jesus speaks the word,
The sea divides, and owns its God;
The stormy floods their Maker know,
Peace, be still, if he bid them now.

The scaly flocks amidst the sea,
To thee the Lord a tribute pay;
The meanest fish that swims the flood,
Leaps up and means a praise to God.

The largest monster of the deep,
On thy commands attendance keep;
By thy commission sport and play,
And slides along the foaming waves.

What scenes of miracles we see,
O God we sing our songs to thee;
Whilst on the seas the sailors ride,
And curse the hand that smooths the tide.

299. Praise to God from All Creatures (C. M.)

GIVE glory to my Maker God,
All heavens, earth, and sea;
And all they that are found in them,
They all belong to him.

How is thy name by all ador'd,
In heaven, earth, and sea;
All that have life, and move and breathe,
Give glory unto thee.

Saints and angels, thy heavenly host,
And men below the skies,
That are born of God, and have receiv'd
The power of the Most High.

But O the sailors on the main,
Who never knew the Lord,
The sons of courage do blaspheme,
Who trade in floating ships.

The men astonished, mount the skies,
And sink in gaping graves;
Each like a staggering drunkard reels,
And finds his courage vain.

300. *For Mariners* (C. M.)

WE bring our mortal powers to God,
And worship with our tongues;
We claim some kindred with the skies,
And join th' angelic songs.

Let every living beast and bird,
And fish that swims the sea,
And rocks, and trees, and every tribe,
Give glory, Lord, to thee.

While sailors climb the wat'ry hills,
And plunge into the deep,
Afraid to hear the tempest roar,
They pant with flattering breath.

They hopeless of the distant shores,
Expect immediate death;
Then to the Lord they raise their cries,
He hears their loud request.

They then rejoice to lose their fears,
And see the storm allay'd;
Now to their eyes the port appears,
There let their vows be paid.

301. *For Mourners* (P. M.)

JESUS, lover of my soul,
We now to thy bosom flee;
Whilst there is no water rolls,
And no tempest in our souls.

We have found an hiding-place,
Where every poor soul may rest;
Safe into that port we got,
Where our souls are fill'd with love.

Other refuge have we none,
Hangs our helpless souls on thee;
Leave us, leave us, not alone,
Still support and comfort all.

All our wants on thee we cast,
All our trust on thee be staid;
Cover my defenceless head,
With the shadow of thy wings.

Thou, O Christ, is all I want,
Fill our hearts with love divine;
When we arrive safe into port,
We'll give all glory to the Lord.

302. *Convinced of Sin* (L. M.)

HIDE them, O gracious Saviour, hide,
All this poor blaspheming crew;
They that do not know thee, the Lord,
O make them know that thou art God.

O let the storm of life be past,
Safe them into the haven guide;
O Lord, receive their souls at last;
O save them by thy grace alone.

Tho' some do plunge in wat'ry graves,
And some drink death among the waves;
Yet the surviving crew blaspheme,
Nor own the God that rescued them.

Lord, for some signal from thy hand,
O shake the sea, and shake the land,
Great God descend with power and grace,
Let sinners see thy frowning face.

Raise now the falling, cheer the faint,
Heal thou the sick, restore the blind;
Thy glory and thy majesty,
May every soul submit to thee.

303. For the Society Meeting (C. M.)

LORD Jesus we now look to thee;
Thy blessings we implore,
We beg for grace and mercy too,
O grant it gracious Lord.

Through thee we now together come,
In singleness of heart;
We meet, O Jesus, in thy name,
We do not wish to part.

Lord Jesus, thy disciples see;
Thy blessings now bestow;
Give us thy Spirit, gracious Lord,
To each thy love bestow.

We know thy presence is within,
But this cannot suffice;
Unless thou plantest in our hearts
A constant paradise.

Come, Holy Ghost, for thee we call,
Thou Spirit of burning, come!
Fill every heart with love divine,
And leave a sweet perfume.

304. The Society Meeting (C. M.)

SEE Jesus, thy dear vessel see,
The promis'd blessing give!
Meet in thy name, we look to thee,
Expecting to receive.

We meet to pray, and praise thy name,
With a poor broken heart,
To do thy will while here below,
In ev'ry believing heart.

Thee we expect with us to join,
With all thy power and grace,
That we may sing thy praise below,
As angels do above.

Breathe on us, Lord, in this our day,
And our poor souls shall live;
Speak peace into our hearts, and say
"The Holy Ghost receive."

Now we are thine, for ever thine,
Our hearts are fill'd with love;
We know that thou art more than wine,
For all seems drunk with love.

305. Society Meeting (S. M.)

WE lift our hearts to thee;
Our hearts and hands are join'd
To praise the blessed Saviour here,
The Saviour of mankind.

We meet, thy grace to take,
Which thou hast freely giv'n;
We meet on earth for thy dear sake,
That we may meet in heaven.

And if no more on earth,
We ever meet at all,
O may we meet around thy throne,
Where parting is no more.

Not in the name of pride,
Nor selfishness we meet;
From nature's paths we turn aside,
And worldly thoughts forget.

Jesus, thy presence is
With us who are thy own;
Now, Lord, let every wounding heart
Thy mighty comforts feel.

306. At Parting (C. M.)

WE bless the Lord that we must
        part
    In body, for a while,
We still continue one in heart,
    Our spirits are all join'd.

Join'd in one spirit to our head,
    Where he appoints, we go;
And still in Jesus' footsteps tread,
    And sing his praise below.

We sing with aching heart, we sing
    With tears in every eye;
We feel his glorious Spirit descend,
    It makes us fit to die.

Oh, may we ever walk in Christ,
    And nothing know besides,
In Christ to live, in Christ to die,
    And then with Christ to fly.

To meet around his dazzling throne,
    Where parting is no more;
There we will sit, and sing with him,
    And make all heaven ring.

307. At Parting (C. M.)

GOOD night, dear friends, now we
        must part,
    Since God has made it so;
We part in body, not in heart,
    Our minds continue one.

May each to each in Jesus join,
    We hand-in-hand go on;
Closer and closer let us walk
    To his belov'd embrace.

Expect his fulness to receive,
    And grace to answer grace;
Nor joy, nor grief, nor time, nor place,
    Nor life, nor death, can part.

If Jesus be with us below,
    We still are one in heart,
We part in body, not in mind,
    Our minds continue one.

Through thee, we now together come
    In singleness of heart;
We meet, dear Jesus, in thy name,
    And in thy name we part.

Appendix 2

Methodists in the New York–New Jersey Area, 1788–1828

The following table is a compilation of membership by race in the Methodist church of New York and New Jersey between 1778 and 1828. Taken from the church's annual minutes, it demonstrates the strength of Methodism in the city and larger towns, but its feebleness in rural areas. Using this table we may follow the efforts of John Jea, George White, and other itinerants as they proselytized on Long Island, in Westchester and Kings counties, and in the farming towns of New Jersey.

In their narratives, Jea and White claimed large attendance at their camp meetings and rallies. As the table shows, the numbers of hearers at those meetings did not automatically translate into membership in the Methodist church. This disparity indicates not indifference to religion, but preference for affiliation with black preachers rather than white denominations. The desire of blacks, long recognized by historians, for clergy of their own race was demonstrated by the estimates Jea and White made of their meetings compared with the actual members.

A second factor was the ability of farm hands and servants to attend meetings. In the city, where distances were minimal blacks could easily walk to weekly services. In the countryside, African Americans joined together from several communities at an occasional meeting but could not commit every Sunday to communal worship.

Third was the separation of the African Methodist church from the parent denomination in 1821. Occurring long after Jea left America, this affected White's ministry. In New York City, black members quickly moved into the newly-independent black church. In the outlying regions, where black churches were rare, black membership in the Methodist church remained low but stable.

Methodists in the New York–New Jersey Area, 1788–1828

White/Black (% Change White/% Change Black)

	New York	New Rochelle	Long Island	Elizabethtown	Middletown	Freehold	Staten Island	Brooklyn	Croton
1788	276/54	522/54	230/9	220/14					
1793	639/154	375/—	271/21	226/8	170/2		77/—		278/6
	(132/185)	(-28/-100)	(18/133)	(3/-43)					
1797	740/141	520/18	325/25	210/—		387/17		23/27	
	(16/-8)	(39/1800)	(20/19)	(-7/-100)					
1801	685/150	736/14*		285/11		336/28		36/28	
	(-7/6)			(36/1100)		(-13/65)		(57/-4)	
1805	700/240	425/13	439/50	455/22		380/31		44/30	420/11
	(2/6)	(-18/-28)	(35/100)	(60/100)		(13/11)		(22/7)	
1809	1531/469	535/62	670/93	656/22	381/20	762/53		152/93	588/19
	(119/95)	(26/377)	(53/86)	(44/0)		(101/71)		(245/210)	(40/73)
1813	1851/627	481/48			317/9	734/43	229/11	179/73	470/17
	(21/34)	(-10/-29)			(-17/-55)	(-4/-19)		(18/-22)	(-20/-11)
1817	2010/843	464/46			111/10	571/42	675/24†	225/80	550/18
	(9/34)	(-4/-4)			(-65/11)	(-22/-2)		(26/10)	(17/6)
1821	2094/61	545/43			177/10	494/21	772/30†	210/6	516/26
	(4/-93)	(17/-7)			(59/0)	(-13/-50)	(14/25)	(-7/-93)	(-6/44)
1825	2567/56	614/36		66/—	193/2	710/29	742/18†	408/6	528/9
	(23/-8)	(13/-16)			(9/-80)	(44/38)	(-14/-44)	(94/0)	(9/67)
1828	3410/67	480/39		88/—	215/1		198/8	444/10	
	(33/20)	(-22/8)		(33/—)	(11/-50)			(9/67)	

*New Rochelle & Croton
†Essex & Staten Island
Source: *Minutes of the Annual Conferences of Methodist Episcopal Church for the Years, 1773–1839*, 2 vol. (New York: Mason & Lane, 1840), vol. 1.

Selected Bibliography

Primary Sources: Unpublished

LIBRARY OF CONGRESS

Carter G. Woodson Papers.
Trenton, New Jersey Circuit of the African Methodist Church, 1828–1848.

NEW-YORK HISTORICAL SOCIETY

African Free School Records, 4 vols.

NEW YORK MUNICIPAL ARCHIVES

New York County Deaths. v. 10 (1836–1840).
"Petition of the African Society on the Subject of Two Lots Purchased for a Burial Ground." June 22, 1795.
Record of Religious Incorporations of the City of New York. v. 1.

NEW YORK PUBLIC LIBRARY

Methodist Episcopal Church Records.
Methodist Marriage Records for the City of New York, 1799–1830. v. 72.
New York State Methodist Episcopal Conference Journals, 1811–1815.
Records of Baptisms, Hudson Street Methodist Church.

PORTSMOUTH, ENGLAND, CENTRAL LIBRARY

Hants Newspaper Clipping File, 6 vols.
Marriage and Death File.

PORTSMOUTH, ENGLAND, CITY RECORD OFFICE
Rate Book, 1814–1829.

TRINITY CHURCH ARCHIVES, NEW YORK CITY
Register of Marriages. v. 1 (1776–1810).

Primary Sources: Published

A Collection of the Most Admired Hymns and Spiritual Songs with the Choruses Affixed as Usually Sung at Camp-Meetings &ct with Others Suited for various Occasions. 1st Edition. New York: John C. Totten, 1809.

African Methodist Episcopal Church Magazine. 2 vols. 1842–1845.

[Allen, Richard]. *The Articles of Association of the African Methodist Episcopal Church of the City of Philadelphia*. Philadelphia: John Ormrod, 1801.

———. *A Collection of Spiritual Songs and Hymns Selected from Various Authors by Richard Allen*. Philadelphia: John Ormrod, 1801.

———. *The Life Experience and Gospel Labours of the Right Reverend Richard Allen, Written by Himself and Published by his Own Request*. Nashville: Abingdon Press, 1960.

Amyto. *Reflections on the Inconsistency of Man Particularly Exemplified in the Practice of Slavery in the United States*. New York: Printed by John Buel, 1796.

Andrews, Charles W. *History of the African Free Schools, from their Establishment in 1787 to the Present Time; Embracing a Period of More than Forty Years: Also a Brief Account of the Successful Labors of the New York Manumission Society*. New York: Mahlon Day & Co., 1830.

Aptheker, Herbert, ed. *"One Continual Cry," David Walker's Appeal to the Colored Citizens of the World. . . .* New York: Humanities Press, 1965.

Bangs, Nathan. *A Vindication of Methodist Episcopacy*. New York: W. A. Mercein, Printer, 1820.

———. *The Life of Freeborn Garretson Compiled from his Printed and Manuscript Journals and other Authentic Documents*. New York: Emory and Waugh, 1829.

Bourne, Hugh. *A General Collection of Hymns and Spiritual Songs for Camp Meetings, Revivals, &ct. . . . New Edition*. Bingham, England: Office of the Primitive Methodist Connexion by J. Bourne, 1819.

———. *History of the Primitive Methodists Giving an Account of Their Rise and Progress up to the Year 1823*. Bemersley, England: J. Bourne, 1823.

Coker, Daniel. *A Dialogue Between a Virginian and an African Minister*. Baltimore: Edes for James, 1810.

———. *Journal of Daniel Coker, A Descendant of Africa from the Time of Leaving New York in the Ship Elizabeth, Captain Sebor on a Voyage for Sherbro in Africa in Company with three agents and about Ninety Persons of Color*. Baltimore: Edward J. Coale, 1820.

Crowder, Jonathan. *A True and Complete Portraiture of Methodism or the History of the Weseleyan Methodists*. New York: Daniel Hitt and Thomas Ware for the Methodist Connexion in the United States, J. Totten, 1813.

[Day, Thomas]. *The Dying Negro A Poetical Epistle from a Black Who Shot Himself on Board a Vessel in the River Thames, to his Intended Wife*, 2nd Edition. London: W. Flexney, 1774.

[Dow, Lorenzo]. *The Dealings of God, Man, and the Devil as Exemplified in the Life, Experience, and Travels of Lorenzo Dow, in a Period of over Half a Century: Together with his Polemic and Miscellaneous Writings Complete to which is Added the Vicissitudes of Life by Peggy Dow*. New York: Sheldon, Lampert and Blakeman, 1849.

Edwards, Paul and Dabydeen, David, eds. *Black Writers in Britain 1760–1890*. Edinburgh, Scotland: University of Edinburgh Press, 1991.

Elliott's Improved New York "Double Director" for 1812. New York: Printed and Sold by William Elliott, 1812.

[Gilbert, Olive]. *Narrative of Sojourner Truth, A Northern Slave Emancipated from Bodily Servitude by the State of New York, in 1828*. Boston: Yearington, 1850.

Hymns for the Use of the Methodist Episcopal Church, Revised Edition. New York: Carleton & Porter, 1849.

[Jea, John]. *A Collection of Hymns Compiled and Selected by John Jea, African Preacher of the Gospel*. Portsea, England: James M. Williams, 1816.

———. *The Life, History, and Unparalleled Sufferings of John Jea, the African Preacher*. Portsea, England: James M. Williams, c. 1815.

Longworth, Thomas. *Longworth's Directory of New York City in the United States of America*. New York: 1800–1834.

Methodist Magazine, 1773–1830.

Minutes of the Annual Conferences of the Methodist Episcopal Church for the years 1773–1839. 2 vols. New York: T. Mason and G. Lane for the Methodist Episcopal Church, 1840.

[New-York Methodist Tract Society]. *Tracts #1–37*. New York: John C. Totten, 1821– .

George Osborn, ed. *The Poetical Works of John and Charles Wesley*, 13 vols. London: Wesleyan-Methodist Conference, 1868–1872.

[Pennington, James W. C.]. *The Fugitive Blacksmith, or Events in the History of James Pennington, Pastor of a Presbyterian Church, New York City*. 2nd Edition. London: Charles Gilpin, 1849.

[Rush, Christopher]. *A Short Account of the Rise and Progress of the African Methodist Episcopal Church in America*. New York: For the author, 1843.

[Sancho, Ignatius]. *Letters of the late Ignatius Sancho, An African. . . .* 5th Edition. London: William Sancho, 1803.

[Spencer, Peter]. *The African Union Hymn Book, Designed as a Companion for the Pious, and Friends of All Denominations, Collected from Different Authors (from the Line of Scriptural Text)Isaiah xlix, 13*. First Edition. Published by Peter Spencer for the African Union Church in the United States. Wilmington, Del.: R. Porter, 1822.

Thirteenth Annual Conference of the New York African Methodist Episcopal Church, 1834. In Dorothy Porter, ed. *Early Negro Writing 1760–1837*. Boston: Beacon Press, 1971.

Totten, John C. *The Moral and Religious Cabinet Containing Short Accounts of Christian Experience together with Instructions and Useful Extracts Intended to Promote Happiness of Pious Minds*. v.1. (January–June, 1808). No further volumes published. New York: John C. Totten, 1808.

[Walford, John]. *Memoirs of the Life and Labours of the late Venerable Hugh Bourne by a Member of the Bourne Family*. London: Bemersley Press, n.d.

Ward, Samuel Ringgold. *Autobiography of a Fugitive Negro: His Anti-Slavery Labours in the United States, Canada, & England*. London: John Snow, 1855.

Wedderburn, Robert. *The Horrors of Slavery and Other Writings*. ed. by Iain McCalman, Princeton, N.J.: Markus Weiner Publishers, 1992.

Wheeler, Peter, *Chains and Freedom or The Life and Adventures of Peter Wheeler, a Colored Man yet Living. A Slave in Chains, a sailor on the Deep, and a Sinner at the Cross*. ed. by Charles E. Lester. New York: E. S. Arnold, 1838.

[White, George]. *A Brief Account of the Life, Experience, Travels and Gospel Labours of George White, An African Written by Himself and Revised by a Friend*. New York: John C. Totten, 1810.

Printed Government Documents

Acts of the General Assembly of the State of New Jersey, 1786 (10th Session). Trenton: Printed for the State, 1787.

Minutes of the Common Council of the City of New York, 1784–1831. 21 vols. New York: Published by the City of New York, 1930.

Newspapers

Hampshire Telegraph, 1810–1820

The Trenton Mercury, and the Weekly Advertiser, 1787.

Books, Articles, and Dissertations

Acholonu, Catherine Obianuju. *The Igbo Roots of Olaudah Equiano*. Owerri, Nigeria: AFA Publications, 1989.

Allen, Michael. "The Dickens Family at Portsmouth, 1807–1814," *The Dickensian*, 77 (1981), 131–44.

Andrews, Doris Elizabeth. "Popular Religion and the Revolution in the Middle Atlantic Ports: The Rise of the Methodists." Ph.D. diss.: University of Pennsylvania, 1986.

Andrews, William L. "African-American Autobiography Criticisms: Retrospect and Prospect," in Eakin, Paul John, ed. *American Autobiography Retrospect and Prospect*. Madison, Wis.: University of Wisconsin Press, 1991.

———. *To Tell a Free Story the First Century of African-American Autobiography, 1760–1865*. Urbana, Ill.: University of Illinois Press, 1986.

Armstrong, Anthony. *The Church of England, the Methodists and Society, 1700–1850*. Totowa, N.J: Rowman and Littlefield, 1973.

Atkinson, Reverend John. *Memorials of Methodism in New Jersey*. Philadelphia: Perkenpine and Higgins, 1860.

Baker, Frank. "The Origins, Character, and Influence of John Wesley's *Thoughts on Slavery*," *Methodist History*, 22 (1984), 75–86.

———. *Representative Verse of Charles Wesley*. Nashville: Abingdon Press, 1962.

Baldwin, Lewis V. *Invisible Strands in African Methodism: A History of the African Union Methodist Church Protestant and Union American Methodist Episcopal Churches, 1805–1980*. Metuchen, N.J.: Scarecrow Press, 1983.

Balmer, Randall H. *A Perfect Babel of Confusion: Dutch Religion and English Culture in the Middle Colonies*. New York: Oxford University Press, 1989.

Barnes, Sandra T. *Africa's Ogun Old World and New*. Bloomington, Ind.: Indiana University Press, 1989.

Berlin, Ira. *Slaves Without Masters: The Free Negro in the Antebellum South*. New York: Pantheon Books, 1974.

Bernard, A. C. "Die Pinksterfees in Die Kerklike Jaar." Ph. D. diss: University of Amsterdam, 1954.

Blackburn, Robin. *The Overthrow of Colonial Slavery, 1776–1848*. London: Verso Books, 1988.

Blackburn, Roderic H. and Piwonicke, Ruth, eds. *Rembrance of Patria: Dutch Arts and Culture in Colonial America, 1609–1776*. Albany: Albany Institute of History and Art, 1988.

Blackmar, Elizabeth. *Manhattan For Rent, 1785–1830*. Ithaca, N.Y.: Cornell University Press, 1989.

Bloch, Ruth. *Visionary Republic: Millenial Themes in American Thought, 1756–1800*. New York: Cambridge University Press, 1985.

Bolster, W. Jeffrey. "'To Feel Like a Man': Black Seamen in the Northern States, 1800–1860," *Journal of American History*, 76 (1990), 1173–99.

Buttrick, George Arthur. *The Interpreter's Bible: The Holy Scriptures in the King James and Revised Standard Versions.* 12 vols. Nashville: Abingdon Press, 1952.

Carwardine, Richard. *Transatlantic Revivalism: Popular Evangelicalism in Britain and America, 1790–1865*. Westport, Conn.: Greenwood Press, 1978.

Clemens, Paul G. E. and Simler, Lucy. "Rural Labor and the Farm Household in

Chester County, Pennsylvania," in Stephen Innes, ed. *Work and Labor in Early America*. Chapel Hill, N.C.: University of North Carolina Press for the Institute of Early American History and Culture, 1988.

Cole, Thomas R. *The Journey of Life: A Cultural History of Aging in America*. New York: Cambridge University Press, 1992.

Cone, James M. *The Spirituals and the Blues: An Interpretation*. Westport Conn.: Greenwood Publishers, 1972.

Cornelius, Janet Duitsman. *When I Can Read My Title Clear: Literacy, Slavery, and Religion in the Antebellum South*. Columbia, S.C.: University of South Carolina Press, 1991.

Costanzo, Angelo. *Surprizing Narrative: Olaudah Equiano and the Beginnings of Black Autobiography*. Westport, Conn.: Greenwood Press, 1987.

Creel, Margaret Washington. *"A Peculiar People": Slave Religion and Community-Culture Among the Gullahs*. New York: New York University Press, 1988.

Cross, F. L. ed. *The Oxford Dictionary of the Christian Church*. New York: Oxford University Press, 1974.

Crudden, Alexander. *Crudden's Complete Concordance to the Old and New Testaments*, ed. by A. D. Adams *et al.* Philadelphia: John G. Winston Company, 1930.

Davidson, Cathy. *Revolution and the Word: The Rise of the Novel in America*. New York: Oxford University Press, 1986.

Dayton, Donald W. *Theological Roots of Pentacostalism*. Metuchen, N.J.: Scarecrow Press, 1987.

Du Bois, W. E. B. *The Negro Church, A Social Study*. Atlanta, Ga.: Atlanta University Press, 1903.

Dunkerly, R. "Lazarus," *New Testament Studies,* 5 (1959), 321–27.

Dye, Ira. "Early American Merchant Seafarers," *Proceedings of the American Philosophical Society*, 120 (1976).

Edwards, Viv and Thomas J. Sienkewicz. *Oral Cultures Past and Present: Rappin' and Homer*. Oxford, U.K.: Basil Blackwell, 1990.

Eicholz, Alice and Rose, James. *Free Black Heads of Household in the New York State Federal Census, 1790–1830*. Detroit: Genealogical Publishers, 1981.

Essig, James D. *Bonds of Wickedness: American Evangelicals Against Slavery, 1770–1808*. Philadelphia: Temple University Press, 1982.

Finke, Roger and Starke, Rodney. "How the Upstart Sects Won America: 1776–1850," *Journal for the Scientific Study of Religion*, 28 (1989), 27–44.

Forde, Daryll. *Efik Traders of Old Callabar*. London: Oxford University Press for the International African Institute, 1956.

Foster, Francis Smith. *Witnessing Slavery: The Development of Antebellum Slave Narratives*. Westport, Conn.: Greenwood Press, 1979.

Freeman, Rhoda Golden. "The Free Negro in Antebellum New York." Ph.D. diss.: Columbia University, 1966.

Frey, Sylvia R. *Water from the Rock: Black Resistance in a Revolutionary Age*. Princeton, N.J.: Princeton University Press, 1991.

Garrett, Clarke. *Spirit Possession and Popular Religion from the Camisards to the Shakers*. Baltimore: Johns Hopkins University Press, 1987.

———. *Respectable Folly: Millenarians and the French Revolution in France and England*. Baltimore: Johns Hopkins University Press, 1975.

Gates, Henry Louis, Jr. *The Signifying Monkey: A Theory of African-American Criticism*. New York: Oxford University Press, 1986.

Gates, William G. *Illustrated History of Portsmouth*. Portsmouth, U.K.: Charpentier and Co., 1900.

Geddes, Alistair. "Portsmouth Murders During the Great French Wars 1700–1800," *Portsmouth Papers*, 9 (1970).

George, Carol V. *Segregated Sabbaths: Richard Allen and the Rise of Independent Black Churches, 1760–1840*. New York: Oxford University Press, 1973.

Goodfriend, Joyce D. *Before the Melting Pot: Society and Culture in Colonial New York City, 1664–1730*. Princeton, N.J.: Princeton University Press, 1992.

Graff, Harvey J. *The Legacies of Literacy: Continuities and Contradictions in Western Culture and Society*. Bloomington, Ind.: Indiana University Press, 1987.

Herbermann, Charles G. *et al. The Catholic Encyclopedia*. 16 vols. New York: Robert Appleton Co., 1907–1914.

Hackett, David G. *The Rude Hand of Innovation Religion and Social Order in Albany, New York, 1652–1826*. New York: Oxford University Press, 1991.

Hackett, Rosalind I. J. *Religion in Calabar: The Religious Life and History of a Nigerian Town*. Berlin, Germany: Mouton de Gruyter, 1989.

Hall, Timothy David. "Contested Boundaries: Itinerancy and the Reshaping of the Colonial American Religious World." Ph.D. diss.: Northwestern University, 1991.

Hatch, Nathan O. *The Democratization of American Christianity*. New Haven: Yale University Press, 1989.

Hempton, David. *Methodism and Politics in British Society*. Stanford, Calif.: Stanford University Press, 1984.

Higginbotham, A. Leon, Jr. *In the Matter of Color, Race & the American Legal Process: The Colonial Period*. New York: Oxford University Press, 1978.

Hill, Christopher. *A Tinker and a Poor Man: John Bunyan and His Church*. New York: Alfred Knopf, 1989.

Hodges, Graham Russell. *African-Americans in Monmouth County, New Jersey, 1784–1860*. Lincroft, N.J. : Monmouth County Park System, 1992.

———. *"Root and Branch": African-Americans in New York and East Jersey, 1613–1863,* forthcoming.

Humez, Jean McMahon. *Gifts of Power: The Writings of Rebecca Jackson, Black Visionary, Shaker Eldress*. Amherst, Mass.: University of Massachusetts Press, 1981.

Isherwood, Laurence. *Christianity Comes to Portsmouth*. Havant, England.: For the author, 1975.

Kent, John. *Holding the Fort: Studies in Victorian Revivalism*. London: Epworth Press, 1978.

Kimbrough, S. T. "Charles Wesley as a Bibilical Interpreter," *Methodist History*, 26 (1988), 139–53.

——— and Beckerlugge, Oliver A. *The Unpublished Poems of Charles Wesley*. 3 vols. Nashville: Kingswood Books, 1988–1992.

Klingberg, Frank. *Anglican Humanitarianism in Colonial New York*. Philadelphia: Church Historical Society, 1940.

Kruger, Vivienne L. "Born to Run: The Slave Family in Early New York, 1626–1827." Ph.D. diss.: Columbia University, 1985.

Lednum, John. *A History of the Rise of Methodism in America from 1736 to 1785*. Philadelphia: For the author, 1859.

Lee, Sidney, ed. *Dictionary of National Biography*. 62 vols. London: Smith, Elder, 1900.

Levine, Lawrence W. *Black Culture and Black Consciousness: Afro-American Folk Thought From Slavery to Freedom*. New York: Oxford Unversity Press, 1977.

Linebaugh, Peter. "All the Atlantic Mountains Shook," *Labour/Le Travialleur*, 10 (1982).

———. *The London Hanged: Crime and Civil Society in the Eighteenth Century*. New York: Cambridge University Press, 1992.

Lovegrove, Deryck W. *Established Church, Sectarian People: Itinerancy and the Transformation of English Dissent, 1780–1830*. New York: Cambridge University Press, 1988.

Lovell, John. *Black Song: The Forge and the Flame, The Story of How the Afro-American Spiritual was Hammered Out*. New York: MacMillan Publishers, 1970.

Luidens, John Pershing. "The Americanization of the Dutch Reformed Church." Ph.D. diss.: University of Oklahoma, 1969.

McCalman, Iain. *Radical Underground Prophets, Revolutionaries and Pornographers in London, 1795–1840*. New York: Cambridge University Press, 1988.

Marini, Stephen A. "Evangelical Itinerancy in Rural New England: New Gloucester, Maine, 1754–1807," in Peter Benes, ed. *Itinerancy in New England and New York*. Boston: Boston University Press, 1986, 65–76.

Martin, David. *Tongues of Fire: The Explosion of Protestantism in Latin America*. Oxford, U.K.: Basil Blackwell, 1990.

Mathews, Donald. *Slavery and Methodism: A Chapter in American Morality, 1780–1845*. Princeton, N.J. : Princeton University Press, 1965.

Mohl, Raymond A. "Education as Social Control in New York City, 1784–1825," *New York History*, 51 (1970), 219–38.

Mosby, Dewey E., ed. *Henry Osawa Tanner*. Philadelphia: Philadelphia Museum of Art, 1991.

Moses, Wilson Jeremiah. *Black Messiahs and Uncle Toms: Social and Literary Manipulations of a Religious Myth*. University Park, Pa.: Pennsylvania State University Press, 1982.

Munsell, Joel, *Annals of Albany*. 10 vols. Albany, N.Y. : J. Munsell, 1855.

Nash, Gary B. "Forging Freedom: The Emancipation Experience in the Northern Seaport Cities, 1775–1820," in Ronald Hoffman and Ira Berlin, eds. *Slavery and Freedom in the Age of the American Revolution*. Charlottesville, Va.: University Press of Virginia, 1983, 3–48.

———. *Forging Freedom: The Formation of Philadelphia's Black Community 1720–1840*. Cambridge, Mass.: Harvard University Press, 1988.

———. *Race and Revolution*. Madison, Wis.: Madison House Publishers, 1990.

Nelson, Dana D. *The Word in Black and White: Reading "Race" in American Literature 1638–1867*. New York: Oxford University Press, 1992.

Nicolls, Charles H. "Slave Narrators and the Picaresque Mode," in Charles T. Davis and Henry Louis Gates, Jr., eds. *The Slave's Narrative*. New York: Oxford University Press, 1985.

Offord, John. *Churches, Chapels and Places of Worship on Portsea Island*. Portsmouth, England: Portsmouth City Record Office, 1989.

Olney, James. *Metaphors of Self: The Meaning of Autobiography*. Princeton, N.J.: Princeton University Press, 1972.

———.*Tell Me Africa: An Approach to African Literature*. Princeton, N.J.: Princeton University Press, 1973.

Ottley, Roi and Weatherby, W. J. *The Negro in New York*. New York: NYPL/ Oceana Publishers, 1967.

Patterson, Orlando. *Slavery and Social Death: A Comparative Study*. Cambridge, Mass.: Harvard University Press, 1982.

Payne, Daniel A. *History of the African Methodist Episcopal Church*, ed. by C. S. Smith. Nashville: A.M.E. Sunday-School Union, 1891.

———. *The Semi-Centenary and Retrospective of the African Methodist Church in the United States of America*. Baltimore: Sherwood and Co., 1866.

Petty, John. *The History of the Primitive Methodist Connexion from its Origins to the Conference of 1859*. London: R. Davies, 1860.

Pointer, Richard W. *Protestant Pluralism and the New York Experience: A Study of Eighteenth-Century Diversity*. Bloomington, Ind.: Indiana University Press, 1988.

Piersen, William D. *Black Yankees: The Development of an Afro-American Subculture in Eighteenth Century New England*. Amherst, Mass.: University of Massachusetts Press, 1988.

Raboteau, Albert J. *Slave Religion: The "Invisible Institution" in the Antebellum South*. New York: Oxford University Press, 1978.

Raybold, G. A. *Reminiscenses of Methodism in West Jersey*. New York: Land and Scott, 1849.

Rediker, Marcus. *Between the Devil and the Deep Blue Sea: Merchant Seamen, Pirates, and the Anglo-American Maritime World, 1700–1750*. New York: Cambridge University Press, 1987.

———."Good Hands, Stout Heart, and Fast Feet: The History and Culture of Working People in Early America," *Labour/Le Travialleur*, 10 (1982).

———and Linebaugh, Peter. "The Many-Headed Hydra": Sailors, Slaves, and the Atlantic Working Class in the Eighteenth Century," *Journal of Historical Sociology*, 3 (1990), 225–82.

Richey, Russell. *Early American Methodism*. Bloomington, Ind.: Indiana University Press, 1991.

Richardson, Harry V. *Dark Salvation: The Story of Methodism as It Developed Among Blacks in America*. Garden City, N.Y.: Doubleday, 1976.

Rock, Howard B. *Artisans of the New Republic: The Tradesmen of New York City in the Age of Jefferson*. New York: New York University Press, 1979.

Roeber, A. G. "'The Origin of Whatever Is Not English among Us': The Dutch-speaking and the German-speaking Peoples of Colonial British America," in Bernard Bailyn, and Philip Morgan, eds. *Strangers in the Realm: Cultural Margins of the First British Empire*. Chapel Hill, N.C.: University of North Carolina Press for the Institute of Early American History and Culture, 1991, 220–83.

Rosenberg, Bruce. *Can These Bones Live?: The Art of the American Folk Preacher*. 2nd Edition. Urbana Ill.: University of Illinois Press, 1988.

Rouget, Gilbert. *Music and Trance: A Theory of the Relations between Music and Possession*. Chicago: University of Chicago Press, 1985.

Sandiford, Keith. *Measuring the Moment: Strategies of Protest in Eighteenth-Century Afro-English Writing*. Selinsgrove, Pa.: Susquehanna University Press, 1988.

Saunders, W. H. *Annals of Portsmouth*. London: Adams and Co., 1850.

Sellers, Ian. *Nineteenth Century Nonconformity*. London: E. Arnold, 1972.

Shea, Daniel B. *Spiritual Autobiography in Early America*. Princeton, N.J.: Princeton University Press, 1968.

Shyllon, Folorin O. *Black Slaves in Britain*. London: Oxford University Press, 1974.

Simpson, Robert Drew, ed. *American Methodist Pioneer: The Life and Journals of the Rev. Freeborn Garretson*. Rutland, Vermont: Academy Books, 1984.

Smith, Billy G. *The "Lower Sort": Philadelphia's Laboring People, 1750–1800*. Ithaca, N.Y.: Cornell University Press, 1990.

Smith, Timothy L. "Slavery and Ideology: The Emergence of Black Christian Consciousness in Nineteenth-Century America," *Church History*, 41 (1972).

Sobel, Mechal. *Trabelin' On: The Slave Journey to an Afro-Baptist Faith*. Westport, Conn.: Greenwood Press, 1979.

Southern, Eileen. *The Music of Black Americans: A History*. New York: W. W. Norton, 1971.

Starling, Marion Wilson. *The Slave Narrative: Its Place in American History.* Washington, D.C.: Howard University Press, 1988.

Stevens, Abel. *The History of the Religious Movement of the Eighteenth Century Called Methodism*. 3 vols. New York: Carleton and Porter, 1858–1864.

Stout, Harry S. *The New England Soul: Preaching and Religious Culture in Colonial New England*. New York: Oxford University Press, 1986.

Stuckey, Sterling. *Slave Culture: Nationalist Theory & the Foundations of Black America*. New York: Oxford University Press, 1987.

Synan, Vinson. *The Holiness-Pentacostal Movement in the United States*. Grand Rapids, Mich.: William B. Eerdmans Publishing Company, 1971.

Tanner, Henry Osawa. "Lazarus," *African Methodist Episcopal Review*, 1898.

Tebell, John C. *A History of Book Publishing in the United States*. 4 vols. New York: R. R. Bowker, 1972.

Thomas, Lamont D. *Rise to be a People: Paul Cuffe, Black Entrepreneur and Pan-Africanist*. Urbana, Ill.: University of Illinois Press, 1986.

Thompson, Edward P. *The Making of the English Working Class*. New York: Pantheon Books, 1963.

Thornton, John. *Africa and Africans in the Making of the Atlantic World, 1400–1680*. New York: Cambridge University Press, 1992.

Tricentenary Studies, 1928, of the Reformed Church in America: A Record of Beginnings. New York: The [Reformed] Church, 1928.

Tyson, John R., ed. *Charles Wesley, A Reader.* New York: Oxford University Press, 1989.

Walls, William J. *The African Methodist Episcopal Zion Church: Reality of the Black Church*. Charlotte, N.C.: African Methodist Episcopal Publishers, 1974.

Wakeley, J. B. *Lost Chapters in the Early History of American Methodism*. New York: Carleton and Porter, 1858.

Walker, James W. St. G. *The Black Loyalists: The Search for the Promised Land in Sierra Leone and Nova Scotia*. New York: Holmes and Mier, 1976.

Ward, A. R. *Religion and Society in England, 1790–1850*. London: Batsford, 1972.

Werner. Julia Stewart. *The Primitive Methodist Connection: Its Background and Early History.* Madison, Wis.: University of Wisconsin Press, 1984.

Wheeler, R. W. "The Booksellers and Booktrade of Portsmouth and Portsea, 1700–1850." Diploma thesis: Portsmouth School of Social and Historical Studies, 1987.

White, Shane. *Somewhat More Independent: The End of Slavery in New York City, 1770–1810*. Athens, Ga.: University of Georgia Press, 1991.

Wilentz, R. Sean. *Chants Democratic: New York City & The Making of the American Working Class, 1788–1850*. New York: Oxford University Press, 1984.

Williams, William Henry. *The Garden of American Methodism: The Delmarva Penninsula, 1769–1820*. Wilmington, Del.: Scholarly Resources, 1984.

Wilson, Ellen. *The Loyal Blacks*. New York: Capricorn Books, 1976.
Wright, Richard R., Jr. *The Centennial Encyclopedia of the African Methodist Episcopal Church*. Philadelphia: A. M. E. Church, 1916.
Wood, Gordon S. *The Radicalism of the American Revolution*. New York: Alfred Knopf, 1992.
Woodson, Carter G. *The History of the Negro Church*. Washington, D.C.: Associated Publishers, 1921.
Zilversmit, Arthur. *The First Emancipation: The Abolition of Slavery in the North*. Chicago: University of Chicago Press, 1967.

Index